FINAL
WARNING

Grant R. Jeffrey

D0979843

HARVEST HOUSE PUBLISHERS
Eugene, Oregon 97402

FINAL WARNING

Copyright © 1996 by Grant R. Jeffrey
Published by Harvest House Publishers
Eugene, Oregon 97402

Library of Congress Cataloging-in-Publication Data
Jeffrey, Grant R.
  Final warning : economic collapse and the coming world government / Grant R. Jeffrey.
    p.   cm.
  Includes bibliographical references (pp. 500–501).
  ISBN 1-56507-479-3
  1. Bible—Prophecies—Depressions. 2. Bible—Prophecies—Economic forecasting. 3. Bible—Prophecies—International organization. 4. Economic history—1990– 5. Depressions—Biblical teaching. 6. Economic forecasting—Biblical teaching. 7. International organization—Biblical teaching. I. Title.
BS649.D42J44   1996
220.1'5—dc20   96-3672
                                                      CIP

Printed in the United States of America.

96 97 98 99 00 / LP / 10 9 8 7 6 5 4 3 2

*To my beloved wife Kaye, who is my
partner in ministry and the joy of my life.*

*She accompanies me in my research tours
around the world and shares my love of the
prophetic truths of Scripture.*

Acknowledgments

Many great Bible scholars have explored the prophetic Scriptures in past centuries. I have obtained many of their old and rare books through countless trips and correspondence with people throughout the world. These volumes contain many insights that have immeasurably assisted my understanding of the deep truths of the ancient prophecies. If we can now see farther than some of the prophecy writers in past centuries, it is because we have stood on their shoulders, building on their insights, to enable us to understand the fascinating prophetic events of our generation.

In addition to these works, the Bible itself is our ultimate source for understanding the prophecies about the return of Jesus Christ to set up His Messianic kingdom. Our highest goal as students of the Scriptures is to clearly understand what the Lord is saying to Christians in this generation. The application of the Bible's truths to our heart, mind, and spirit and our obedience to that revelation should be the focus of our studies in prophecy.

✦   ✦   ✦

Notice to the reader about *Final Warning*
Final Warning offers only general investment observations based on the author's experience, and makes no specific recommendations.

Contents

Part 4: The Coming Economic Crisis

Part 5: Escaping the Economic Chaos to Come

Part 6: New Insights from the Ancient World

Introduction

The world's economy is already beginning to feel the first tremors of the coming economic collapse that will set the stage for the rise of the Antichrist. This tyrant will rule the earth during the final seven years of history leading to the Battle of Armageddon.

As Christians we are commanded by the Bible to live in holiness and to witness to those around us as though the Lord could return at any moment. At the same time we must continue to plan and work as though He may not return for 100 years. If the Lord delays His return, then we may have to live through the greatest economic collapse in history. As we who are Christians consider these dangerous economic times in which we live, we may want to obtain information and advice about biblically based financial strategies that will protect our family assets and businesses in light of the rapid move toward an economic New World Order.

Final Warning will explore the economic agenda of the elite globalist groups that are conspiring to force America and Canada to join the coming one-world government. We will examine the financial strategies that will allow us to survive the economic roller coaster awaiting us in the years ahead. *Final Warning* also reveals the fascinating catastrophic political, economic, and military crises that will unfold as we rush toward the new millennium.

The elite financial interests who are planning a one-world government to replace the nation states of the past are quite aware that an economic collapse is the best way to force nations to surrender their sovereignty and abdicate their power to the elite leaders of the New World Order. There are a number of excellent books that outline the economic agenda of the New World Order and the dangers of a coming economic collapse.[1] However, there is currently very little in the way of biblically based financial information that lays out a practical financial strategy for Christians to survive the difficult times that lie ahead.

Prior to publishing my first book, *Armageddon*, in 1988, I spent 18 years as a professional financial planner doing pensions, tax planning, insurance brokerage, will preparation, and estate planning. As a Chartered Life Underwriter and financial planner I worked with thousands of professionals and business owners developing plans to help them achieve their goals of financial independence and preserve their estates as they transferred their businesses to their children. During those years I conducted numerous financial planning seminars for secular and Christian audiences.

In 1988 the Lord led my wife Kaye and I to enter into full-time ministry and focus on the exciting prophesies that point to the nearness of the second coming of Jesus Christ. *Final Warning* represents over 30 years of economic and prophetic research while dealing with the practical economic problems facing Christians in the 1990s. In this book I will share what my latest research reveals about the exciting events that will culminate in the return of our Lord and Savior Jesus Christ. For example, recently there have been some fascinating archaeological discoveries in Israel, such as the tombs of first-century Christians mentioned in the New Testament, including Sapphira (Acts 5), and the son of Simon of Cyrene, who carried Christ's cross.[2] Most astonishing of all, you will read a long-lost report from 1872 that details the discovery of the stone coffins of Mary, Martha, and Lazarus in a cave cemetery under the ancient city of Bethany.

Any careful inquirer into the truths of Scripture is confronted with the fact that over one-quarter of all the verses in the Bible are concerned with prophecy. We are commanded by the Lord to teach the "whole counsel of God," not to simply pick and choose the parts of His divine revelation that we find comfortable. One-quarter of God's "whole counsel" and revelation to mankind consists of prophetic passages. Therefore we must examine these passages carefully to determine their meanings.

There are four major reasons why prophecy is vital to the church in our generation: 1) Prophecy authenticates the Bible as the inspired Word of God to an unbelieving generation; 2) the message of the prophets calls the church to live in purity and holiness in these latter days in light of Christ's imminent return; 3) the prophetic message of the soon coming of Jesus motivates us to witness to those who have never accepted Christ as their personal Savior; 4) the message of prophecy is the best single evangelism tool we have to reach the lost with the claims of Christ.

Let's look at each of these elements one by one.

1. Prophecy Authenticates the Inspired Word of God

Fulfilled biblical prophecy is a powerful proof to an unbelieving world that the Bible is the inspired Word of God. Therefore, it can be relied upon when the Scriptures record that Jesus Christ said, "I am the way, the truth, and the life. No one comes to the Father except through Me" (John 14:6). Careful examination of the ancient prophecies about the destruction of Tyre and Babylon; the incredibly detailed predictions about the life, death, and resurrection of Jesus of Nazareth; and hundreds of other fulfilled prophecies provide incontrovertible proof that the Bible was inspired by God and thus we can rely upon its teaching about the destiny of our eternal souls.

Sir Isaac Newton, the greatest scientist in history, wrote about the fascinating prophecies of the Bible. As a Christian, Newton believed that a comparison of the fulfillments of prophecy with the original prophecies provided a powerful proof of the inspiration of the Scriptures. He wrote, "For the event [outcome] of things predicted many ages before, will then be a convincing argument that the world is governed by providence."

In this book, as well as in my previous books, including *Armageddon—Appointment with Destiny*, I will and have provided ample proof that the predictions made in the Scriptures hundreds of years before their fulfillment provide overwhelming proof that the Bible is the reliable and inspired Word of God.

2. Prophecy Calls on the Church to Live Holy Lives

The prophet John revealed that the hope of Christ's return was the motivation for Christians to live in holiness and expectation. "Beloved, now we are the children of God; and it has not yet been revealed what we shall be, but we know that when He is revealed, we shall be like Him, for we shall see Him as He is. And everyone who has this hope in Him purifies himself, just as He is pure" (1 John 3:2,3). At a time when moral standards are falling everywhere, the unchanging message of Bible prophecy is that we as Christians must resist the devil and walk in holiness. Someday, every believer will give an account of every idle deed and word to God. Living expectantly in the light of Christ's soon return will have a profound effect on our commitment to personal holiness and sanctification before our Lord.

3. Prophecy Motivates Us to Witness

The soon coming of Jesus Christ motivates us to witness to those who have never accepted Christ as their Savior. Every one of us has been placed by God in a unique family, work environment, or school where we may be the only Christian witness. We are commanded by our Lord to share the good news of salvation with everyone we meet. Jesus warned that "whoever confesses Me before men, him I will also

confess before My Father who is in heaven. But whoever denies Me before men, him I will also deny before
My Father who is in heaven" (Matthew 10:32,33).

Witnessing is not just an option for Christians.
Someday, every believer will have to render an account of his or her faithfulness or unfaithfulness to
our Lord's command when we see Jesus face to face in
heaven. The prophetic message of the nearness of
Christ's return reminds us that we need to witness
while there is still an opportunity to do so. "I must
work the works of Him who sent Me while it is day;
the night is coming when no one can work" (John 9:4).

4. Prophecy Is a Tool to Reach the Lost

We Christians who live in North America and
Europe are living in a generation of appalling spiritual complacency. Non-Christians around us are
simply not interested in theology, the church, or the
history of the faith. In fact, the only topic I have
found that is consistently fascinating to unbelievers
is that of Bible prophecy. The most skeptical of cyn-
ics today still possesses a profound curiosity about
the future. If while we are in a friendly conversation
on current events we introduce the fact that ancient
biblical prophecies actually foretold the major
geopolitical events of the last days, we will often find
ourselves involved in an open-ended discussion of
the Bible and our faith. There is an inborn curiosity
in the hearts of men and women about the future
that prompts them to discuss prophecy. In recent
years both CBS and NBC have carried prime-time

documentaries that deal with prophecy and the Bible. To the surprise of the networks, both shows received number-one Nielson ratings. NBC received more than 40,000 phone calls after running its show.

If you have read my books before, you know that every one contains the plan of salvation and an invitation for readers to accept Christ as their personal Savior. I encourage Christians to purchase any of my six prophecy books and give them away to unbelievers. Every week we receive letters from people who have led a friend or family member to faith in Christ through the use of these books.

Even hardened prisoners have read my prophecy books out of curiosity and, as a result, found faith in Jesus Christ. One man who had accepted Christ while in prison wrote to let me know that my books had been instrumental in winning a convicted murderer to faith in Christ.

In all the literature of mankind, the Bible has stood alone over thousands of years in its overwhelming influence on the thinking and behavior of billions of souls. While all other books were written to inform us, the Bible was uniquely written to transform us through its divine message. As we carefully examine the message of the Bible it will change us as we are touched by the Holy Spirit of God, who inspired human authors to communicate His message to His creation. Our attitude should always be as a student carefully searching the Holy Word of God to learn its truths. We should all remain lifelong students of the Bible, ever seeking to learn more until our graduation day when each of us will meet the

Author face to face. As David Livingstone, the great missionary and explorer of Africa, wrote, "All that I am I owe to Jesus Christ, revealed to me in His Divine Book."[3]

The greatest minds of the last 2,000 years have studied the Bible and declared the overwhelming importance of Scripture and its significance in the life of mankind. The great Christian writer Saint Augustine explored the writings of the classical authors in his search for truth before he found an abiding faith in Jesus Christ. Indicating the profound difference between the Word of God and the writings of men, Augustine wrote: "I have read in Plato and Cicero sayings that are very wise and very beautiful: but I never read in either of them: 'Come unto me all ye that labour and are heavy laden.' "[4] In a similar vein, the writer Charles Lamb described the enormous difference between Jesus Christ and Shakespeare, the greatest writer in the history of the English language, as follows: "If Shakespeare should come into this room, we would all rise; but if Jesus Christ should come in, we would all kneel."

PART 1

A Survey of End-Times Prophecies

CHAPTER 1

Daniel: The Prophet Who Saw Through Time

Daniel is the greatest of the ancient prophets of Israel, both in his unblemished character as a man of God and in the unparalleled revelations God gave him so he could see through the veil of time to describe the future. It is impossible to exaggerate Daniel's importance in terms of his influence on the prophetic views of both Jews and Christians during the last 2,000 years. Sir Isaac Newton, the great physicist, was so fascinated by the prophecies of Daniel that he wrote a book about them. Newton wrote, "To reject Daniel is to reject the Christian religion,"[1] indicating the fundamental role of Daniel's prophecies in Christian thought. Joseph Poule, a German theologian who lived from 1852 to 1920, noted the vital importance of prophecy in theology: "Eschatology is the crown and capstone of dogmatic theology."[2]

The main themes of biblical eschatology were developed by the great prophets of the Old Testament (particularly Daniel) and the various New Testament prophecies that built on the prophetic themes found in Daniel. It is significant that the Dead Sea Scrolls reveal that those who lived at Qumran gave the prophecies of Daniel the highest place of honor in their theology and Messianic expectation.

Attacks on the Book of Daniel

There is probably no other book of the Bible that has sustained more continuing attacks over the centuries than the book of Daniel. The reason is simple. Daniel provides the strongest evidence a person could ask for to prove the inspiration of Scripture, the identification of Jesus and the Messiah, and the promise of Christ's return to establish His Kingdom on earth.

The author of Daniel declares that he received these prophetic visions from God while advising the Kings of Babylon (606–536 B.C.). These prophecies are so precise and awe-inspiring that we are faced with only two possible alternatives: 1) Daniel was written, as it claims, before 536 B.C. and therefore is truly an inspired prophetic book worthy of diligent study, or 2) Daniel was written by a brilliant imposter who fraudulently wrote these "prophecies" around 168 B.C., after the prophesied events had already occurred. It is vital that we determine which alternative is correct because the prophetic message in Daniel is central to the gospel's message of the coming redemption of the earth. Let's consider the historical and textual evidence for both alternatives.

Criticisms Against the Book of Daniel

The higher critical school of Bible scholars in the last century hated the supernatural miracles and divine prophecies found throughout the Word of God. These negative unbelieving critics boasted that their greatest accomplishment was their decision to categorically deny the authenticity of Daniel's prophecies. One unbelieving critic, Dr. David Williams, a theologian from the nineteenth century, wrote in his Essays about the critics' rejection of the authority of Daniel's writings: "It is one of the highest triumphs and most saving facts of the more recent criticism, to have proved that the book of Daniel belongs to the time of Antiochus Epiphanes (168 B.C.)."[3]

Tragically, many seminary professors, pastors, and Bible commentaries today accept the argument of the higher critical and unbelieving school of scholars who reject the authenticity of Daniel's prophecies without considering the evidence. This rejection of Daniel's authority has inevitably weakened the belief of many people in the inspiration of Scripture. It has also eroded belief in Bible prophecy as God's genuine message to the church today. In his excellent defense of the authenticity of Daniel's prophecies, *The Prophet Daniel*, E.B. Pusey wrote the following in 1863: "The faith can receive no real injury except from its defenders. . . . If the faith shall be (God forbid!) destroyed in England, it will not be by open assailants, but by those who think they defend it, while they themselves lost it."[4]

Professor Pusey knew that the greatest danger to the faith of Christians did not come from external attacks by open enemies of the church. The real danger comes from trusted pastors and theologians who have privately abandoned their confidence in the prophecies of the Bible. Over the last few generations, the leaders of many mainline churches have progressively abandoned the "faith once delivered to our fathers" until the difference between those critics attacking the faith and the theologians defending it became blurred. The "salt" had definitely lost its savor. "Salt is good; but if the salt has lost its flavor, how shall it be seasoned?" (Luke 14:34).

A Response to the Critics

A careful examination of the historical, archaeological, linguistic, and biblical evidence proves categorically that the book of Daniel was a genuine prophecy composed before 536 B.C., as it claims.

In the past centuries, Jewish sages and the Christian church unanimously agreed that the prophecies of Daniel were legitimate and genuine. The pagan Greek writer Porphyry in the third century after Christ was the first who rejected Daniel's prophecy. Porphyry despised biblical prophecy and his hatred of the supernatural forced him to conclude that prediction of future events was simply impossible. He pointed to the incredibly accurate fulfillment of Daniel's prophecies as proof that these visions must have been written by an impostor at some point after the events had taken place.

In response to the critics, E.B. Pusey articulated the clear choice that faces us: "The book of Daniel is either Divine . . . or an imposture."[5] Professor Pusey understood the secret motives of most of those who denied the inspiration of the book of Daniel as well as those who declared that Daniel's prophecies must have been written by an impersonator in 168 B.C. These critics have determined in their own mind, before considering the evidence, that it is impossible that Daniel's prophecy could be genuine. Professor Pusey described their thinking as follows: "It is manifest from the writers themselves, that their central argument is this: 'Almighty God does not or cannot work miracles, or reveal the future to His creatures. Therefore, since miracles or prophecy are impossible, a book which contains an account of miracles must be written long after the alleged miracles are related to have been worked; a book containing predictions beyond the unaided sagacity of man must have been written after the events which are predicted.' "[6]

People who refuse to believe the supernatural are generally unwilling to truly examine the evidence. Professor Pusey correctly pointed out the origin of their criticism. "They overlooked the historical point that the disbelief had been antecedent [previous] to the criticism. Disbelief had been the parent, not the offspring of their criticism; their starting point, not the winning point of their course."[7] These critics have already adopted the conclusion that predictive prophecy and the supernatural are impossible. However, for those who will examine the question objectively, the evidence is overwhelming that the historical Daniel wrote the prophecies in his book between 606 B.C. and 536 B.C., centuries before the events he prophesied actually occurred.

Evidence for the Authenticity of Daniel

A century ago, skeptics rejected the biblically declared date of 606 B.C. to 538 B.C. for the writing of Daniel on the basis that three Greek words for musical instruments appeared in the manuscript. These critics believed that the presence of these Greek words was inconsistent with the claim that Daniel was written in Babylon centuries before the time of Alexander the Great's Grecian conquest of the Middle East. However, recent historical and archaeological evidence has proven that the Greeks traveled widely throughout the area of Babylon centuries before the time of Daniel. That would account for Daniel's knowledge of Greek names for these musical instruments.

Despite the fact that the critics' basic arguments were demolished decades ago, many modern Bible commentaries still parrot the old higher critical assumption that the book of Daniel "must have been written around 168 B.C." to encourage the Jews during the persecutions led by Antiochus Epiphanes. However, the critics' argument against the early date for the writing and the genuineness of Daniel's prophecy is untenable in the face of the historical and manuscript evidence.

The Septuagint   Numerous references to the prophecies of Daniel appear in documents that were written long before the 168 B.C. Maccabean revolt against Antiochus Epiphanes. For example, the Greek translation of the Hebrew Old Testament, the Septuagint, translated by seventy Jewish scholars during the reign of Pharaoh Ptolemy Philadelphus

(283–247 B.C.), included Daniel as one of the inspired books in the Bible.

The Book of Ezekiel   The prophet Ezekiel, a contemporary of Daniel and a captive in Babylon, indicated that Daniel was well known to the Jewish captives. Ezekiel wrote his book around 550 B.C. and referred to Daniel in two passages. In the first one Ezekiel records that God declared that a land that persistently sinned against Him would be punished "though even Noah, Daniel and Job were in it" (14:14,20). And then in chapter 28, Ezekiel, reporting how God described Satan before he fell into sin, wrote, "Behold, you [Satan] are wiser than Daniel! There is no secret that can be hidden from you!" (verse 3). In the face of these references to Daniel almost four centuries before 168 B.C, it defies understanding how a serious critic can honestly believe that Daniel was composed by an impostor.

The First Book of Maccabees   The *First Book of the Maccabees*, written about 168 B.C, records that the dying general Mattathias reminded his sons of the great heroes of the faith in Israel's history. Mattathias referred to Daniel's three companions "Ananias, Azarias, and Misael having believed, were saved out of the flame." Mattathias also reminded his sons of the great faith of the prophet Daniel in his hour of crisis: "Daniel for his innocency, was delivered from the mouth of lions" (1 Maccabees ii. 59,60). These statements provide the strongest proof that the writer of First Maccabees in 168 B.C was familiar with Daniel's writings from the Bible and believed Daniel's account was historically accurate. These statements would not have been made if the book of Daniel was composed, as the critics contend, in that same period—around 168 B.C

Jesus Christ   Jesus Christ Himself mentioned Daniel by name and endorsed his work as that of an inspired prophet of God. In His sermon on the signs of the end of the age Christ declared, "Therefore when you see the 'abomination of desolation,' spoken of by Daniel the prophet, standing in the holy place (whoever reads, let him understand), 'then let those who are in Judea flee to the mountains'" (Matthew 24:15,16). In this unusual declaration, Jesus affirmed that Daniel was a true prophet of God and confirmed the authority of Daniel's prophecies forever for all who accept the deity of Christ and the inspiration of Scripture. In addition, our Lord commanded believers to read and understand the words of Daniel's prophecy.

Both Paul and John draw repeatedly on the prophetic themes first articulated by Daniel six centuries earlier. The apostles believed that the redemptive plan of God would be prophetically fulfilled in two great pivotal redemptive events: first, Christ's life, death, and resurrection; second, His return to earth as the Messiah King to redeem mankind and the earth from the curse of sin. The writers of the New Testament saw these two redemptive acts as two parts of God's great redemptive plan for mankind.

The History of Daniel

The Jewish name *Daniel* means "God is my judge." And one of the most important passages in the book appears in chapter seven, where Daniel described his awesome vision of God as the Ancient of Days, sitting in judgment on all mankind. Daniel's prophetic theme is the absolute certainty that regardless of appearances that evil is triumphing, God will finally judge both individual sinners and wicked nations. God's people will then be vindicated; the saints will be resurrected to enjoy the righteous government of God's eternal kingdom. Daniel's book began with God's judgment against apostate Israel when the armies of Babylon captured Jerusalem. Significantly, the book concluded with God's final judgment on the wicked nations and their powerful leader, the Antichrist, at the Battle of Armageddon.

Daniel was taken captive as a young man during the conquest of Jerusalem in 606 B.C. He was taken by the Babylonian general, Prince Nebuchadnezzar, who was acting under the order of his father, King Nabopolassar. Daniel, along with the Jewish King Jehoiachim, was part of the first group of captives carried to Babylon. According to Daniel 1:3,5, Daniel descended from the princely blood of Israel. The Jewish historian Josephus declared that Daniel descended from the family of Zedekiah; Saadiah Gaon in his commentary of Daniel 1:5 claimed the prophet descended from the seed of King Hezekiah in fulfillment of 2 Kings 20:18. The Jewish Haggadah and the Chronicon Syriacum 27 also stated that Daniel was a descendant of the kings of Judah.

Daniel and His Friends Taken Captive

When the princely and noble Jewish captives were taken in chains to Babylon by the armies of

Nebuchadnezzar, their names, following the oriental custom, were changed to demonstrate the absolute power of their conqueror. The prophet Daniel's original Hebrew name meaning "God is my judge" was now changed to *Belteshazzar*, "Bel's treasurer," in honor of Bel, the pagan god of Babylon. Hananiah's original name, meaning "God is gracious to me," was changed to *Shadrach*, meaning "the messenger of the sun." Azariah's name meant "the Lord helped" but was changed to *Abednego*, meaning "the servant of Nego," another of the pagan gods of Babylon. It was a Babylonian custom to take captives from the best noble families of the conquered nations and to train them as future advisors to the royal court.

Archaeologists recently discovered, next to the ruined palace in Babylon, the elaborate ruins of the special schools for training the "wise men." In these special schools the best and the brightest of the noble captives would be taught the language skills and knowledge they would need to advise a future ruler. Massive libraries in Babylon held hundreds of thousands of documents inscribed on clay tablets, which were learning resources for these special students.

Within several years of their captivity, Daniel and his friends became major officials in the kingdom of Babylon. They were probably about 16 years old when they first entered the palace. These captives were "young men in whom there was no blemish, but good-looking, gifted in all wisdom, possessing knowledge and quick to understand, who had ability to serve in the king's palace, and whom they might teach the language and literature of the Chaldeans" (Daniel 1:4).

When Daniel and his royal companions were captured, it is possible that they were made eunuchs. The
Babylonians often did this to the noble captives they
intended to train as future advisors of the Babylonian
court. Daniel 1:3 tells us that the prisoners, including
Daniel and his three friends, were under the control of
the master of the eunuchs. The prophet Isaiah foretold
this centuries earlier to King Hezekiah of Israel:

> "Behold, the days are coming when all that is in your house,
> and what your fathers have accumulated until this day, shall
> be carried to Babylon; nothing shall be left," says the LORD.
> "And they shall take away some of your sons who will de-
> scend from you, whom you will beget; and they shall be eu-
> nuchs in the palace of the king of Babylon" (Isaiah 39:6,7).

The Jewish historian Josephus recorded this in his
Antiquities of the Jews (X.10.1):

> He also made some of them to be eunuchs. . . . Now among
> these were four of the family of Zedekiah, of most excellent
> dispositions; the one of whom was called Daniel, another
> Ananias, another Misael, and the fourth Azarias; and the king
> of Babylon changed their names.

The Refusals to Compromise

The Babylonians routinely dedicated their food to
their pagan idols (Exodus 34:15). In addition, they
served animals with the blood still in the carcass
(Leviticus 19:26). Millions of Jewish captives were

forced to eat this polluted food—a tragic fulfillment of the prophecy of Hosea: "They . . . shall eat unclean things in Assyria" (Hosea 9:3).

The Bible tells us that Daniel and his friends refused to eat the spiritually polluted royal food that was offered to them. As a result of their uncompromising faithfulness, God caused these four righteous sons of Israel to flourish and become more robust than those captives who ate the rich food from the king's table. What Daniel and his friends did may seem a small matter, but the Bible stresses the importance of a lifelong building of our character so that we will be able to stand when the real challenges of life come. "If you faint in the day of adversity, your strength is small" (Proverbs 24:10).

King Nebuchadnezzar promoted the Jewish counselors. His action aroused the jealousy of several Babylonian court officials, who developed a plan to destroy them. They remembered that Nebuchadnezzar had decreed that no one could pray to anyone other than a 90-foot-high golden statue that the proud king had erected in the plain of Dura. When Shadrach, Meshach, and Abednego were found praying to their God, the pagan counselors brought them before the king. In his rage, Nebuchadnezzar commanded that the three Hebrew ministers bow before the idol or be burned in the fiery furnace. They refused the king's command to join in his pagan worship. In their admirable and courageous response, they committed their lives into the hands of their God, saying, "O Nebuchadnezzar, we have no need to answer you in this matter. If that is the case, our

God whom we serve is able to deliver us from the burning fiery furnace, and He will deliver us from your hand, O king. But if not, let it be known to you, O king, that we do not serve your gods, nor will we worship the gold image which you have set up" (Daniel 3:16-18).

When the three Israelites were thrown into the furnace, the king was astonished to see the Son of God walking in the fire with them, protecting them from danger (*see* Daniel 3:25). It is often true in the life of a Christian that God does not appear until we are thrown into the fire of life's experience. Then, when we need God the most, He displays His power to assist us in our extremity. Someone has wisely said, "Man's extremity is God's opportunity."

Some people have wondered why Daniel's three friends were accused and not Daniel himself. In this type of religious inquisition it is normal that only those who are specifically accused are brought to the king for punishment. Daniel may have been traveling safely outside of Babylon taking care of business for the king. However, a more likely reason may be found in the nature of court politics. It is common in oriental court schemes of this kind for the enemy to launch an attack on the less powerful friends of their main target—in this case, Daniel. If they had been successful, they would then have dared to risk an attack on Daniel, who by now was a close friend and advisor to King Nebuchadnezzar.

In the last century, an archaeologist discovered an intriguing signet in Babylon's ruins containing a scene that is in striking accord and corroboration of this Scriptural record. There are three figures in an enclosure, which seems to represent a furnace; not far off is a gigantic figure or idol; devotees or worshippers are seen on the plain without; while several other minute representations appear among these. Whether this actually refers to "the three Hebrew worthies," or to some other similar ordeal, certain it is that the Bible scene could hardly be represented more unequivocally and completely on so small a space (*Truth of Revelation Demonstrated*, Murray, p. 24).[8]

Another significant archaeological discovery is reported by Professor Rawlinson in *Smith's Bible Dictionary*. An explorer named M. Oppert discovered the remains of an enormous "pedestal of colossal statute" in the plain of Dura, southwest of Babylon's ruins, a century ago.[9]

While Daniel was always bold in his stand for God, he revealed a very humble and tender spirit when Nebuchadnezzar called on him to interpret his prophetic dream concerning the destruction of the great tree (Daniel 4). This vision foretold that a terrible madness would afflict the king of Babylon for seven years. With the most gentle respect and loyal concern for his monarch, Daniel records his emotional reaction: "Then Daniel . . . was astonished for a time, and his thoughts troubled him" (Daniel 4:19). After the king encouraged Daniel to have confidence and proceed with his explanation, the prophet said, "My lord, may the dream concern those who hate you, and its interpretation concern your enemies!" (Daniel 4:19). Daniel was distressed that his king would now be humbled and lose his kingdom to his enemies.

Upon faithfully revealing the meaning of the prophecy, Daniel entreated the king to repent of his sinful pride in the hope that the threatened judgment might still be averted: "Therefore, O king, let my counsel be acceptable to you; break off your sins by being righteous, and your iniquities by showing mercy to the poor. Perhaps there may be a lengthening of your prosperity" (Daniel 4:27). This incident shows that though Daniel and his people had been violently taken captive to a pagan, foreign land, he did not harbor bitterness or hatred for his oppressors.

The biblical account tells us that the king of Babylon refused to repent of his pride. Twelve months later, forgetting God's warning, the king was "walking about the royal palace of Babylon" (Daniel 4:29), proudly admiring the beautiful, massive buildings which he had built in the greatest city of the ancient world. Nebuchadnezzar boastfully spoke in sinful pride, "Is not this great Babylon, that I have built for a royal dwelling by my mighty power and for the honor of my majesty?" (Daniel 4:30). The prophet Daniel faithfully recorded the immediate judgment God sent because of the king's arrogant claim that the glory of his kingdom was a result of his own power instead of a gift and trust given to him by God. "While the word was still in the king's mouth, a voice fell from heaven: 'King Nebuchadnezzar, to you it is spoken: the kingdom has departed from you! And they shall drive you from me, and your dwelling shall be with the beasts of the field'" (Daniel 4:31,32). That very hour, Nebuchadnezzar fell from his powerful position as the greatest monarch the world had ever known and became a madman reduced to eating grass in the palace garden. This isn't the only time God sent such a judgment; many times throughout history, powerful individuals have ignored God's blessings and gifts, believing that these accomplishments came solely due to their own efforts. Yet, as they proudly boasted of their works, everything turned to dust in their mouth. Nebuchadnezzar's example should remind each of us that all of our possessions, gifts, and accomplishments are simply a trust to be faithfully administered for our Lord. Someday we will all render an accounting of how we used the talents and possessions that the Lord placed in our hands during our life on earth.

Daniel's Extraordinary Character

Daniel displayed the highest spiritual character of any of the human personalities that appear in the biblical narrative. Daniel's character did not change or waver throughout his whole life, despite constant challenges, trials, afflictions, and great honors granted to him by the two most powerful empires of his day. Despite his incredible rise from slavery to become the prime minister of two pagan empires, Daniel never lost his humility and unwavering faith in God's mercy. He recorded the events of his extraordinary life without exaggeration. The divine visions and prophecies God gave him were simply recorded without embellishment. Daniel gave God all the glory. When he was offered the highest honors a pagan monarch could give him, Daniel responded by directing the king to worship and thank God. It was God who received the glory, never Daniel.

Daniel serves as an example for each of us today. We live in a spiritually deceptive time when Satan attempts to divert our attention on to individual teachers rather than on the Word of God and Jesus Christ. The prophet Isaiah warned that God will not share His glory with His servants: "For My own sake, for My own sake, I will do it; for how should My name be profaned? And I will not give My glory to another" (Isaiah 48:11).

Daniel was trained in all the wisdom of the great and powerful pagan culture of Babylon, just as Moses had been trained earlier in the highest knowledge attained by the magicians of ancient Egypt. And like Moses and Joseph, Daniel began as a slave with fewer rights than a prisoner in our lowest jails today. However, under the supernatural guidance of God's hand, Daniel quickly rose to become the powerful prime minister of the greatest empire in the ancient world. Through his obedience to the revealed will of God, Daniel received the interpretation of the emperor's prophetic dreams and thereby shamed the famous magicians and wise men of Babylon. Three times the angel Gabriel declared he was a man "greatly beloved" of God (Daniel 9:23; 10:11,19).

Whoever can endure the trials of adversity with fortitude and honor will usually be able to bear the challenge of prosperity with equal greatness. The soul that cannot be defeated by sickness, attacks, and trials will usually not succumb to the temptations of wealth. The adversities that afflicted Daniel and his friends did not make them strong; rather, the challenges they faced revealed the great strength of character that each possessed as a result of his life-long faith in God.

Even the queen of Babylon testified to the purity of Daniel's character, wisdom, and excellent spirit. When no one else could interpret the writing of the palace wall at Belshazzar's feast, the queen mother suggested that they call for Daniel. "Inasmuch as an excellent spirit, knowledge, understanding, interpreting dreams, solving riddles, and explaining enigmas were found in this Daniel, whom the king named Belteshazzar, now let Daniel be called, and he will give the interpretation" (Daniel 5:12).

As a result of his incredible giftedness from God, Daniel became the chief administrator of the great pagan scholars and royal advisors in Babylon (Daniel 2:48). Despite his working for decades with pagan associates and the obvious temptation to use magic, Daniel never joined in the superstitious rites of the Chaldeans. He would not compromise his faith in God.

Daniel in the Lions' Den

Toward the end of his life, after the rising Media-Persian empire had conquered Babylon in 538 B.C., the officials of the new empire began to hate Daniel because he was trusted and respected by the conqueror, King Darius. Apparently Daniel adhered to such high principles that even his enemies recognized his courage and spiritual greatness (Daniel 6:22-28). Despite ruling

Daniel = God is my Judge

two pagan empires for over six decades as the foreign Jewish prime minister in the midst of unceasing oriental court intrigues, Daniel's enemies were unable to accuse him of any wrongdoing. "So the governors and satraps sought to find charge against Daniel concerning the kingdom; but they could find no charge of fault, because he was faithful; nor was there any error or fault found in him" (Daniel 6:4). They found nothing wrong "because he was faithful." What a wonderful testimony to Daniel's unblemished character and career!

While under the rule of King Darius, several administrators plotted a new scheme against Daniel. These jealous officials slyly approached the king with a proposal: Pass a law forbidding every person under threat of death, to pray to anyone other than the king for the next 30 days. King Darius signed the decree, apparently unaware that this new law would threaten the life of his best counselor.

Despite the threat to his life, Daniel continued his lifelong habit of prayerful devotion to his Lord. "When Daniel knew that the writing was signed, he went home. And in his upper room, with his windows open toward Jerusalem, he knelt down on his knees three times that day, and prayed and gave thanks before his God, as was his custom" (Daniel 6:10). The simple phrases "toward Jerusalem" and "as was his custom" speak volumes about Daniel's character and his lifelong love of Jerusalem, the Holy City of his fathers.

Centuries earlier, when Jerusalem and Israel flourished during the golden age of King Solomon, the king had prophesied that those who prayed towards the walls of the Temple would have their prayers heard by Almighty God:

> When they come to themselves in the land where they were carried captive, and repent, and make supplication to You . . . and pray to You toward their land which You gave to their fathers, the city which You have chosen and the temple which I have built for Your name: then hear in heaven Your dwelling place their prayer and their supplication, and maintain their cause (1 Kings 8:47-49).

Obedience to God's command to pray toward the Temple, the dwelling place of God's *Shekinah* glory, demonstrated that Daniel and the other captives believed that their Lord had not abandoned His chosen people in their long exile in Babylon. Even today, thousands of Jews come to pray at the sacred Western Wall of the Temple Mount in Jerusalem, knowing that God's command to pray toward His sanctuary has never been rescinded.

When the evil officials discovered Daniel praying to God, they brought him before King Darius, who had no choice but to sentence Daniel to the lion's den for execution. It is fascinating to note that a century ago an explorer named Captain Mignan discovered, in the ruins of Babylon, monuments that depict prisoners being eaten by wild lions. Another inscription and stone carving of lions killing prisoners was discovered near the tomb of Daniel at Susa, Iraq.

Daniel trusted the Lord to protect him from the hungry lions that had been trained by the Babylonians to kill and eat their prisoners. To illustrate his

unflinching faith, after committing his life to the
care of his God, Daniel lay down to sleep on a fur-
lined couch in the dungeon of Babylon. He trusted
that the same God who created the lions was also
able to restrain their natural inclination to kill
him. The next morning, the king hurried to the
dungeon. He discovered his faithful servant still
alive and testifying to the glory of his God. " 'My
God sent His angel and shut the lions' mouths, so
that they have not hurt me, because I was found innocent before Him; and also, O king, I have done
no wrong before you.' Then the king was exceedingly glad for him, and commanded that they
should take Daniel up out of the den. So Daniel
was taken up out of the den, and no injury whatever was found on him, because he believed in his
God" (Daniel 6:22,23).

The simple statement "no injury whatever was
found on him, because he believed in his God"
contains the secret of the true confidence that
every Christian can acquire by placing his complete faith in the hands of God. No real and lasting
injury can afflict us when we place our lives in the
care of our heavenly Father. While our bodies may
be destroyed, our true eternal destiny is in heaven,
so we should not fear what man or life's trials can
do to us.

Daniel's Legacy

Daniel had an enormous impact on the people of his
time as well as those who would follow in succeeding

generations. His prophecies influenced the concepts
and language of later prophets, including Zechariah and
Haggai, and had a role in the writings of the apostles
Paul and John.

The article on Daniel in *Smith's Bible Dictionary*
declares, "There can be no doubt that it [the book of
Daniel] exercised a greater influence upon the early
Christian church than any other writing of the Old
Testament." Any objective study of Western culture
and attitudes will conclude that the apocalyptic ideas
of Christianity and Judaism have permeated the
thoughts and expectations of all educated Western-
ers. The prophetic expectations of both Jews and
Christians have been shaped to a large degree by their
understanding of the prophecies of Daniel. And
today, the prophetic hopes and fears of *millions* of
people are still shaped by the predictions of this ancient prophet of Israel.

Daniel himself foretold that wise men who understood the prophetic Scriptures would arise in the last
days and "turn many to righteousness." In Daniel
12:3, the prophet wrote, "Those who are wise shall
shine like the brightness of the firmament, and those
who turn many to righteousness like the stars forever
and ever." Daniel's prophecies are of vital importance
to anyone who wants to understand the events of the
last days. The apostle Peter declared that these
prophecies are "things which angels desire to look
into." He wrote, "Of this salvation the prophets have
inquired and searched diligently, who prophesied of
the grace that would come to you, searching what, or
what manner of time, the Spirit of Christ who was in

them was indicating when He testified beforehand the sufferings of Christ and the glories that would follow. To them it was revealed that, not to themselves, but to us they were ministering the things which now have been reported to you through those who have preached the gospel to you by the Holy Spirit sent from heaven—things which angels desire to look into" (1 Peter 1:10-12).

According to the closing words of Daniel's prophecy an angel commanded the prophet to "shut up the words, and seal the book until the time of the end; many shall run to and fro, and knowledge shall increase" (Daniel 12:4). If you read carefully, you'll notice that God never intended that Daniel's prophecies should be sealed forever. Rather, the angel said these prophecies were to be sealed only "until the time of the end." When the "time of the end" arrives, Daniel's prophecies will finally be unsealed. Then students of the Scriptures will be able to understand the mysterious predictions about the incredible events that will transpire in the last days.

I believe Daniel's prophecies clearly indicate that we are approaching the "time of the end." Indeed the unsealing of these prophecies in our lifetime foreshadows the return of Jesus Christ as the Messiah King.

CHAPTER 2

The Rise and Fall of World Empires

God's original plan was for Israel to be first among the nations and bless all the peoples of the earth. After 400 years of captivity in Egypt and 40 years of wandering in the wilderness, Joshua and the chosen people crossed the Jordan River to establish their nation in the Promised Land of Canaan. For the first 450 years Israel was governed under the direct rule of God's appointed judges. However, Israel rejected God's government system and demanded a king "to judge us like all the nations" (1 Samuel 8:4). The Lord allowed Israel to have a monarchy, but he warned the people that it would lead to national disaster.

Following the righteous reign of King David, Israel began to sink into idolatry under David's son Solomon and his unrighteous royal descendants. The first major crisis occurred when the ten northern tribes rebelled against the heavy demands of King

Rehoboam, Solomon's son. This split the nation into two kingdoms: Israel and Judah. In the centuries that followed, both the northern kingdom of Israel and the southern kingdom of Judah progressively abandoned righteous government and the worship of God.

During the next four centuries, Israel and Judah sank deeper and deeper into pagan worship, compromise, and idolatry. Despite continuous warnings from the prophets of God, both leaders and people generally ignored God's commands and openly indulged in licentious worship. After centuries of depravity, God's patience with Israel finally came to an end. In fulfillment of Jeremiah's prophecy, the Lord raised up the new Babylonian Empire to conquer Assyria. The triumphant armies of Prince Nebuchadnezzar then conquered all of the nations of the Middle East, including the disobedient nation of Israel.

At the time of the conquest, the prophet Jeremiah met in Jerusalem with the ambassadors assembled from the surrounding nations. Following God's command, he wore a yoke around his neck and announced,

Thus says the *Lord* . . . "I have given all these lands into the hand of Nebuchadnezzar the king of Babylon, My servant; and the beasts of the field I have also given him to serve him. So all nations shall serve him and his son and his son's son, until the time of his land comes; and then many nations and great kings shall make him serve them. And it shall be, that the nation and kingdom which will not serve Nebuchadnezzar the king of Babylon, and which will not put its neck under the yoke of the king of Babylon, that nation I will punish," says the LORD, "with the sword, the famine, and the pestilence, until I have consumed them by his hand" (Jeremiah 27:6-8).

God placed all of the nations under the yoke of the Babylonian Empire—the first of four gentile empires destined to rule the earth until the Messiah comes to establish His eternal kingdom. At that time (606 B.C.) the Lord transferred the sovereignty of the world from Israel to the Gentiles, commencing a period Luke called "the times of the Gentiles" (Luke 21:24), which will continue until Jesus returns.

The King's Vision

One day King Nebuchadnezzar was dreaming about what would happen to his kingdom after he died. As he dreamed, the monarch received an incredible prophetic vision from the Lord. When the king awoke, he was disturbed because he could not remember the details of his dream. He demanded that his wise men and advisors not only recall his dream but that they interpret it all as well or he would execute all of them. When Daniel heard about the king's threat, he asked the king "to give him time, that he might tell the king the interpretation" of the dream (Daniel 2:16). God then revealed the details of the king's dream and its interpretation to the prophet. The king's vision outlined in great detail the future political-military destiny of the series of empires that would rule the world for the next 2,500 years (see Daniel 2).

Nebuchadnezzar's vision was of a gigantic human figure comprised of four distinct metals: a head of gold, both arms and chest of silver, its thighs and torso of bronze, its legs of iron, and the feet and ten toes were a combination of iron and clay. The metals symbolized the course of worldwide gentile rule for the next 2,500 years. The progression from gold to silver to bronze to iron indicated that each of the empires would be progressively stronger in military power but of lesser value as they degenerated from a monarchy to military rule and finally ended with democracy and dictatorship.

The conclusion of Nebuchadnezzar's dream revealed a "stone" that "was cut out without hands, which struck the image on its feet of iron and clay, and broke them in pieces" (Daniel 2:34). This magnificent image was suddenly destroyed when the supernatural stone pulverized the feet of iron and clay. The stone then expanded to become a great mountain that filled the entire earth. This stone represents the coming eternal Messianic kingdom of Christ that will replace the pagan gentile empires of the world. Daniel interpreted Nebuchadnezzar's dream as a clear prophetic representation of the future kingdoms that will rule the earth from 606 B.C until the time Messiah comes to set up His eternal kingdom at the end of this age.

Incredibly, Daniel accurately prophesied that only four empires would rule the known world during the time between King Nebuchadnezzar's rule until Christ's return. Within the first 500 years following his prophetic vision, all four empires appeared on the

stage of world history in the exact order predicted by
Daniel. No new kingdoms have appeared on the
scene since the fall of the Roman Empire. Despite repeated efforts by various conquerors over the last 1,200
years, including Charlemagne, Frederick Barbarossa,
Napolean, Adolph Hitler, and Joseph Stalin, no one
has succeeded in establishing a fifth world empire to
replace the fourth world empire of Rome.

Daniel interpreted Nebuchadnezzar's prophetic
vision as shown on page 51 (*see* Daniel 2:38-44).

The Head of Gold—Babylonian Empire

Beginning in 608 B.C. the Babylonian Empire, led by
King Nebuchadnezzar, became the head of gold that
represented overwhelming wealth and power. Seventy years later the confident but wicked kingdom of
Babylon fell to the Medes and Persians. One night
while the Media-Persian armies surrounded the huge
walls of Babylon, King Belshazzar held a profane and
drunken feast, allowing his guests to drink from the
gold and silver vessels that had been taken from the
Temple of Jerusalem. Suddenly, a hand and fingers appeared and wrote on the wall of the banquet hall:
"MENE, MENE, TEKEL, UPHARSIN" (Daniel 5:25).
The dinner guests began to panic, and none of the
king's wise men could interpret the message. Daniel,
now an old retired official, had been forgotten after
King Nebuchadnezzar died, but the old queen mother
remembered his great abilities and called on him to
interpret the writing. Daniel told King Belshazzar the

Prophetic Element	Empire	Details of Prophecy
Head of Gold	Babylon	"you are this head of gold"
Chest of Silver	Med-Persia	"after you shall arise another kingdom inferior to yours"
Belly of Bronze	Greece	"third kingdom of bronze, which shall rule over all the earth"
Legs of Iron	Rome	"the fourth kingdom shall be as strong as iron . . . and . . . will break in pieces and crush all the others"
Toes of Iron and Clay	Ten nations will arise out of the Roman Empire	"the kingdom shall be divided . . . . partly strong and partly fragile"
Stone Cut Without Hands	The Messianic kingdom	"in the days of these kings the God of heaven will set up a kingdom which shall never be destroyed"

Daniel's prophecies in Daniel 2:38-44

meaning of the supernatural words: "God has num-
bered your kingdom, and finished it. . . . You have
been weighed in the balances, and found wanting.
. . . Your kingdom has been divided, and given to the
Medes and Persians" (Daniel 5:26-28). That very
night in October 538 B.C. the rebel Media-Persian
army of Darius conquered Babylon. Precisely as the
prophet Jeremiah had foretold, the brilliant but short-
lived Babylonian Empire lasted only 70 years. "Then
it will come to pass, when seventy years are completed, that I will punish the king of Babylon and that
nation, the land of the Chaldeans, for their iniquity,
says the LORD; and I will make it a perpetual desolation"
(Jeremiah 25:12).

The Chest of Silver—Media-Persian Empire

The second world empire, represented by the chest of
silver, would be stronger than the golden Babylonian
Empire because silver is stronger than gold. At the
same time, it is of lesser value.

History records that the Media-Persian Empire
raised enormous armies, including the army that
King Xerxes mobilized for his unsuccessful attack on
Greece. Greek historians reported that it took an entire day for the more than one-million-man Persian
army to pass before Xerxes' throne, which was set
high on a hill. Yet this huge empire laced the nobility
and impact of Babylon. After only 207 years, the
Media-Persian Empire was destroyed by Greece at
the climactic Battle of Arbela in 331 B.C. Alexander
the Great exacted his revenge on the Persians for

Xerxes' earlier attack on Greece by utilizing revolutionary new tactics of rapid attacks, well-trained troops, and brilliant military strategies. Daniel had a separate vision about the Greek Empire in Daniel 8:20,21, where we read about a rapidly moving male goat (representing the Greek empire) that destroys the slower two-horned ram that represents the Media-Persian empire.

The Belly of Bronze—Greek Empire

The third world empire, the Greek kingdom of bronze, was stronger than that of Media-Persia, just as bronze is a stronger metal than silver. In only a few years the young King Alexander conquered the whole known world from the Mediterranean Sea to India with only 32,000 men.

The Jewish historian Josephus, a contemporary of the apostle Paul, wrote in his history, *Antiquities of the Jews*, that Daniel's prophecies actually saved the Holy City from destruction by the armies of Alexander the Great. After Alexander conquered the ancient seaport of Tyre in 332 B.C. he moved south to destroy Jerusalem when he learned that the Jews had unwisely resisted his demands to surrender their city. Miraculously, as Alexander approached the city with his army, the Jewish high priest came out of the city wearing beautiful white Temple robes to meet the young conqueror. Alexander was shocked when the high priest proceeded to tell him that Jewish Scriptures had foretold his invasion and military success. The high priest told Alexander that God had revealed to the prophet Daniel some 300 years earlier that a great king would arise from Greece and subdue the entire world. When the priest showed Alexander these exact prophecies in the ancient Scriptures, Alexander was so moved that he worshiped in the Temple and gave orders not to destroy Jerusalem or the surrounding countryside.

Despite Alexander's great abilities, the Greek Empire was unable to remain united after Alexander's death. Daniel prophesied that at the peak of Alexander's power, "the large horn [of the male goat] was broken, and in place of it four notable ones came up toward the four winds of heaven" (Daniel 8:8). When Alexander died suddenly at a young age, he had no legal heir to succeed him. His huge empire, based on the democratic government of city-states, was divided among his top four generals, just as Daniel had predicted 300 years earlier.

The Greek Empire made great inroads in converting the world to their form of culture and civilization. In 285 B.C., Egypt's King Ptolemy Philadelphus, who had an enormous love of knowledge, wanted a copy of the Hebrew Scriptures in his own Greek language. The king arranged for a group of 70 Jewish scholars in Egypt to translate the ancient Hebrew texts into the Greek tongue. The resulting translation is called the LXX, or the Septuagint, from the Greek word for "seventy." This is the translation of the Old Testament that Jesus and the apostles quoted as recorded in the New Testament. In addition, the entire New Testament was written in Greek.

As a result of Alexander the Great's success, Greek became the universal language throughout the known world. This common language greatly facilitated the rapid spread of Christianity.

The two strongest of the four kingdoms that once made up the Greek Empire were Syria and Egypt. The Greek general Seleucus Nicator controlled the area north of the Promised Land, and General Ptolemy I Soter controlled the Egyptian kingdom to the south. These two kingdoms battled each other for supremacy in Israel. After several centuries of warfare, Israel established its independence through a successful Jewish rebellion led by Judas Maccabaeus, "the Hammer of God," against the Syrian King Antiochus IV, also known as Epiphanes. Antiochus IV had attacked the Jewish Temple and slaughtered tens of thousands of Jewish believers. Through a series of miraculous victories, the Jewish forces succeeded in defeating the Syrian armies.

After its victory in 165 B.C., Israel recovered a strong measure of its independence. The descendants of Judas, known as the Maccabees, oversaw what was called the Hasmonaean Dynasty. They ruled Israel peacefully for 100 years using a variety of foreign alliances until the legions of the rising Roman Empire invaded the Middle East.

The divided Greek Empire continued to rule from 331 B.C. until the year 63 B.C. The powerful new empire of Rome, led by General Pompey, conquered the independent Jewish kingdom and captured the Temple. Pompey impudently entered the Holy of Holies and instilled his Roman garrisons throughout Palestine. The Romans took over the fortress north of the Temple to maintain control

over Jerusalem. Herod the Great later renamed it
the Tower of Antonia in honor of his friend and pa-
tron Mark Anthony.

The Legs of Iron—Roman Empire

In Nebuchadnezzar's dream, the fourth world empire,
Rome, was represented by two strong legs of iron that
broke into pieces all that stood before it. Rome consolidated the various nations of the huge empire into
an enormous military machine that was virtually
invincible. One of the unique characteristics of the
Roman Empire was its incredible military might,
which, combined with an efficient police and judicial
system, completely supplanted the preceding kingdoms. Even today, after 2,000 years, many of our governmental institutions, legislative procedures, and
judicial codes find their origin in the Roman Empire.

Exactly as the prophetic dream foretold, the Roman
Empire divided into two kingdoms following the
reign of Emperor Constantine. The western empire
was based in Rome, and the eastern empire set up its
capital in Constantinople (Istanbul, Turkey). The iron
kingdom of Rome ruled the known world far longer
than any other. The western empire finally ceased to
exist as a major force when barbarians defeated Rome
in A.D. 476. However, the eastern empire, known as
the Byzantine Empire, continued for another 1,000
years until its defeat by the Turks in A.D. 1453.

The Toes of Iron and Clay—Ten Nations

The last part of Nebuchadnezzar's dream portrayed
the final world empire—Rome revived as a ten-nation

confederacy, represented by the ten toes made up of iron and clay. During the last 1,500 years many kings and conquerors have tried and failed to revive the glories of Rome. Yet God clearly predicted that, in the days immediately preceding the return of Jesus Christ to set up His Messianic "stone kingdom" (*see* Daniel 2:34), there would be a final empire comprised of ten nations based on the old Roman empire. These nations will be united in a confederacy.

One of the most startling features of world politics since the 1948 rebirth of Israel is the rapid revival of the Roman Empire in a reunited Europe. In 1957 the Treaty of Rome accelerated the move to gather the nations of Europe together into a multinational superstate. The European Union, as of this writing, includes 15 member states, with many additional nations waiting to join. Thus the most powerful colossus of economic, political, and military power in history is being created in Europe. These nations have agreed to create a European Defense Army together with a common European Foreign Policy.

Daniel foretold that there would come a day when the leader of a revived Roman Empire will make a seven-year treaty with Israel. For the first time in 2,000 years, it is actually possible that this united Europe will be able to fulfill Daniel's prophecy.

The Times of the Gentiles

In the Gospel of Luke, Jesus prophesied, "They will fall by the edge of the sword, and be led away captive into all nations. And Jerusalem will be trampled by

Gentiles until the times of the Gentiles are fulfilled" (Luke 21:24). The New Testament uses two Greek words that are translated "times." One word is *chronoi*, meaning "times," and the other is *kairoi*, which means "seasons." *Chronoi* refers to duration or length of time. However, *kairoi* denotes seasons of time involving certain events such as we imply by the word "epoch." The phrase "the times of the Gentiles" uses the word *kairoi*, indicating that we should understand Christ's phrase as "the seasons of the Gentiles." This implies that the times of the Gentiles will end upon the completion of certain prophesied events.

The "times of the Gentiles" began with the conquest of Jerusalem and Israel by the gentile Babylonian King Nebuchadnezzar in 606 B.C.:

> They burned the house of God, broke down the wall of Jerusalem, burned all its palaces with fire, and destroyed all its precious possessions. And those who escaped from the sword he carried away to Babylon, where they became servants to him and his sons until the reign of the kingdom of Persia, to fulfill the word of the LORD by the mouth of Jeremiah, until the land had enjoyed her Sabbaths. As long as she lay desolate she kept Sabbath, to fulfill seventy years (2 Chronicles 36:19-21).

This period known as "the times of the Gentiles" extends over the greater part of human history from the time of Babylon's glory until the final victory of the Messiah over the Antichrist at the end of this age. The conclusion of the "times of the Gentiles" will forever end the domination of the world by the wicked gentile kingdoms. The Messiah will gloriously descend upon the Mount of Olives to defeat the Antichrist's final attack on Jerusalem. Jesus Himself will then end the "treading down" (Isaiah 22:5) of Jerusalem, the gentile oppression that the Holy City has endured for 2,000 years. When Christ defeats the armies of the Antichrist, He will enter Jerusalem through the sealed Eastern Gate and usher in His Messianic kingdom as prophesied by Ezekiel: "The glory of the LORD came into the temple by way of the gate which faces toward the east" (Ezekiel 43:4).

The "times of the Gentiles" that began thousands of years ago under King Nebuchadnezzar was symbolized by his demand that all men must worship his golden image or face death. This golden image was a foretaste of the final "abomination of desolation." This "abomination" will be a satanic idol of the Antichrist that the False Prophet will create during the three-and-a-half-year Great Tribulation. He will demand that all men on the earth worship the Antichrist and his image. It is significant that the "times of the Gentiles" will witness a revival of pagan idolatry and image worship during the last days leading to the Battle of Armageddon. A prominent feature of almost every one of the gentile empires throughout history has been the deification of man, usually in the form of emperor worship. It began with the Babylonian worship of the image of Nebuchadnezzar. Then came the demand that no one pray to any god by the Media-Persian King Darius. This continued with the demand that all men worship the mad Greek King Antiochus Epiphanes, and finally developed into full-fledged emperor worship under the Caesars of Rome.

A Key Distinction

There is a difference in meaning between the scriptural expression "the times of the Gentiles" (Luke 21:24) and the phrase "the fullness of the Gentiles" in Romans 11:25: "For I do not desire, brethren, that you should be ignorant of this mystery, lest you should be wise in your own opinion, that hardening in part has happened to Israel until the fullness of the Gentiles has come in" (Romans 11:25). The phrase "the fullness of the Gentiles" refers to the complete number of people that God will draw out from gentile nations to be part of His "royal priesthood" and "special people" of 1 Peter 2:9.

Acts 15:14,15 alludes to us that the Lord knows in advance how many will ultimately join the Bride of Christ: "Simon has declared how God at the first visited the Gentiles to take out of them a people for His name. And with this the words of the prophets agreed, just as it is written." Just as a shepherd knows his sheep, the Lord knows the number of those who follow Him.

This period, "the fullness of the Gentiles," will end at the rapture. Then during the seven-year Tribulation period that Daniel called "the seventieth week," the Lord will again call Israel to become a "light to the nations." At the conclusion of the Tribulation period, the "times of the Gentiles" will finally end the gentile domination of Jerusalem and the world.

It is interesting that the Bible's prophecies uses wild "beasts" to symbolize the gentile empires of the world, illustrating their unruly violence and base passions for power and greed. In this regard, it is significant that a number of nations have usually chosen wild beasts as their national symbols: Britain—the lion; Greece—the leopard; Russia—the bear; America—the eagle; Austria—the double-headed eagle; Italy—the wolf.

Babylon the Great

The name *Babylon* evokes a powerful image of the greatest city of the ancient world. The name is derived from *Babil*, which means "the gate of God." Located approximately 56 miles south of Baghdad in modern Iraq, it grew in power until it became the most important city in the Middle East.

Babylon was originally known by the name *Summer*, the fertile country lying between the Tigris and Euphrates Rivers. The first mention of Babylon in Genesis reveals that the city of Babel was founded by Nimrod, the "mighty hunter," the son of Cush. "Cush begot Nimrod; he began to be a mighty one on the earth. He was a mighty hunter before the LORD. . . . And the beginning of his kingdom was Babel" (Genesis 10:8-10).

The Tower of Babel

After the Flood, the next major rebellion against God took place at Babel. The sinfully arrogant men of that ancient city, in an attempt to make themselves famous, built a high tower "whose top is in the heavens." The Bible records their actions and motives: "They said, 'Come, let us build ourselves a city, and a tower whose top is in the heavens; let us make a name for ourselves, lest we be scattered abroad over the face of the whole earth'" (Genesis 11:4).

God's response to their rebellion was to "confuse their language, that they may not understand one another's speech" (Geneses 11:7). In the total confusion that resulted from the people's inability to understand each other, "the LORD scattered them abroad from there over the face of all the earth, and they ceased building the city" (verse 8).

Centuries later, around 1760 B.C., the great King Hammurabi made Babylon the political and religious capital of his immensely powerful empire. Hammurabi combined astute diplomacy with superb military leadership to defeat the other kingdoms of Mesopotamia. He became the ruler of the first united Babylonian Empire, which extended from the Persian Gulf to the Habur River.

Babylon's First Demise

In the centuries that followed, the first Babylonian Empire faded away until it was succeeded by another rising power. The Assyrians had the most brutal armies the world had yet seen. Their standard practices included skinning captives alive and cutting off the noses of their prisoners of war.

Nineveh, in the far north of the kingdom, became the Assyrian capital. Assyria conquered most of the Middle East under the leadership of a series of powerful kings. Shalmaneser II fought Israel's King Ahab while Tiglath-pileser III carried the people of northern Israel into captivity. The Assyrian kings Shalmaneser IV and Sargon II completed Israel's destruction and captivity during Jewish King Hoshea's rule, destroying Israel's capital city of Samaria. The Assyrian armies of Sennacherib destroyed the city of Babylon. Esarhaddon and Ashurbanipal dominated Babylon despite continuous rebellion. For two centuries, from the eighth century B.C. till the sixth century B.C., Babylon gradually declined in power, becoming merely a regional administrative center. Many of these kings listed above are recorded in the Bible's history describing the centuries of continual Assyrian invasions of the Holy Land.

Despite Assyria's overwhelming power, God's prophets warned that the wicked empire of Assyria and its capital Nineveh were doomed to certain destruction. The reluctant prophet Jonah warned of the judgment that would come unless the Assyrians repented of their great wickedness and idolatry. "Yet forty days, and Nineveh shall be overthrown!" (Jonah 3:4). However, in one of the more marvelous miracles recorded in the Bible, the whole city of Nineveh repented and confessed their sins. As a result of their repentance, God withheld the threatened judgment. Yet a century later, after Nineveh had forgotten God and again indulged in utterly pagan worship, God's judgment fell on the wicked city. Around 630 B.C., the prophet Zephaniah arose to warn of God's coming judgment on the Assyrian kingdom that had oppressed the children of God for so long: "He will stretch out His hand against the north, destroy Assyria, and make Nineveh a desolation, as dry as the wilderness" (Zephaniah 2:13).

The Babylonian Empire

By 626 B.C., Assyria fell into political and military disarray. A powerful Chaldean ruler named Nabopolassar proclaimed himself king of the Assyrian province of Babylonia and defeated the demoralized Assyrian armies. He then destroyed the Assyrian capital of Nineveh in 612 B.C. Towards the end of his reign, King Nabopolassar left his army in the hands of his capable son, Prince Nebuchadnezzar, defeated the remnants of the Assyrian army and pushed their Egyptian allies out of Syria. As Nebuchadnezzar began his invasion of Egypt, he learned of his father's death and the possible threat of rivals stealing his throne. In a daring and dangerous march across the desolate Arabian desert, a journey no one thought possible, Nebuchadnezzar speedily returned to Babylon to secure his throne.

When the Egyptian pharaoh Necho knew that Assyria was no longer a military threat, he moved Egypt's armies into Palestine and Syria. At this time Judah had undergone a major spiritual revival under the leadership of King Josiah, culminating in the glorious Passover in the eighteenth year of his reign (2 Chronicles 35:1-19). Soon afterward, however, King Josiah was killed when he attempted to defeat the Egyptian armies as they marched through the Valley of Megiddo in northern Israel. Although Pharaoh Necho warned Josiah against fighting him, the Scriptures record that the Jewish king rejected "the words of Necho from the mouth of God. So he came to fight in the Valley of Megiddo" (2 Chronicles 35:22). King

Josiah fought the battle in disguise and was mortally wounded by an arrow. "So he died, and was buried in one of the tombs of his fathers. And all Judah and Jerusalem mourned for Josiah. Jeremiah also lamented for Josiah" (2 Chronicles 35:24,25).

In 605 B.C., Prince Nebuchadnezzar and his Babylonian armies attacked the Egyptian forces and defeated them decisively at the historic Battle of Carchemish. This victory established the Babylonian Empire as the supreme world power.

During this campaign, Nebuchadnezzar also conquered Jerusalem and Judah in 606 B.C., taking a group of nobles captive back to Babylon, including Daniel and his companions. This defeat of Judah began the prophesied Babylonian captivity that was to last for 70 years (Jeremiah 25:11). When Judah rebelled a second time in 598 B.C., Nebuchadnezzar's army took 10,000 additional captives to Babylon, including the prophet Ezekiel. The Jewish King Zedekiah rebelled a third (and final) time against the king of Babylon in violation of God's command revealed through the words of His prophet Jeremiah (Jeremiah 38:17-23). After a bitter siege of several years, Nebuchadnezzar's armies conquered and burned the city of Jerusalem and the Temple of Solomon on the ninth day of the Jewish month Av, 587 B.C.

The City of Babylon

King Nebuchadnezzar, a brilliant general, expanded his vibrant new empire until his armies conquered the entire Middle East. He rebuilt the old imperial

capital of Babylon to become the largest city in the
known world. Massive new temples and palaces were
built, along with impressive processional boulevards
in honor of his pagan gods, Marduk, Asshur, and
Ishtar. Daniel, Ezekiel, and hundreds of thousands of
Jewish captives were marched in chains down these
boulevards through the Ishtar Gate. This historic gate
was discovered in the last century and taken to Germany, where it was rebuilt in the Berlin Museum.

Babylon was strategically located on the most important trade routes in the Middle East, the Tigris and
Euphrates Rivers, which flowed from Assyria south
to the Persian Gulf. Under King Nebuchadnezzar
Babylon became the greatest and most populous city
in the ancient world with great walls and a ziggurat,
gates and temples, and its fabled hanging gardens.
Babylon, in the midst of a large plain, was divided by
the Euphrates River, which flowed north to south
through the center of the city carrying rich alluvial
soil from the mountains far to the north. This created a fertile plain of deep, rich topsoil. The old city on
the eastern bank had palaces and temples; the new city
grew in grandeur on the western bank of the river. The
temple of Marduk, the major Babylonian deity, was
built near the center of the capital. North of the city
the engineers built a ziggurat, a seven-storied edifice,
that some scholars believe may be related to the ancient Tower of Babel.

The Greek historian Herodotus described Babylon's dimensions as follows: The four sides of the
city were defended by huge double walls, each 14
miles long. These walls measured an astonishing 56

miles in circumference, enclosing a city that covered 196 square miles of land. The walls were of truly extraordinary strength. The outer walls stood over thirty stories tall (310 feet) and were wide enough to allow eight chariots to ride abreast at the top (87 feet wide). The builders used brick that was cemented with bitumen, a kind of asphalt that bubbled up through the earth from an immense underground lake of oil and bitumen that lay underneath Babylon. This bitumen became as hard as rock once it was exposed to the air.

The walls were surrounded by a 30-foot-wide moat. Once the moat was filled with water diverted from the Euphrates, the defenders of the city could easily attack an invading army with a continuous deadly rain of arrows shot from the high walls. The Babylonian sentries stood in observation towers that were 400 feet high and could see an army approaching from over 25 miles away. The city was also guarded by a hundred massive gates composed of solid brass.

Babylon was divided into sections by 50 major boulevards, each 15 miles in length and 50 yards wide. Half of these streets ran north-south and the other half ran east-west. These huge streets, lined with magnificent houses and government buildings, began at the 25 gates on each wall and intersected one another at right angles. The city was divided by these 50 boulevards into 676 squares, creating individual distinct neighborhoods. The inner sections of these squares were used as gardens and common recreation areas.

The Euphrates River brought merchandise into the city, which, in turn, made the city rich. The wealth of

Babylon was staggering, with gold and silver almost as common as base materials in other cities. We can get an idea of the magnitude of this wealth when we see what Nebuchadnezzar did when he fell in love with a beautiful princess from the northern mountain areas of Media. When she married him and moved to Babylon she became depressed by the flat land with no natural mountains in sight. Overwhelmed with love for his new wife, Nebuchadnezzar built an artificial mountain with terraced hanging gardens in the midst of his capital city to provide her with a beautiful view. Early in this century, German archaeologists discovered the ruins of a group of palaces and fortifications in the northwest corner of the old city. These may have been the foundations of the hanging gardens of Babylon, one of the seven wonders of the ancient world.

The Euphrates River was lined on each bank by a high, thick brick wall similar to the walls surrounding the city. Immense gates of brass were placed in these walls at the end of each of the major east-west streets. People going through these gates would walk down steps to landing places that allowed them to easily cross from one side of the city to the other in boats. In the center of Babylon an enormous bridge, 30 feet wide and built of huge stones fastened by iron chains, crossed the river. A magnificent palace stood at each end of the bridge. (Many of the scenes described in the book of Daniel occurred within these two palaces.) Engineers had built a subterranean tunnel beneath the river connecting these two palaces. An elaborately designed system of canals insured that excess floodwaters would be diverted away from the city during seasonal flooding. During the construction of these canals the engineers created a huge artificial reservoir some 40 miles square and ten yards deep, to the west of the city to hold the river water while they built the interior walls along the riverbanks. Once the walls were finished, the Euphrates was restored to its original course.

During Nebuchadnezzar's 43-year reign, he extended Babylon's control over the Middle East. However, despite its immense military power, the neo-Babylonian Empire of Nebuchadnezzar and his successors was short-lived. After Nebuchadnezzar's death in 562 B.C., his empire began to decline in power. Nabonidus, one of the governors of the empire, rose to become king of Babylonia in 556 B.C. After a few years, King Nabonidus left the capital of Babylon and moved to the city of Harran. He left his son King Belshazzar to rule in his stead as "the second ruler" of the empire. This unusual situation explains why Belshazzar was only able to name Daniel as "the third ruler" in the kingdom when he wanted to offer him honors for reading the writing on the wall of the palace (Daniel 5:16).

Babylon's Destruction

The Bible warned that Babylon, the most magnificent empire the world had ever seen, would last only 70 years because of the nation's cruelty against Israel and their pagan worship: "'Then it will come to pass, when seventy years are completed, that I will punish the king of Babylon and that nation, the land of the Chaldeans, for their iniquity,' says the LORD; 'and I will make it a perpetual desolation'" (Jeremiah 25:12). At the same time, Jeremiah also warned the Jews about their approaching 70-year captivity in Babylon because of their sinful rebellion against God's commands: "And this whole land shall be a desolation and an astonishment, and these nations shall serve the king of Babylon seventy years" (Jeremiah 25:11). The prophet Daniel revealed in his writing that he was aware of Jeremiah's prophecy and knew that the 70 years of Babylon's triumph over the nations was about to end. "In the first year of his reign I, Daniel, understood by the books the number of the years specified by the word of the LORD, given through Jeremiah the prophet, that He would accomplish seventy years in the desolations of Jerusalem" (Daniel 9:2).

Cyrus the Great, the king of Persia, founded the Persian Empire and ruled it from 549 to 530 B.C. After he conquered the Iranians, the Lydians (Turkey), and the Greek city-states on the Aegean coast, Cyrus brought his armies to the gates of Babylon. As prophesied by Daniel, under the leadership of Cyrus the Great, the armies of Media-Persia captured Babylon in 539 B.C. and incorporated the territories of Babylonia into the rising new Persian Empire, the second gentile world empire, the "kingdom of silver."

On October 13, 538 B.C., the very night that the fingers supernaturally wrote the doom of Babylon on the walls of Belshazzar's palace, the Persian army captured Babylon. The Babylonian king and his guests ignored the Persian armies besieging the city because they were confident that the massive city defenses and 30-story-high walls would keep out the invaders. But their confidence was misplaced, for nothing could keep God's prophesied plan from taking place. A hundred and fifty years before Cyrus was born, the prophet Isaiah, inspired by God, prophesied that a king called Cyrus would be led by God to subdue the nations, including Babylon.

Thus says the LORD to His anointed, to Cyrus, whose right hand I have held—to subdue nations before him and loose the armor of kings, to open before him the double doors, so that the gates will not be shut: "I will go before you and make the crooked places straight; I will break in pieces the gates of bronze and cut the bars of iron. I will give you the treasures of darkness and hidden riches of secret places, that you may know that I, the LORD, who call you by your name, am the God of Israel" (Isaiah 45:1-3).

Furthermore, Isaiah foretold the exact manner of King Cyrus's brilliant military strategy to conquer the impregnable city of Babylon. After digging an artificial canal to drain the river's flow, Cyrus entered the city by marching his elite troops along the dry river bed. The soldiers were able to wrench open the immense brass gates from below the normal water level and enter the city near the palace, conquering all before them.

The ancient historian Herodotus confirmed the accuracy of Isaiah's prophecy.

Cyrus . . . placed a portion of his army at the point where the river enters the city, and another body at the back of the place where it issues forth, with orders to march into the town by the bed of the stream, as soon as the water became shallow enough: he then himself drew off with the unwarlike portion of his host, and made for the place where Nitocris dug the basin for the river, where he did exactly what was done formerly: he turned the Euphrates by a canal into the basin, which was then a marsh; on which, the river sank to such an extent that the natural bed of the stream became fordable. Hereupon the Persians who had been left for the purpose at Babylon by the riverside, entered the stream, which had now sunk so as to reach about midway up a man's thigh, and thus got into the town. (This occurred in the dead of night.) Had the Babylonians been apprised of what Cyrus was about, or had they noticed their danger, they would not have allowed the entrance of the Persians within the city, which was what ruined them utterly, but would have made fast all the street-gates which gave upon the river, and mounting upon the walls along both sides of the stream, would so have caught the enemy as it were in a trap. But, as it was, the Persians came upon them by surprise, and so took the city (Herodotus, lib.i.,c.190, 191).

The Greek historian Xenophon also confirmed the accuracy of Isaiah's prophecy about the "hidden riches" (Kaiah 54:3).

On taking Babylon Cyrus became at once the possessor of its immense wealth. . . . Having assembled his principal officers, he publicly applauded their courage and prudence, their zeal and attachment to his person, and distributed rewards to his whole army.

Babylon's Second Demise

After the collapse of its armies, Babylon became a part of the Persian Empire and lost its independence forever. The conquest of Babylon in 539 B.C. made Cyrus the undisputed ruler of a vast kingdom covering the known world. Cyrus immediately freed the Jewish captives in Babylon, as the Scriptures had prophesied he would, and allowed them to return to Israel.

> Now in the first year of Cyrus king of Persia, that the word of the LORD spoken by the mouth of Jeremiah might be fulfilled, the LORD stirred up the spirit of Cyrus king of Persia, so that he made a proclamation throughout all his kingdom, and also put it in writing, saying. . . . Who is there among you of all His people? May his God be with him! Now let him go up to Jerusalem, which is in Judah, and build the house of the LORD God of Israel (He is God), which is in Jerusalem (Ezra 1:1,3).

Two centuries later, in 330 B.C., the third world empire, the "kingdom of bronze" prophesied by Daniel, arose under the leadership of Alexander the Great to capture the city of Babylon. Alexander planned to rebuild Babylon and make it the central capital of his vast new empire, but his premature death prevented his plans from being carried out. As Daniel had foretold, the Grecian empire was divided between the four horns (Daniel 8:8)—the four generals of Alexander—following the death of their brilliant leader.

Babylon became a capital for the Seleucid dynasty, one of the "four horns," for a period of time after 312 B.C. But later the majority of Babylon's population moved to the new capital, Seleucia. The massive building blocks and materials of Babylon were removed to be used in building projects in surrounding cities. While some of the temples remained as ruins testifying to its former grandeur, Babylon faded into insignificance until it virtually disappeared under the desert sands by the time of the Islamic conquest in the seventh century A.D. The legacy and cultural achievements of Babylon made a deep impression on the ancient world, especially Israel and Greece. Babylon has also left its lasting mark on today's culture in the fields of geometry and astronomy.

The Future of Babylon

After 1,000 years of silence, the ruins of Babylon were discovered beneath the sands of the Iraqi desert during the early years of the nineteenth century. The excavations confirmed many of the historic details recorded in the book of Daniel. Thousands of brick inscriptions were found containing the names of King Nebuchadnezzar and other mighty monarchs of the ancient biblical past. However, the amazing story of Babylon is not yet completed. The prophecies of Isaiah and Revelation reveal that Babylon will be rebuilt in the last days and will become a major economic power. As I documented with photos in my earlier books *Messiah* and *Prince of Darkness*, the Iraqi Department of Antiquities has carried out major restoration work under the instructions of Saddam Hussein. During the last decade they have rebuilt the city at a cost of over $900 million to date.

This rebuilt city of Babylon will become one of the capitals of the future Antichrist, as indicated by one of his prophetic titles, the "king of Babylon" (Isaiah 14:4). Prophecies reveal that this ancient city will once again become a den of satanic witchcraft and will be destroyed by supernatural fire from heaven. The prophet Isaiah foretold the final destruction of this city, which has been the center of satanic opposition to God from the opening pages of Genesis with the Tower of Babel until its final destruction in the future by God during the Great Day of the Lord: "And Babylon, the glory of kingdoms, the beauty of the Chaldeans' pride, will be as when God overthrew Sodom and Gomorrah" (Isaiah 13:19). You'll recall that earlier we learned that deep beneath the foundations of the now-rebuilt city lies an enormous lake of bitumen and oil that bubbles up through the sand during the summer months. It is very possible that God has placed this fuel in a position where He can use it to fulfill His prophecy of Babylon's final judgment and destruction.

CHAPTER 3

The Roman Empire Will Rise Again

The fourth kingdom shall be as strong as iron, inasmuch as iron breaks in pieces and shatters all things; and like iron that crushes, that kingdom will break in pieces and crush all the others" (Daniel 2:40). Daniel's prophetic interpretation of King Nebuchadnezzar's dream was later followed by a vision of his own: "After this I saw in the night visions, and behold, a fourth beast, dreadful and terrible, exceedingly strong. It had huge iron teeth; it was devouring, breaking in pieces, and trampling the residue with its feet" (Daniel 7:7).

The Old Roman Empire

Nebuchadnezzar's dream of the great metallic image (Daniel 2) and Daniel's vision of the four great wild beasts (Daniel 7) are different prophetic views of the same successive series of four world empires that would rule the world until the coming of Jesus Christ as the Messiah King.

Rome, the fourth world empire, began as an insignificant city-state but quickly rose to master all of Italy in the third century before Christ. Rome had an ongoing rivalry with Carthage in North Africa and eventually conquered most of northern Africa as well as the Greek Empire during the second century before Christ. As one nation after another fell before the disciplined and brutal legions of Rome, the Caesars came to rule virtually the whole of the known world by the time of Christ. In 65 B.C. Pompey's legions first conquered Syria. Then he led his armies to Judea and the Holy City. During Pompey's siege of Jerusalem, the Roman army slaughtered 12,000 Jewish soldiers in the final assault on the Temple fortress. The blood ran as high as a man's ankles in the Court of the Israelites as the Jewish defenders fought to the last against the Roman troops trying to enter the Holy Place. Under Caesar Augustus, who ruled Rome during the life of Christ, the Romans expanded their empire to include present-day Romania, Bulgaria, Hungary, and Yugoslavia. By A.D. 58, Roman ensigns flew over the northern nations of Europe, including the territories of England, Switzerland, France, and Belgium.

In all of history no other empire has ever ruled so vast a territory for such an extensive period of time as the iron kingdom of Rome. Unlike other empires that often absorbed the cultures and traditions of its conquered peoples, Rome crushed every nation beneath the feet of its deadly legions, destroying existing cultures and replacing them. Over 1,000 years have passed since the glory days of Roman power, yet even today, the nations of Europe, the Mediterranean, and even North America have forms of government, language, culture, and laws that are clearly derived from ancient Rome.

Prophecy and the Revived Roman Empire

The metallic image in Daniel 2 had "feet and toes, partly of potter's clay and partly of iron, the kingdom shall be divided; yet the strength of the iron shall be in it, just as you saw the iron mixed with ceramic clay" (Daniel 2:41). We read more about this divided kingdom in Daniel 7, where we read about "a fourth beast, dreadful and terrible," "had ten horns." These horns represent the ten nations that would arise from the territory of the ancient Roman Empire (Daniel 7:7). Both of these prophetic visions reveal that the fourth world empire, Rome, will be revived in the last days in the form of ten nations occupying its ancient historic territory. This tenfold division of the Roman Empire describes the embryonic power base of the Antichrist's world government at the close of "the times of the Gentiles" and immediately prior to the second coming of Christ. Scripture tells us about the kingdom that will succeed the revived empire:

> You watched while a stone was cut out without hands, which struck the image on its feet of iron and clay, and broke them in pieces. Then the iron, the clay, the bronze, the silver, and the gold were crushed together, and became like chaff from the summer threshing floors; the wind carried them away so that no trace of them was found. And the stone that struck the image became a great mountain and filled the whole earth. . . . And in the days of these kings the God of heaven will set up a kingdom which shall never be destroyed; and the kingdom shall not be left to other people; it shall break in pieces and consume all these kingdoms, and it shall stand forever. Inasmuch as you saw that the stone was cut out of the mountain without hands, and that it broke in pieces the iron, the bronze, the clay, the silver, and the gold—the great God has made known to the king what will come to pass after this. The dream is certain, and its interpretation is sure (Daniel 2:34-35,44,45).

Ancient Jewish Writers and the Revived Roman Empire

Ancient Jewish sages believed that the "stone . . . cut out without hands" was an emblem of the coming Messiah. The ancient writings of Rabbi Simeon Ben Jochai and Saadiah Gaon declared that "the stone" of Daniel 2:34-45 represents the Messiah referred to in Genesis 49:24, who is called "the Shepherd, Stone of

Israel." The ancient Jewish Midrash *Bemidbar Rabba* (sect. 13. fol. 209.4) also stated that the stone was a symbol of the coming Messiah. The ancient Jewish commentary on Genesis, *Zohar* (fol. 85.4), states, "In the time of the King Messiah, Israel shall be one nation in the earth, and one people to the holy blessed God; as it is written, in the days of these kings shall the God of heaven set up a kingdom."

In yet another writing, *Pirke Eliezer* (c.30.fol. 31.2), we find this interesting statement: "The Ishmaelites shall do fifteen things in the earth in the last days; the last of which mentioned is, they shall erect an edifice in the Temple; at length two brothers shall rise up against them, and in their days shall spring up the branch of the son of David." In the Bible, the word "branch" is used as a title of the Messiah. "Then speak to him, saying, 'Thus says the LORD of hosts, saying: "Behold, the Man whose name is the Branch! From His place He shall branch out, and He shall build the temple of the LORD'"" (Zechariah 6:12).

Two ancient Jewish sages, Jarchi and Aben Ezra, claimed that the stone kingdom represents the kingdom of the Messiah who will rule forever. The great rabbi Rashi wrote that the ten horns represent ten kings who will rule the territory of the Roman Empire before the destruction of the Holy Temple. Another sage, Malbim, stated that these ten horns are ten kingdoms that will develop in the last days as major powers within the outlines of the ancient Roman Empire.

The ancient book of Zohar declared, "In the times of the Messiah, Israel shall be one people to the Lord, and he shall make them one nation in the earth, and they shall rule above and below; as it is written, and in the days of these kings shall the God of heaven set up a kingdom which shall never be destroyed." The Jewish sage Saadiah, in his commentary on Daniel 7:27, wrote, "The kingdom of the King Messiah is an everlasting kingdom, and his government is to generations and generation, and all dominions shall serve and obey him." This eternal kingdom of the Messiah, which will begin with the 1,000-year Millennium on the existing earth, will continue forever on the new earth after it is renewed by heaven's fire.

In Joseph Mede's Works (page 903) he recorded that one of the ancient Jewish sages, Rabbi Abraham Sebah, described the role of Rome and the timing of the last days in his commentary on Genesis 1. He commented, "Rabbi Sebah declared, 'In the course of sixth millennium of the world, Rome will be destroyed and the Jews restored.'"

Ancient Christian Writers and the Revived Roman Empire

Christian writers in the early centuries following Christ believed that the Bible taught that the Roman Empire would be divided into ten kingdoms when it reappeared in its final form at the end of the age. Some writers today challenge that concept. However, there is overwhelming evidence that the Scriptures as well as post-apostolic church writers affirm this doctrinal view.

The *Epistle of Barnabas* (A.D. 110) quoted from the book of Daniel concerning the rise of the ten kingdoms from the former Roman Empire. The writer revealed that these ten confederate nations would join forces at the end of the present age. Irenaeus, an early Christian writer who lived between A.D. 120–202, was a disciple of Polycarp, the companion of the apostle John. Following the same interpretation as the Jewish sages, Irenaeus wrote:

> The great God hath signified by Daniel things to come, and he hath confirmed them by the Son; and Christ is the stone which is cut out without hands, who shall destroy temporal kingdoms, and bring in an everlasting one, which is the resurrection of the just; for he saith, the God of heaven shall raise up a kingdom which shall never be destroyed (*Against Heresies* 1.5.c.26).

Irenaeus also observed that the ten toes are ten kings, among whom the kingdom will be divided. Tertullian, another contemporary of Irenaeus, wrote that "the disintegration and dispersion of the Roman State among the ten kings will produce Antichrist, and then shall be revealed that Wicked One, whom the Lord Jesus shall slay with the breath of His mouth and destroy by the brightness of His manifestation."

Hippolytus, one of the most brilliant of early Christian writers and a follower of Irenaeus, wrote about the ultimate division of the Roman Empire

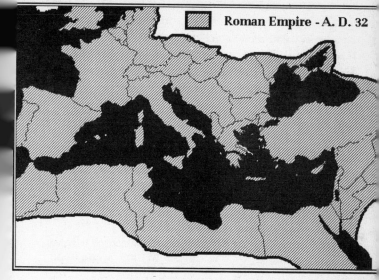

Roman Empire - A. D. 32

The Revived Roman Empire

into ten nations at the end of the age in his *Treatise on Christ and Antichrist* (about A.D. 250): "The legs of iron and the beast dreadful and terrible, expressed the Romans, who hold the sovereignty at present; the toes of the feet which were part clay and part iron, and the ten horns, were emblems of the kingdoms that are yet to rise; the other little horn that grows up among them meant the Antichrist in their midst." Another key theologian, Lactantius (A.D. 310), wrote:

> The Empire will be subdivided, and the powers of government, after being frittered away and shared among many, will

be undermined. Civil discords will then ensue, nor will there be respite from destructive wars, until ten kings arise at once, who will divide the world among themselves to consume rather than govern it.

Bishop Cyril, the head of the Jerusalem church in A.D. 350, quoted from Daniel's vision about the future Roman Empire and its tenfold division, implying that this teaching was widespread throughout the churches. Jerome (A.D. 400) declared that "at the end of the world, when the kingdom of the Romans is to be destroyed, there will be ten kings to divide the Roman world among themselves." Theodoret and others during the fifth century made reference to the revived Roman Empire. These writers were unanimous in their view that, in the future, the Roman Empire would revive as ten confederate nations.

Irenaeus interpreted the "little horn" of Daniel 7:8 to be the future Antichrist. He wrote:

Daniel having respect to the end of the last kingdom, that is, the last ten kings, among whom their kingdom should be divided, upon whom the son of perdition shall come he says; that ten horns shall be upon the beast, and another little horn should rise up in the midst of them; and three horns of the first be rooted out before him.

In another passage, Irenaeus declared,

John the disciple of the Lord in the Revelation hath yet more manifestly signified of the last time, and of those ten kings in it, among whom the empire that now reigns [the Roman Empire] shall be divided; declaring what shall be the ten horns, which were seen by Daniel.

The Christian theologian of the fourth century, Jerome, wrote,

When the Roman Empire is destroyed, there shall be ten kings who shall divide it among them; and an eleventh shall arise, a little king, who shall conquer three of the ten kings; and having slain them, the other seven shall submit their necks to the conqueror (*Observations of Daniel*, pp. 75-89).

A History of Failure

Over the last 2,000 years, many people have tried but all have failed to revive the glorious Roman Empire. In A.D. 800, Charlemagne, also known as Charles the Great, tried to reunite the nations of Europe under his leadership in a Holy Roman Empire. However, despite his valiant efforts, it was doomed to failure. As historians have wryly noted, his conquered nations were neither "Holy," "Roman," nor was it a true "Empire." A thousand years later, in A.D. 1800, the brilliant general Napolean conquered half of Europe but failed to unite these nations into a cohesive empire that would last longer than his own lifetime.

The recurrent longing for a revival of the glories of Rome was also expressed by the noted French novelist Victor Hugo, who wrote, "Let us have the United States of Europe. Let us have a continental federation." In our century both Adolph Hitler and Mussolini tried and failed to recreate the Roman Empire. Although Montesque, the French philosopher, was a proponent of the reunification of Europe, he also noted, "Whenever in the past Europe has been united by force, the unity lasted no longer than the space of a single reign."

A Significant Attempt

In the 1920s and 1930s the fascist party of Mussolini rose to power in Italy under a program that promised to revive the ancient Roman Empire. This initial success by Mussolini inspired Adolph Hitler to seize power in Germany and attempt the creation of his Third Reich, which was yet another attempt to revive the Roman Empire. If anyone doubts that these dictators consciously intended to bring back the Roman Empire they should consider the wording of Mussolini's Fascist Creed. The religious magazine *Dawn* reported in February 1926 that the Bishop of Brescia, as authorized by the consent of the Vatican, read the Fascist Creed to his congregation. This amazing catechism was taught in Mussolini's Balilla, the young boys' Fascist training centers, which were organized throughout the cities of Italy. The Fascist creed consists of twelve articles:

1. I believe in Rome Eternal, the mother of my Fatherland.
2. And in Italy, her first-born;
3. Who was born of her virgin womb by the grace of God;
4. Who suffered under the barbarian invader, was crucified, slain and buried;
5. Who descended into the sepulchre, and rose again from the dead in the nineteenth century;
6. Who ascended to Heaven in her glory in 1918 and 1922 (by the Fascist march on Rome);
7. Who is seated at the right hand of mother Rome;
8. Who will come thence to judge the quick and the dead;
9. I believe in the genius of Mussolini;
10. In our Holy Father Fascism and in the Communion of its martyrs;
11. In the conversion of the Italians; and
12. In the resurrection of the Empire. Amen.

The Italian dictator Mussolini is reported to have said, "Within five years Rome must become the most wonderful city in the world in the eyes of all people of the globe. . . . Vast, well-ordered, powerful as in the days of the first empire of Augustus, Rome must again become the wonder of the whole world."

The great British statesman Winston Churchill wrote a prophetic letter to his cabinet in the darkest days of World War II in October 1942: "Hard as it is to say now, I trust that the European family may act unitedly as one under a Council of Europe. I took forward to a United States of Europe." After the war, Churchill and other key leaders helped formulate various committees in Europe and the United States in an attempt to further the plans to unite Europe. Significantly, the leadership of many of these committees came from the intelligence community. The American Committee on a United Europe was created in 1949. William Donovan, the former director of the Office of Strategic Services (OSS), the predecessor of the CIA, was its chairman and Allen Dulles, director of the CIA, was vice-chairman. Detailed research reveals that the western intelligence agencies financially assisted many of the elitist groups that worked toward creating a world government.[1]

The European Union and the New Roman Empire

Beginning with the 1957 Treaty of Rome, the initial six nations of the current European Union began to move toward their goal of European unity and, ultimately, world government. These six nations were Italy, Germany, France, Belgium, the Netherlands, and Luxembourg. The United Kingdom, Denmark, and Ireland joined in the 1970s. Then Greece voted to enter the European Community in May 1979, making it a ten-nation confederacy. In 1986 Spain and Portugal were added to the group, raising the membership to 12 nations which by this time represented the greatest alliance of economic power and, potentially, the most powerful military force on earth. As we consider the prophetic significance of this union, we need to keep in mind that the ancient Roman Empire also included territories in southeastern Europe, Turkey, the Middle East, and the northern coast of Africa. The two iron legs of the great image in Daniel 2 foretold the division of the original Roman Empire into eastern and western halves. That occurred in A.D. 376. And the ten toes, partly iron and partly clay, suggest that the revived empire may include nations from both the eastern and western portions of the ancient Roman Empire. This would involve the nations of Turkey, Syria, Egypt, Libya, Algeria, and so on.

Now, Daniel's prophecy does not require that every single inch of territory in the original Roman Empire must once again be incorporated into the newly revived empire of the last days. However, it is more than probable that the final Roman Empire will involve ten nations, including countries from both the eastern and western divisions of the ancient Roman empires.

Sweden, Austria, and Finland recently voted to enter the European Union, which as of this writing includes 15 nations. It is possible that the union will grow to more than 25 nations. However, we can already see a trend toward the creation of a three-tier system. Edouard Balladur, the prime minister of France, announced the possibility of a three-tier Europe in a speech given on August 30, 1994. The inner core of this new European Union will be nations "committed to full-blooded monetary, military and social union." The Germans have openly called for the creation of such a tiered super-state structure in their document *Reflections on European Policy*. Germany and France have openly backed the creation of a core of member states that want to form an inner ring of fully integrated nations. These "inner states" are now determined to press ahead at full speed with European integration whether or not their other partners agree. Germany, France, Belgium, the Netherlands, and Luxembourg currently form the inner ring of nations that are committed to relinquishing their sovereignty. Britain, Italy, and Spain form a second group, an outer ring of less committed nations, that wish to benefit economically but still retain some measure of their sovereignty. The third group, the outermost ring of countries at the periphery of the continent, includes Denmark, Greece, Portugal, Ireland, and the nations of eastern Europe that are now negotiating to join the Union. These nations want the economic benefits of the union with no surrender of their sovereignty.

The inner ring of five nations, who all signed the Treaty of Rome in 1957, now want to rapidly unite their countries into a transnational superstate with one currency, one army, one parliament, and one foreign policy. The *European* newspaper reported on September 8, 1994, a significant statement by Balladur, the French prime minister: "A small number of EU member states must build an organization better structured, monetarily as well as militarily. Later we'll need to work to turn these three circles into two, perhaps, much later into a single one."

The Antichrist and the
New Roman Empire

When the inner circle of five nations expands to include ten states, the white horseman of the Apocalypse (as prophesied by the apostle John in Revelation 6:2) will arise to seize power over this alliance. This horseman, the Antichrist, will make a seven-year treaty with Israel as part of his strategy to "destroy the mighty, and also the holy people" (Daniel 8:24). Daniel's prophecy that "the people of the prince who is to come shall destroy the city and the sanctuary" (Daniel 9:26) spoke of two distinct destructions of Jerusalem within a single prophecy. The first destruction occurred in A.D. 70 when the Roman Empire and its armies burned Jerusalem and destroyed the Temple. The second destruction will be an attack on Jerusalem at the end of the seven-year treaty in the last days. Daniel's statement "the people of the prince who is to come" reveals that the future prince will come out of the *revived* Roman Empire. This future Roman emperor will rule the ten-nation European confederacy of the last days.

In Daniel 8:23,24, the prophet further describes the Antichrist: "In the latter time of their kingdom, when the transgressors have reached their fullness, a king shall arise, having fierce features, who understands sinister schemes. His power shall be might, but not by his own power." In other words, this Antichrist with "fierce features" will receive supernatural power from Satan so he can achieve spectacular results in politics, economics, and war.

During the terrible rebellion of the last days this satanically possessed tyrant will "prosper and thrive; he shall destroy the mighty, and also the holy people" (Daniel 8:24). Initially, this coming world leader will produce economic prosperity to gain favor in his rapid rise to power. His brilliant economic policies will produce massive wealth so that he "shall cause deceit to prosper under his hand" (verse 25). When the nations are enjoying their peace and prosperity, the Roman Antichrist "shall destroy many in their prosperity" (or "peace" according to the authorized King James Version).

The Antichrist's initial success will motivate him to "magnify himself in his heart" and "even rise against the Prince of princes" (Daniel 9:25). As John warns in the book of Revelation, the white horseman of the Apocalypse, the Antichrist, will initially conquer many nations by means of false peace treaties. Then he will seek to expand his power worldwide through military conquest, which is symbolized by the second horseman of the Apocalypse, the red horseman of war. In the same manner as the previous antichrists throughout history, this last Antichrist will hate the Jewish people because they bear God's holy name and remain His chosen people.

Despite the Antichrist's satanic powers, he will meet his doom when he battles with Jesus Christ and the armies of heaven at Armageddon. He will be captured, and the Lord will cast both the Antichrist and the False Prophet into the lake of fire forever (Revelation 19:20).

CHAPTER 4

Daniel's Vision of the 70 Weeks

The Jewish historian Josephus declared that Daniel was one of the greatest of the prophets since he not only predicted future events accurately but he also determined the time when these prophecies would come to pass. And through the centuries, Jewish sages have believed that only two of the great men in the Bible were given precise information about the time of the end: Daniel and Jacob. They have claimed that "there are two men to whom the end was revealed, and afterwards it was hidden from them" (*Bereshit Rabba*, sect. 93. fol. 84.4). It is fascinating to note that Rabbi Mehumiah, who lived some 50 years before the time of Jesus Christ, concluded, based on Daniel's prophecy, that the coming of the Messiah could not be deferred longer than 50 years (apud Grotium, *de Ver. Relig. Christ.* 1.5. sect. 14).

The Final Seven Years

The prophecy of Daniel 9:27 tells us about the final
seven years of the Antichrist's rule: "Then he shall
confirm a covenant with many for one week; but in
the middle of the week He shall bring an end to sacrifice and offering. And on the wing of abominations
shall be one who makes desolate, even until the consummation, which is determined, is poured out on
the desolate." The preceding verse, Daniel 9:26,
described the identity of the one who will make a
seven-year "covenant" or treaty with the "many,"
the Jews who have returned from exile to establish
the state of Israel. The verse describes the Antichrist
and his origin as follows: "After the sixty-two weeks
Messiah shall be cut off, but not for Himself; and
the people of the prince who is to come shall destroy
the city and the sanctuary. The end of it shall be with
a flood, and till the end of the war desolations are
determined."

Daniel's curious expression "the people of the
prince who is to come" indicates clearly that the
Antichrist, "the prince who is to come," will come
out of and lead the "people . . . [who] shall destroy
the city and the sanctuary." History reveals that it
was the legions of the Roman Empire that destroyed
"the city," Jerusalem, and "the sanctuary," the Temple,
in A.D. 70. Therefore, the Antichrist, "the prince,"
must rise out of the territories and nations of the
ancient Roman Empire to lead its armies in a relentless campaign to conquer the nations of the whole
earth in the last days.

The great Jewish commentator Shlomo ben Yitzchk, known as "Rashi," commented on the phrase "but his end shall come like a flood" in these words: "The end of the Romans who destroyed Jerusalem will be total destruction through the promised Messianic King." He also said the phrase "the people of the prince who comes" refers to "the legions of Vespasian and Titus." Commenting on the prophesies about Jerusalem's continuous history of invasion and burning, Rashi wrote around A.D. 1100 that the phrase "and till the end of the war desolation are determined" means, "Till after the final wars waged by the Messianic King and the war of Gog and Magog, desolations are decreed for the city." He interpreted the passage in Daniel 9:27, "He shall confirm a covenant with many for one week," as follows: "The Roman Emperor will make a firm covenant with the Jewish nation for seven years. The 'great ones' [the many] means the Jewish rulers, rather than its more common usage of 'many.'" The commentary of *Daniel* in the *Art Scroll Tanach Series* said this about the prophecy in Daniel 9:24-27: "According to Ibn Ezra's interpretation of the seventy weeks, this last week of the seventy weeks is not included in the sixty-two weeks mentioned before. . . . This week is set apart."

It is fascinating to note that the modern Jewish commentary on the prophecies of Daniel, the *Art Scroll Tanach Series* on Daniel produced by Mesorah Publications, Ltd., interprets these prophecies of Daniel to teach that this false messiah will stop the "daily sacrifice" in the Temple. In regard to the teaching of the Jewish rabbi Rashi and Metzudos on Daniel 8:12-13, it states, "The daily sacrifice is destined to be taken away for a specific period of time." Rashi also said, "An idol, which is mute as a rock, will replace the daily sacrifice in the Temple." This Jewish interpretation is all the more fascinating when we compare it with the prophecy found in the book of Revelation that the false prophet will create an idol or statue of the Antichrist and demand that all men worship the idol or die.

Jewish commentaries, including the Seder Olam (ch. 28) and Ibn Ezra's *Commentary on Daniel, Perush HaKatzer* (A.D. 1150) interpret Daniel's words "seventy weeks" to mean 490 years, a period of 70 sevens (weeks) of years. In an astonishing admission, the commentary on the prophecy of Daniel 9:24-27 in the *Art Scroll Tanach Series* reveals that the Jewish writing *Mayenei HaYeshuah* declares that "if the Jews had repented during this period [the 490 years] the Messianic king would have come at its termination." The great Jewish sage Moses Maimonides agreed, saying this in his observations on Leviticus 26:16: "Had the Jews not sinned again during this period, the complete redemption would have occurred upon its completion." These significant comments on Daniel's prophecy reveal the Jewish commentators' understanding that the prophet had predicted that the Messiah would be revealed at the very time Jesus Christ was born in Bethlehem.

Ancient Jewish writings also remark that "the Holy Ark, the altars and the holy vessels will be revealed through the Messianic king." The sages acknowledge that "the Ark was not present in the second Temple" and the prophecy that the Messiah will "anoint the Holy of Holies" (Daniel 9:24) "refers to the Third Temple, which in contradistinction to the Second Temple, will be anointed." The sages (*Yoma* 21b) tell us that "the Second Temple, which was not anointed (*Tosefta Sotan* 13:2), lacked five things, among them the Shechinah Glory, the evident Presence of the Living God. But the Third Temple will be anointed."

Daniel's Vision of the Future

Daniel's vision of the 70 weeks contains a brief outline of the future history of the world:

Seventy weeks [490 years] are determined for your people and for your holy city, to finish the transgression, to make an end of sins, to make reconciliation for iniquity, to bring in everlasting righteousness, to seal up vision and prophecy, and to anoint the Most Holy.

Know therefore and understand, that from the going forth of the command to restore and build Jerusalem until Messiah the Prince, there shall be seven weeks and sixty-two weeks; the streets shall be built again, and the wall, even in troublesome times.

And after the sixty-two weeks Messiah shall be cut off, but not for Himself; and the people of the prince who is to come shall destroy the city and the sanctuary. The end of it shall be with a flood, and till the end of the war desolations are determined. Then he shall confirm a covenant with many for one week; but in the middle of the week He shall bring an end to sacrifice and offering (Daniel 9:24-27).

After the Babylonian invasion and occupation in Jerusalem in 606 B.C., the prophet Jeremiah declared to the Jewish people that "this whole land shall be a desolation and an astonishment, and these nations shall serve the king of Babylon seventy years" (Jeremiah 25:11). Daniel read Jeremiah's prediction in 538 B.C. and knew that the 70 years of the captivity in Babylon would end two years later in 536 B.C. He began to pray and ask God to show him the future of the Jewish people.

While Daniel was prayerfully interceding on behalf of his people and the Holy City, God sent His angel Gabriel to give Daniel "skill and understanding" about the future course of world history. As a result of this prayer, Daniel received one of the most amazing visions ever given to man. This vision of the 70 weeks foretold to the precise day centuries later when Israel would reject and "cut off" their promised Messiah. Daniel's vision also prophesied about the appearance of the Roman Antichrist who, at the end of the age, would make a seven-year treaty with Israel. Daniel's vision was an unusual biblical prophecy because the time elements were given so precisely.

An important but often ignored factor in the chronology of prophecy is that of the proper length of the prophetic year. The Jewish year, during biblical times, was lunar-solar and had only 360 days. The solar year of 365.25 days, which we currently use, was unknown to the nations of the Old Testament. According to the articles on chronology in the *Encyclopaedia Britannica* and *Smith's Bible Dictionary*, Abraham continued to use the 360-day year of his original Chaldean homeland when he migrated to Canaan. The biblical record of Noah's flood in the book of Genesis confirms that a 30-day month was in use. The Genesis account recorded that the interval between the seventeenth day of the second month to the seventeenth day of the seventh month was precisely 150 days, which tells us that the five months contained exactly 30 days each. Therefore, the Jewish year in Bible times contained 12 months of 30 days, totalling 360 days.

According to the *Encyclopaedia Britannica*, Sir Isaac Newton related that "all nations, before the just length of the solar year was known, reckoned months by the course of the moon, and years by the return of winter and summer, spring and autumn; and in making calendars for their festivals, they reckoned thirty days to a lunar month, and twelve lunar months to a year, taking the nearest round numbers, whence came the division of the ecliptic into 360 degrees."

Therefore, if we wish to understand the precise times involved in the fulfillment of prophecy, we need to base our calculations on the lunar-solar year of 360 days that the prophets themselves used. In the book of Revelation, John's vision of the Great Tribulation described the last three-and-one-half years as being exactly 1260 days (Revelation 12:6), "a time and times and half a time" (a time = a year of 360 days; verse 14), and "forty-two months" of 30 days each (13:5). These references confirm that in Bible times, both historically and prophetically, a year contained precisely 360 days.

Daniel's prophecy of the 70 weeks began with these words: "From the going forth of the command to restore and build Jerusalem until Messiah the Prince, there shall be seven weeks [sevens], and sixty-two weeks [sevens]" (Daniel 9:25). The prophecy was tragically fulfilled to the precise day 483 years after it commenced. This "command to restore and build the walls of Jerusalem" was issued by the Persian King Artaxerxes Longimanus "in the month of Nisan, in the twentieth year" of his reign (Nehemiah 2:1). According to the Talmud (a collection of ancient Jewish religious writing and law), "The first day of the month of Nisan is the New Year for the computation of the reign of kings and for festivals." In other words, when no other date is given, we assume the event occurred on the first day of Nisan. The Royal Observatory in Greenwich, the United Kingdom, has calculated that the first of Nisan in the twentieth year of the reign of King Artaxerxes occurred on March 14, 445 B.C.

Daniel's prophecy indicated that the period "from the going forth from the command to restore and build Jerusalem," given on March 14, 445 B.C., a period

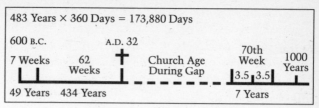

Daniel's Vision of the 70 Weeks

of seven weeks (7 × 7 = 49 years) and a period of an additional sixty-two weeks (62 × 7 = 434 years), totalled 69 weeks of years equalling 483 biblical years (69 × 7 years = 483 biblical years). This period of 69 weeks of years, or 483 biblical years, contains precisely 173,880 days (483 × 360 days = 173,880 days). According to Daniel's prophecy, at the end of the 69 weeks (483 years or 173,880 days), the "Messiah shall be cut off." A careful calculation reveals that a period of precisely 173,880 days or 483 biblical years from the beginning point of March 14, 445 B.C. ended precisely to the day on Palm Sunday, the tenth day of the Jewish month Nisan, or April 6, A.D. 32, in fulfillment of Daniel's prophecy. On the exact day foretold centuries earlier, Jesus Christ entered Jerusalem through the Eastern Gate and presented Himself to Israel as their promised Messiah. (For further information regarding this calculation, see "The date of Christ's ministry and crucifixion" in the Appendix to my book *Armageddon* [Toronto, Canada: Frontier Research Publications, Inc. 1988].)

To sum up these calculations, Daniel's vision spoke of a total of 70 "sevens" or 70 "weeks" of years, equalling 490 years. This period of time, spanning from the command to rebuild the walls of Jerusalem (March 14, 445 B.C.) until the Messiah was to be "cut off" (April 6, A.D. 32, the tenth of Nisan) is seven "sevens" plus 62 "sevens," equalling a total of 69 "weeks of years" (173,880 days). This prophecy was fulfilled to the exact day. (Note: In calculating the duration in years between any date in B.C.—Before Christ, to any date in A.D.— *Anno Domini*, "in the year of our Lord," one year must always be omitted. The time elapsed between the Passover in 1 B.C. and the next Passover in A.D. 1 was only one year, not two years. There was no such year as Zero B.C.). To simplify this even further, the period from March 14, 445 B.C. to March 14, A.D. 32 adds up to 476 years of 365 days each—173,740 days. Add the 24 days from March 14, A.D. 32 until April 6, A.D. 32. Then add the 116 leap days which occurred during that 476-year period. Add those figures together (173,740 + 24 + 116 = 173,880), and you will get the same total of 173,880 days. The first 69 "weeks" of Daniel's vision of the 70 weeks ended with the cutting off of the Messiah and were fulfilled to the precise day. However, the seventieth "week" of Daniel's prophecy, the final seven years of this age, remains to be fulfilled in our generation. In light of the incredible accuracy of the first part of Daniel's prophecy, we can be confident that the remaining "week" of seven years, the Tribulation period occupying the seventieth week of years, will be fulfilled just as precisely.

The Seventieth Week—The Tribulation

The final seven-year "week" of Daniel 9:27 will culminate with the terror of the tyranny of Antichrist
and the Tribulation period with the Mark of the
Beast system. When Israel rejected Jesus Christ as
their promised Messiah on Palm Sunday, April 6,
A.D. 32, concluding Daniel's sixty-ninth week, God's
prophetic clock stopped ticking. As a consequence of
Israel's rejection of their Messiah, the Lord postponed Israel's prophesied kingdom for what has now
been almost 2,000 years. At the beginning of this interval between Daniel's sixty-ninth week and the
final seventieth week at the end of this age, the Lord
created a church composed of both Jews and Gentiles
from all nations. His plan for the church is that its
members witness to the world about His offer of salvation to any who will accept Jesus Christ as their
personal Lord and Savior. Also, Daniel's prophecy
foretold that war and desolations would continue
during this interval until the end of this age.

Daniel's prophecy declared that "seventy weeks"
were decreed for "your people," the Jews (Daniel
9:24). The first 69 weeks of years focused exclusively upon God's dealing with "your people"—the
Jewish people. In the seventieth week, God's focus
will return to dealing with Israel. Thus the Lord
will never leave this world without a witness. Before His death, Christ promised that "this gospel of
the kingdom will be preached in all the world as a
witness to all the nations, and then the end will
come" (Matthew 24:14). This "gospel of the kingdom"

will resemble the message that both John the Baptist and Jesus preached during their years of ministry on earth. John the Baptist preached the message, "Repent, for the kingdom of heaven is at hand! For this is he who was spoken of by the prophet Isaiah, saying, 'the voice of one crying in the wilderness: "Prepare the way of the Lord, make His paths straight" (Matthew 3:2,3). Jesus also taught this same message: "From that time Jesus began to preach and to say, 'Repent: for the kingdom of heaven is at hand'" (Matthew 4:17).

The Abomination of Desolation

In Matthew 24:15 Jesus warned, "When you see the 'abomination of desolation,' spoken of by Daniel the prophet, standing in the holy place (whoever reads, let him understand), then let those who are in Judea flee to the mountains." In this prophecy Christ confirmed Daniel's prediction that the Antichrist will defile the rebuilt Temple during the last days. He will do this by committing an act of supreme spiritual defiance against heaven—an act that the Lord called the "abomination of desolation." Evidently the Antichrist will spiritually defile the Holy of Holies of the future Temple in Jerusalem by committing some act that will express his contempt and blasphemy against Almighty God. Jesus declared that during this event the Antichrist will be "standing in the holy place." The apostle Paul, in 2 Thessalonians 2:3-4, described this event: "The man of sin is revealed, the son of perdition, who opposes and exalts himself above all that is called God or that is worshiped, so that he sits as God in the temple of God, showing himself that he is God."

This rebellion expressed by the Antichrist will not be anything new. From that point in the dateless past when Satan first rebelled against God he has continued in his sinful pride in an attempt to usurp God's position in heaven. The prophet Ezekiel described the first appearance of sin in the universe in his description of Satan's original rebellion. Addressing Satan as "the prince of Tyre," the Lord declared, "Son of man, say to the prince of Tyre, 'Thus says Lord GOD: "Because your heart is lifted up, and you say, 'I am a god, I sit in the seat of gods, in the midst of the seas,' yet you are a man, and not a god, though you set your heart as the heart of god" (Ezekiel 28:2). Then in verses 8 through 10, God describes the terrible punishment that awaits Satan in his final judgment.

The Mistaken Calculation

Over the years, many people have asked why the Jewish calendar says we are 5,751 years from the creation of Adam while it appears from the Christian calendar that we are approaching the year 6000 from Adam. The reason for the difference is because of two significant errors that the ancient Jewish sages committed in their calculations. Part of the difference can be accounted for by an ancient copyist error from the list of ages of the patriarchs found in Greek Septuagint text of Genesis 5. The other part of the problem is

found in the Jewish sages' interpretation of Daniel's
vision of the 70 weeks.

One of the curious features of Jewish chronology
involves the Jewish sages' traditional interpretation
of Daniel's 70 weeks, which concluded that there
were only 490 years between the time the first
Temple was destroyed by Babylon and the second
Temple was burned by the Roman armies of General
Titus. A careful analysis, however, reveals that the
Babylonians burned the first Temple on the ninth day
of Av (August) in 587 B.C., while the Roman armies
destroyed the second Temple on the very same day,
the ninth day of Av, in A.D. 70, exactly 656 years to
the day later. Remember: There is only one year
between ninth Av, 1 B.C. and ninth Av, A.D. 1 since
there is no year Zero. The problem with the Jewish
sages' calculation that there were only 490 years
between these two events leaves us with 166 years
unaccounted for.

Another major error occurred when the sages were
misled by a copyist's textual error in the Septuagint
Greek translation of the Bible in Genesis 5, which re-
counts the ages of the descendants of Adam. The Septuagint text, which was almost universally accepted
by the ancient Jewish sages, differs from the Hebrew
text in the years given for the duration of the lifetimes
of a number of the descendants of Adam. When we
combine the number of incorrect years introduced in
the Septuagint chronology to the 166-year error from
the sages' misunderstanding of Daniel 9:24-27, we can

account for the Jewish calendar's mistaken calculation that (in 1995) it should be the Jewish year 5751.

Early Church Writings on the Seventieth Week

Some modern scholars have attacked the futurist interpretation of prophecy by claiming that until the
last few centuries, no one had ever interpreted
Daniel's prophecy as pointing to a future Antichrist
and seven-year Tribulation period. These scholars
have claimed that no one ever wrote about this "gap"
or parenthesis of time encompassing the church age of
grace between the sixty-ninth and the seventieth
week of Daniel 9:24-27 until quite recently. However,
these scholars are wrong. Early church writers often
wrote about the prophetic portions of Scripture. A
number of early-church commentaries clearly reveal
that the writers understood that Daniel's vision of the
seventieth week would not be fulfilled until the last
seven years of this age leading up to the Battle of Armageddon. In *The Epistle of Barnabas*, written within
100 years of Christ's resurrection, we find a clear
statement that the seventieth week of Daniel will be
fulfilled only when the Jews return to rebuild their
Temple, which was in ruins at the time that Barnabas
wrote his letter. The passage read, "And it shall come
to pass, when the week is being accomplished, the
temple of God shall be built gloriously in the name of
the Lord" (*The Epistle of Barnabas* 16:24).

Another early writer was Ephraem the Syrian, who was a major theologian and poet in the fourth century A.D. He had a significant influence in the early church and his works are still read to this day in the Greek Orthodox Church. (In a later chapter that deals with the pre-tribulation rapture, we will examine my discovery of Ephraem's clear teaching of the pre-tribulation rapture.) One of Ephraem's books, entitled *The Cave of Treasures*, written in A.D. 370, included a section on the genealogy of Christ. Ephraem taught that the sixty-ninth week of Daniel 9:24-27 ended at the rejection and crucifixion of Jesus the Messiah. He wrote, "The Jews have no longer among them a king, or a priest, or a prophet, or a Passover, even as Daniel prophesied concerning them, saying 'After two and sixty weeks Christ shall be slain, and the city of holiness shall be laid waste until the completion of thing decreed' (Daniel 9:26). That is to say, for ever and ever" (*The Cave of Treasures*, p. 235).

In a later section of his book dealing with the future war of Gog and Magog, Ephraem wrote about the remaining (seventieth) week of Daniel as follows:

At the end of the world and at the final consummation.... Suddenly the gates of the north shall be opened.... They will destroy the earth, and there will be none able to stand before them. After one week of that sore affliction [Tribulation], they will all be destroyed in the plain of Joppa.... Then will the son of perdition appear, of the seed and of the tribe of Dan.... He will go into Jerusalem and will sit upon a throne in the

Temple saying, 'I am the Christ,' and he will be borne aloft by legions of devils like a king and a lawgiver, naming himself god. . . . The time of the error of the Antichrist will last two years and a half, but others say three years and six months.

In that passage Ephraem reveals that commentators from the fourth century of the Christian era understood that the seventieth week of Daniel would be fulfilled when a Jewish Antichrist would defile a rebuilt Temple during the last seven years of this age. Although there are some puzzling elements in Ephraem's fragmented description of the prophetic events of the last days, it is clear that he believed that the seventieth week would be fulfilled in the final days of the age, at which time the Antichrist would appear. Furthermore, it is fascinating to note that Ephraem also taught that Ezekiel's prophecy of the war of Gog and Magog would occur before the seven-year Tribulation period. This is also the position I have arrived at after many years of study.

With all that in mind, let's now explore the incredible developments that are leading us inexorably toward the coming world government prophesied to rule the world in the last days.

PART 2

Setting the Stage for the Final World Empire

CHAPTER 5

The New
World Order

In his book *Surviving the Future*, historian Arnold Toynbee wrote these stunning words:

> We are approaching the point at which the only effective scale for operations of any importance will be the global scale. The local states ought to be deprived of their sovereignty and subordinated to the sovereignty of a global world government. I think the world state will still need an armed police [and the] world government will have to command sufficient force to be able to impose peace.... The people of each local sovereign state will have to renounce their state's sovereignty and subordinate it to the paramount sovereignty of a literally worldwide world government.... I want to see a world government established.[1]

Today, Toynbee's opinions are no longer revolutionary. His rejection of the nation state is now shared by the financial and political elites who are planning to create a new world government. In the distant past, all the peoples on earth lived as one common community. However, the wicked men of that day, in their sinful pride and rebellion against their Creator, joined together to create an astonishing engineering feat—the Tower of Babel in ancient Mesopotamia. The Lord intervened and miraculously confused their language, which prevented them from communicating or understanding one another. God destroyed their project by supernaturally creating a multitude of new languages and forcing the population to separate into separate language groupings that have continued for thousands of years.

Through God's direct intervention at the Tower of Babel, ethnic groupings and nation-states were created. The nation-state is part of God's plan to preserve the ethnic, language, and cultural diversity of mankind forever. The prophecy of Revelation tells us that multiple nations will still continue to exist on the New Earth after the completion of the Millennium: "The nations of those who are saved shall walk in its light, and the kings of the earth bring their glory and honor into it" (Revelation 21:24).

Now, after thousands of years of national independence, elite power groups are planning for a New World Order that will unite all the nations on earth into a one-world government. This will effectively destroy the sovereignty of individual countries.

Why would anyone want to create a one-world government? The horrors of World War I and the resulting deaths of tens of millions of citizens and soldiers shocked political leaders of Europe and America. After the guns were finally silenced, key business, financial, intellectual, and political leaders formed a number of semi-secret organizations to lay the foundation for a future one-world government that would prevent another devastating world war. These elite leaders also saw such an arrangement as a tremendous opportunity to assure themselves and their associates of untold power and wealth.

The Organizations Behind the Scenes

Beginning at the turn of the century the secret powers that truly controlled world events from behind the scenes began to create organizations that would enable them to dominate future world events and ultimately produce the one-world government they desired. Their secret polls and in-depth studies revealed that very few citizens were willing to surrender the sovereignty of their country and constitution to the foreign domination that is inherent in a world government. Consequently, these men decided to form the secret legal foundation and institutions needed for a future world government. They knew that the only way to achieve their goal was to organize surreptitiously and impose their totalitarian world government on the world during a future moment of crisis.

Although the individuals who started these groups were already immensely wealthy and powerful, their insatiable greed and desire to dominate other free men motivated them to join forces to create a socialistic world government that would allow them to rule forever. The documented evidence of the concerted action of these groups over the last seven decades provides overwhelming proof that we are engaged in a spiritual, economic, and political life-and-death struggle for the control of the earth and the destiny of the souls of men. Ancient prophets warned that, in the last days, the nations would join together in federation to create a government that will ultimately be dominated by the most terrifying dictator the world has ever seen. However, the Bible also promises that those who trust in the Lord will be victorious. In addition, the prophecies declare that this tyrant, the Antichrist, will rule for only seven terrifying years. After that, his end will come with his total defeat and destruction at the hands of the returning Messiah Jesus Christ.

America, with its powerful economy and military forces, has been a key target for the people who are planning the future world government. Their plans cannot succeed unless America is weakened to the point where she can be forced to relinquish her freedom and sovereignty. The first step was taken in 1913 with the creation of the U.S. Federal Reserve Banking System. This system created, for the first time, a central bank in America. A central bank, a well-known feature of European power structures for centuries, was repugnant to America's founding fathers and statesmen. The financial elite knew that they had little public support for such an idea. Therefore, their plan to create a central bank that would control U.S. currency was implemented by stealth while Congress was recessing for Christmas in 1913. In one fell swoop, control of the U.S. economy and monetary system was removed from Congress, which was given this power by the Constitution. From that moment on, the economy was controlled by secret bankers and financiers as shareholders that "own" the private banking system, the Federal Reserve System. Amazingly, this incredibly powerful private institution has never been audited in its 82-year history.

The next step, in 1920, after the conclusion of World War I, was the creation of the League of Nations. This was the first serious attempt to establish a future world government. Although Colonel Edward House, Woodrow Wilson's political advisor, did everything possible to lure America into joining the Geneva-based League of Nations, the U.S. Senate recognized the dangers of foreign entanglement and domination. The Senate refused to ratify America's membership and kept the U.S. out of the international system until the end of World War II. This rejection by the Senate postponed the globalist agenda for several decades.

The Council of Foreign Relations

On May 30, 1919, several delegates to the Paris Peace Conference met at the Hotel Majestic in Paris to plan the steps that would ultimately lead to a world government. Officially their purpose was to create an international group of private business and financial leaders who would advise their respective governments on economic policy and international relations.

The United States was represented by Colonel House, who gathered a group of top financial and multinational interest in 1921 to create the Council of Foreign Relations (CFR). In addition, parallel organizations were established in other countries to bring these nations into line with the growing plans for a world government. In London, England, similar elite formed the Royal Institute of International Affairs (Chatham House Group), while the French representatives created the Centre d'Etudes de Politicque Etrangere in Paris. The group in Hamburg, Germany created the Institut fur Auswartige Politik to coordinate European interest with the American CFR.

Beginning with only 273 members in 1921, the "old boy network" of the CFR consolidated their influence in key areas to direct government policy. During the Great Depression of the 1930s members of the council comprised the backbone of the Roosevelt administration and created the New Deal legislation that socialized major aspects of the American economy. During World War II, some council members rose to prominent positions of power within the Roosevelt administration until they achieved total control of the government agenda. The United Nations was virtually created by the Council of Foreign Relations. Within the 14 member United Nations U.S. planning committee, ten people were members of the CFR, including Alger Hiss, who was later revealed to be a Soviet spy. Hiss became the secretary-general of the United Nations founding conference. Fifty-seven of the U.S. delegates to the conference that founded the United

Nations were members of the CFR. Interestingly, Rockefeller, another key CFR member, gave the United Nations a tract of land valued at over $8.5 million for its headquarters in New York.

At the time of his writing, the chairman of the council is Peter Peterson and the president is Leslie Gelb. The CFR group, headquartered in New York, has grown to include 2,700 members who "advise" the U.S. president and his administration regarding government policy. The CFR admits that one of its goals is to replace the U.S. Constitution with a new "model" constitution.[2] Their proposed constitution would allow the president to dismiss Congress at any time and rule as a dictator by executive order. The proposed CFR constitution has no bill of rights, no right for citizens to bear arms, and no right to freedom of religion or freedom of assembly. Another stated goal of the CFR is to merge the United States of America with other nations into a one-world government.

The True Secret Government   It is not an exaggeration to state that the membership of this elite group has formed the true secret government of the United States since 1945. Their membership includes the business, financial, intellectual, military, and political elite of the country, including the leadership of both the Republican and Democratic parties. During the 1992 presidential election, Americans were allowed to choose whichever flavor of president the Council on Foreign Relations presented to them. In the *Council of Foreign Relations*

Annual Report for 1993, chairman Peter Peterson proudly pointed out that all three of the presidential candidates, George Bush, Bill Clinton, and Ross Perot, were members of the Council on Foreign Relations. Chairman Peterson also congratulated his membership on the fact that every single member of President Clinton's cabinet and most of the subcabinet members also belonged to their elite group. When George Bush was president, virtually all of his cabinet members were also drawn from the ranks of the CFR. Oftentimes CFR members will resign from the council during the years they serve in cabinet positions; however, they still attend council meetings and resume their official membership when they return to private life.

I am not suggesting that there is no difference between the Bush and Clinton administrations. In any group of almost 3,000 members, such as the CFR, there will be a range of political opinion that includes both a liberal and a conservative wing. However, regardless of whether the Democrats or the Republicans control the White House or Congress, members of the Council on Foreign Relations will form the real government of the United States. Consider, for example the recent General Agreement on Trade and Tariffs (GATT) legislation passed in a special December session by Congress after many of the Democrats lost their seats in the November 1994 election. This agreement was crafted and wholeheartedly supported by the CFR. Despite the voters' overwhelming repudiation of the philosophy behind this New World Order legislation, the leadership of Congress responded to the wishes of their real bosses, the secret financial elite who will provide huge financial and social benefits to compliant members of Congress once they leave office. The new Republican Speaker of the House, Newt Gingrich, a longtime member of the Council on Foreign Relations, did his duty and joined with Bob Dole and the defeated Democrats to pass this legislation that moves us a huge step closer to the coming world government.

To get a better idea of what is happening here, consider this hypothetical situation: A number of large churches in North America have 2,000 to 3,000 members. Imagine for a moment that the press discovered that the president and everyone in his cabinet were secretly members of the same large church. Furthermore, imagine that researchers discovered that virtually all of the presidents and cabinet members of both the Republican and Democratic administrations during the last 40 years had also been secret members of this same large church. Then imagine that almost every key military, academic, business, and media leader in America during this period also belonged to this one church. Can you imagine the response of the media and America's citizens? They would be outraged to find that one small closed group of people had a total lock on the government of their so-called democracy. Yet this is precisely the situation that prevails in the United States and most other major countries of Western Europe today.

Of course, the members of the CFR do not belong to a single church. They are individuals who, motivated by their desire for power and money, are dedicated to advancing their own secret agenda to bring America into a one-world government despite the fact that their fellow citizens have no such desire.

According to the official membership list published by the council in their annual reports, the following key leaders during the last four decades were all CFR members: Arthur Burns, Henry Cabot Lodge, Henry Kissinger, W. Averell Harriman, Dean Rusk, Robert McNamara (president of the World Bank), Anthony M. Solomon (the U.S. Treasury), James Baker (Secretary of State), Paul Volcker (Federal Reserve), George Shultz, Casper Weinberger, William Casey (CIA), Alan Greenspan (Federal Reserve chairman), Michael Blumenthal (U.S. Treasury), John D. Rockefeller IV, General Walter Bedell Smith, Alexander Haig, William Simon, Cyrus Vance, Andrew Young, William D. Ruckelshaus, Brent Scowcroft, and Rodman Rockefeller. In addition, presidents Richard Nixon, Jimmy Carter, George Bush, and Bill Clinton have been or are on the membership list. Both Newt Gingrich and General Colin Powell are also members of the council.

The Demand for Total Secrecy   The CFR demands that their members maintain total secrecy regarding the views and opinions expressed during their private council meetings and conferences.

Article II of the CFR by-laws says this:

It is an express condition of membership in the Council, to which condition every member accedes by virtue of his or her membership, that members will observe such rules and regulations as may be prescribed from time to time by the Board of Directors concerning the conduct of Council meetings or the attribution of statements made therein, and that any disclosure, publication, or other action by a member in contravention thereof may be regarded by the Board of Directors in its sole discretion as ground for termination or suspension of membership pursuant to Article I of the By-Laws.[3]

On page 182 of the CFR's 1990 annual report, we read that . . .

it would not be in compliance with the organization's non-attribution rule for a meeting participant (i) to publish a speaker's statement in attributed form in a newspaper; (ii) to repeat it on television or radio, or on a speaker's platform, or in a classroom; or (iii) to go beyond a memo of limited circulation, by distributing the attributed statement in a company or government agency newsletter. . . . A meeting participant is forbidden knowingly to transmit the attributed statement to a newspaper reporter or other such person who is likely to publish it in a public medium. The essence of the Rule . . . is simple enough: participants in Council meetings should not pass along an attributed statement in circumstances where there is substantial risk that it will promptly be widely circulated or published.[4]

In other words, "Never say anything!"

In more than 70 years only one person has left the CFR and spoken publicly about its secret agenda. Obviously, the sanctions against speaking out— such as the total social, business, and political rejection of anyone who would dare to break the code of silence—have been quite effective. Even the Mafia has not been as successful in keeping its secrets from becoming public.

In his testimony before the U.S. Senate Foreign Relations Subcommittee on February 17, 1950, the international banker James P. Warburg (CFR) warned, "We shall have world government, whether or not we like it. The question is only whether world government will be achieved by consent or by conquest." In an April 1974 article in *Foreign Affairs*, the CFR quarterly journal, Richard Gardner wrote this about creating the New World Order: ". . . an end run around national sovereignty, eroding it piece by piece, will accomplish much more than the old-fashioned frontal assault."[5] Dan Smoot, an FBI agent and a researcher who spent years examining the CFR, wrote, "The ultimate aim of the Council on Foreign Relations . . . is . . . to create a one-world socialist system and make the United States an official part of it."[6]

The Trilateral Commission

In 1973, Zbigniew Brzezinski, the national security advisor to President Jimmy Carter, and David Rockefeller, both members of the CFR, created a new coordinating group, the Trilateral Commission

(TC). Their purpose was to coordinate their plans for a world government between the three elite groups now controlling the United States, Japan, and Western Europe. Initially their membership consisted of 300 people who made up the elite leadership of the three great regions that dominate the planet. The *Trilateral Commission: Questions and Answers* (1980) described the group in these words: "The founders of the Commission believed it important that cooperation among Western Europe, North American (including Canada) and Japan be sustained and strengthened—not only on issues among these regions but in a global framework as well."[7] The purpose of the TC is "close Trilateral cooperation in keeping the peace, in managing the world economy, in fostering economic redevelopment and alleviating world poverty which will improve the chances of a smooth and peaceful evolution of the global system."[8]

Ultimately, the plan is for each of the three geopolitical groups to create a political, military, and economic alliance in their respective hemisphere. Once they consolidate control in their own sphere, the final step will be to merge the three hemispheres into a one-world government.

Who are among the key players behind the Trilateral Commission? David Rockefeller, head of the Chase Manhattan Bank and the Rockefeller fortune, is the North American chairman. Deputy chairmen have included Canadians such as Mitchell Sharp, the former Canadian Minister of External Affairs, and Jack Warren, former chairman of the Bank of

Montreal and Canada's ambassador to the United States from 1975–1977.

The Trilateral Commission came into public view for the first time during President Carter's administration. The media noted then that 20 of his highest officials and cabinet members belonged to the Trilateral Commission, including the president himself, Vice-President Mondale, and the head of the CIA. In a revealing article in the *Atlantic Monthly*, we discover that "although the Commission's primary concern is economic, the Trilateralists pinpointed a vital political objective: to gain control of the American presidency."

More light is shed on the Trilateral Commission in a book about the inner workings of the Carter presidency called *Cartergate: The Death of Democracy*. In this fascinating book we read this:

> The presidency of the United States and the key cabinet departments of the federal government have been taken over by a private organization dedicated to the subordination of the domestic interests of the United States to the international interests of the multinational banks and corporations. It would be unfair to say that the Trilateral Commission dominates the Carter Administration. The Trilateral Commission is the Carter Administration.

In the last two decades since the 1970s, members of the Trilateral Commission and the Council on Foreign Relations have consolidated their grip on the levers of power throughout the governments of

America, Canada, Europe and Asia. In a rare public criticism of the Trilateral Commission, the *Manchester Union Leader* ran an editorial during the 1979 presidential primaries that warned: "It is quite clear that this group of extremely powerful men is out to control the world."

Other key members of the Trilateral Commission include: Baron Edmund de Rothschild, Henry Kissinger, Casper Weinberger, Robert McNamara, Paul Volcker, Michael Blumenthal, Alan Cranston, Senator John Glenn, Thomas Foley, Alan Greenspan, and George Bush. The founding group included 74 Japanese members representing the elite business, intellectual, and political spheres. Three of Japan's foreign ministers were members. Despite President Ronald Reagan's genuine conservative position on many issues, it is undeniable that his administration was riddled with at least 225 CFR and TC members. The Bush administration was also overwhelmingly represented by CFR and Trilateral members, including every member of the cabinet except James Baker. When President Bill Clinton took office, every officer in his new cabinet and subcabinet were drawn exclusively from the membership of the CFR and TC.

The Bilderbergers/The Alliance

The most secretive of the private international councils planning for a one-world government is the Bilderbergers. This group holds closed meetings and seeks to avoid all media scrutiny. Although most commentators call the group the Bilderbergers, the members themselves call their group "The Alliance." They impose very strict rules of censorship on their members in relation to discussing their plans and policies. This may be related to the fact that the Bilderbergers were financed from the beginning by the Central Intelligence Agency.[9]

This council began when, in May 1952, the political and financial leadership of Europe gathered at the Hotel de Bilderberg in Oosterbeek, Holland, to plan the necessary steps required to unify their nations. These men, led by His Royal Highness Prince Bernhard of the Netherlands (formerly an officer in the Nazi SS in the 1930s) and General Walter Bedell Smith (director of the CIA), became known as the Bilderberger Group. Other key founding members included Colin Gubbins, head of British intelligence, Stansfield Turner, director of the CIA, Henry Kissinger, Lord Rothschild, and Lawrence Rockefeller. Currently, this council meets twice a year to coordinate the efforts of their European and American members who are working to create the "United States of Europe." While their main headquarters is in The Hague, the Netherlands, the American headquarters is located at 345 East 46th Street, New York City. Interestingly, if anyone doubted the alliance between these groups, this building also houses the headquarters of the Trilateral Commission and the Carnegie Endowment for International Peace. There are persistent reports that guests from the former U.S.S.R. (now Russia) are also invited to attend planning sessions from time to time.

The members of the Bilderberger group include the following: Baron Edmund de Rothschild, David Rockefeller, Robert McNamara, and Pierce Paul Schweitzer of the International Monetary Fund. Associated groups include the Round Table, the Royal Institute of International Affairs, and the Pilgrims Society.

Although primarily European, the group does include a number of key American and Canadian members, but no Japanese members. The majority of the 900 members over the last four decades came from the European Union. However, members have also come from Switzerland, Turkey, Australia, and Iceland. Many of the key members of The Alliance are also members of the Council on Foreign Relations and the Trilateral Commission.

Beginning with the pivotal 1957 Treaty of Rome, the European Common Market gradually evolved into the European Union, the most powerful economic and political power on earth. Significantly, the former American ambassador to West Germany, George McGhee, wrote, "The Treaty of Rome which brought the Common Market into being was nurtured at the Bilderberg meetings."[10]

In 1971 an exposé to the *Manchester Union Leader* alleged that members of the Bilderbergers were given illegal advance insider notice of President Nixon's New Economic Policy. This article alleged that these individuals received insider information that enabled their members to make more than $20 billion in illegal profits by trading on this special knowledge before the general public and stock markets knew of the massive monetary changes that Nixon would introduce.

John Foster Dulles, who later became director of the CIA, was one of the key players behind the scenes in the move toward creating the Bilderberger Group and its consolidation with the Council of Foreign Relations. On October 28, 1939, he made a speech in which he indicated that he supported a one-world government to replace national sovereignty.

> The fundamental fact is that the nationalist system of wholly independent sovereign states is complete in its cycle of usefulness. Today, more than ever before, are the defects of the sovereignty system magnified, until now it is not consonant with either peace or justice. It is imperative that there be a transition to a new order. This has, indeed, become inevitable; for the present system is rapidly encompassing its own destruction. The real problem is not whether there will be a transition, but how can transition be made, and to what.[11]

Consider the implications of these statements and memberships in these secret globalist groups by men who have been entrusted with sensitive national security information that is intended to protect their nation's best interests. In their own words, these men proclaim that they are no longer loyal to the United States or Canada as sovereign nations. Instead, they are secretly working for the elimination of the countries that have appointed them to high positions in their desire to merge every nation into the coming one-world government.

The Council of Europe

The Council of Europe is one of the day institutions involved in the consolidation and unification of the revived Roman Empire. The official goals of the council are to strengthen democratic institutions, promote human rights, and develop a single unifying European cultural identity for the new "United States of Europe." In 1949 the Council of Europe was founded with ten original nations, which included most of the key provinces of the ancient Roman Empire.

Today the Council of Europe has grown to 32 member states with the addition of nine new member states from Eastern Europe, including the former Soviet republics of Lithuania and Estonia. By 1997 they expect to add Russia to the council, bringing the emerging Russian empire into pan-European union. On September 29, 1994, the *European* newspaper quoted Daniel Tarschys, the new secretary-general of the council, as declaring, "I feel sure Russia will meet the requirements to join our family of nations." This action represents Europe's seal of acceptance on Russia's so-called "democratic reforms." And recently, council leaders met to negotiate the entrance of Bulgaria, Romania, Poland, Hungary, Slovakia, Latvia, and the Czech Republic. The former Soviet republics of Moldavia, Belarus, and the Ukraine have also applied to join the group.

Remember, the Bible indicates that the Antichrist will rise to power within a ten-nation confederacy in a revived Roman Empire. Then, after he secures his power base, he will expand his dominion to include many more nations through peace treaties and, finally, military action. The European Union and the Council of Europe, then, may very well play significant roles in the unfolding prophetic events of the last days.

The Club of Rome

The Club of Rome (COB) was founded by Aurelio Peccei in 1968 as an institute committed to advancing the globalist agenda. The purpose of the Club of Rome was to be a think tank to focus on solving problems and developing proposals for a one-world government. It is one of the most successful propaganda operations in this century. Significantly, the COR has suggested the need for a massive economic revolution, transferring wealth from those who produce it to those in need. The club has convinced millions of people that our only hope of human survival is to surrender our rights, freedoms, and sovereignty to achieve world government.

Aurelio Peccei, the president of COR, has gone so far as to call for a world dictator:

A charismatic leader—scientific, political, or religious— would be the world's only salvation from the social and economic upheavals that threaten to destroy civilization. Such a leader would have to override national and international interests as well as political and economic structures in order to lead humanity away from the maladies that afflict it. . . . Only a revolution, the substitution of a new world economic order can save us.[12]

In his fascinating book *Mankind at the Turning Point*, Peccei describes "their world model, based on new developments of the multi-level hierarchical systems theory, divides the world into ten interdependent and mutually interacting regions of political, economic or environmental coherence."[13] Interestingly, Peccei has proposed a goal whereby these ten regions of the world would be consolidated into a one-world government by the year 2000.

The Ten Regions of the New World Government

Region 1 — Canada and the United States of America

Region 2 — European Union — Western Europe

Region 3 — Japan

Region 4 — Australia, New Zealand, South Africa, Israel, and Pacific Islands

Region 5 — Eastern Europe

Region 6 — Latin America — Mexico, Central and South America

Region 7 — North Africa and the Middle East (Moslems)

Region 8 — Central Africa

Region 9 — South and Southeast Asia

Region 10 — Central Asia

Some writers have suggested that these ten proposed regions or "kingdoms" may be the ten nations in Daniel's prophecy of the "ten toes" or the "ten horns" of the fourth world empire, the revived Roman Empire. However, a careful examination of Daniel's prophecy reveals that these ten toes and ten horns refer to ten nations that will occupy territory that was formerly part of the historical Roman Empire. Scripture clearly indicates that ancient Rome will arise in the last days as a ten-nation confederacy in the Europe-Mediterranean area. Interestingly,the prophet describes this union as initially weak—it will be made up of several strong nations represented by "toes of iron" and several weaker states represented by the "toes of clay." However, in Daniel's vision of the beast with ten horns, the "eleventh horn," the Antichrist, will arise at some point in time after the ten nations unite. Then the Antichrist will violently "rip up three" of "the horns" representing three of the nations and impose his satanic will on the ten-nation confederacy. From that moment on, according to Daniel, the revived Roman Empire will become the most destructive empire in history, crushing anyone that stands in its way.

The World Federalist Movement

The actor Peter Ustinov is president of the World Federalist Movement, an international group that supports the transformation of the United Nations into a powerful world federation with a mandate to protect the environment and to put an end to war and terrorism. Ustinov states that world government is "inevitable." He claims, "It's a logical ending to a long road of intolerance and battle and all sorts of wretched things in the past."[14] John Anderson, the former independent U.S. presidential candidate, is the head of the sister organization in the United States. He said the organization's goal is not far-fetched. "We just think that the only way to achieve world peace is through a world government."[15]

Both groups were formed in 1947. The U.S. organization, based in Washington, has more than 10,000 members and has groups in more than 80 cities. The international group, which is headquartered in Amsterdam, includes groups in more than 20 nations. These two groups are part of a well planned and funded propaganda campaign aimed at eliminating the nation-state and creating a world government.

The European Union is now undergoing major changes. Jacques Santer was recently chosen as the new president of the powerful unelected Executive Commission. Santer will replace Jacques Delors, his strong-willed predecessor, who led Europe for the last ten years. At the same time that Europe transforms its laws, regulations, and customs to implement the Maastricht Treaty, the directly elected members of the European parliament have gotten a new president: Klaus Hansch. Over 60 percent of the members of the European parliament are serving for the first time. Many of them want to exercise the new enlarged powers delegated to them by the Maastricht Treaty. They want to break down the oppressive levels of bureaucratic secrecy that were built up over the last two decades. The parliament is now removing 62 legal barriers to the free movement of goods and people in Europe.[16]

The most important issue on the agenda of both the European Union's new president, Jacques Santer, and the members of the European parliament is to welcome into the fold a number of new member states from Eastern Europe. In addition to the four nations that joined in January 1995, Poland, Slovakia, Hungary, and the Czech Republic were also offered full membership. And negotiations are continuing with the Ukraine, Belarus, and several of the Baltic states—Estonia, Latvia, and Lithuania.

The Asia-Pacific Economic Community

The Pacific Rim nations are expanding their economies and industrial capacities at an astounding rate. South Korea has developed an industrial base that is exceeded only by Japan. Taiwan's economy has grown at a sustained rate of over six percent per year for the last 20 years. Two of the key reasons for the astonishing growth in these countries are their industrious populations and their incredible savings rate. In Singapore, for example, the average citizen saves an amazing 46 percent of every $100 earned. This awesome rate of personal savings has produced a huge capital base that helps to fuel the engine of the economies in the Pacific Rim. In the last ten years the capitalization of the Pacific Rim stock markets has grown 600 percent from $600 million to $3.8 billion.

The Asia-Pacific Economic Community (APEC) was recently founded to create a true Asia-Pacific Economic Community in cooperation with GATT. Their major goal is the creation of a free trade zone with virtually no tariffs throughout the Pacific region. An Eminent Persons Group was formed to make recommendations for future policy directions for APEC:

> Our Eminent Persons Group believes that the time has come for APEC to adopt a bold and ambitious vision for the twenty-first century: the creation of a true Asia Pacific Economic Community. That Community should seek to achieve free trade in the region. It should do so in ways that strengthen the global trading and economic system. APEC should agree upon these goals ... set a date certain, perhaps 1996, for deciding the target date and timetable for achieving the goal of free trade in the Asia Pacific.[17]

One of the goals of this community is to establish a new institutional infrastructure that will coordinate the consolidation of the policies of all countries in the region.

It's interesting to note that China's economy is exploding with sustained growth rates exceeding 10 percent yearly. The ancient nations that are prophetically called "the kings of the East" in the book of Revelation are quickly rising to become the greatest economic, political, and military powers in the history of Asia. According to the Bible's prophecies, this dynamic confederacy of powerful Asian nations will arise in the last days to fight against the Western nations (who will be under the control of the Antichrist) in the climactic Battle of Armageddon.

America Is Preparing the Way

The President's Powers

Some writers have questioned how America could relinquish her sovereignty and join the coming world government in light of the constitutional safeguards that were created by the founding fathers. However, since World War II, the U.S. Congress has passed a number of laws giving the president awesome executive powers that grant him sole control of the government and military forces in the event of nuclear war or some other national emergency. In such situations, it is obvious that the president needs legal authority to direct and control the resources of the nation to protect its citizens. However, these executive orders are a loaded gun that a future president could use to legally establish a dictatorship that brings America to join a world government. Some people have suggested that an "emergency" could be created in the future as an excuse to enact legislation that Congress would never pass in normal times.

The range of dictatorial powers available to a president during a declared national emergency are equal to or greater than the legal powers that were held by Adolph Hitler or Joseph Stalin during their dictatorships. The legislation allows a president to suspend the Constitution and exercise these powers whenever he alone determines that the nation faces a "national emergency." The term "national emergency" is not defined by the laws in question. It is left solely to the president to determine when a national emergency exists.

The following are just a few of the national security laws that a president could exercise during a national emergency without any further reference to Congress:

10995 Seizure of all print and electronic communications media in the United States.

10997 Seizure of all electric power, fuels, and minerals, public and private.

10998 Seizure of food supplies and resources, public and private, including farms and equipment.

10999 Seizure of all means of transportation, including cars, trucks or any other vehicles, including control over highways, harbors, and waterways.

11000 Seizure of all American people for work forces under federal supervision; it allows the government to split up families if they believe it is necessary.

11001 Seizure of all health, education and welfare facilities, public and private.

11002 Registration by the Postmaster General of all men, women, and children for government service.

11003 Seizure of all airports and aircraft.

11004 Seizure of all housing and finance authorities; authority to establish forced relocation and to
designate areas that must be abandoned as "un-
safe." Establishment of new locations for population groups; building of new housing on public
land.

11005 Seizure of all railroads, inland waterways,
and storage warehouses, public and private.

11051 Authorize the Office of Emergency Planning
to put the above order into effect in times of increased international tension or financial crisis.[18]

Please note that these draconian dictatorial powers can be legally invoked by the president alone
whenever he feels there is a time of increased international tension or financial crisis. Every western
democracy has similar laws that were set up to provide for the continuity of government in the event
of a nuclear war. In both Canada and the United
Kingdom, these laws are called Orders in Council
and were passed secretly by the Privy Council under
the authority of the prime minister.

The Washington Report recently pointed out that
Operation Dragnet can be implemented under the
McCarran Act—Title II. Under this legislation the
president can legally suspend the U.S. Constitution
and Bill of Rights with a single phone call and impose
martial law. A number of reliable sources have reported that U.S. government agencies have accumulated the names of over one million American

citizens in a high-speed Univac computer in Washington as possible targets for arrest during a future time of national emergency.[19] Some sources suggest these lists contain names of prominent Christians and other patriots who have publicly expressed concerns about the move toward the New World Order. Federal agencies could quickly arrest the people named on these lists and hold them in detention camps. Numerous sources confirm that such detention camps exist in several states.[20] These camps may be connected to President Reagan's "Rex 84" national security program, which created eleven federal detention centers in Florida, Virginia, Georgia, New York, Pennsylvania, Wisconsin, Arkansas, Arizona, and California.

Numerous confidential sources have confirmed that National Guard units and regular army units are training—in mock-ups of American cities, which are built on large army bases—to attack, seize, and complete door-to-door searches for weapons. A former special-forces officer told me that his unit was training in a live ammunition drill on a firing range recently. During the exercise, agents from the Alcohol, Tobacco and Firearms Agency, who were using the next firing range, began to quietly interview the troops. These agents asked repeatedly if the soldiers would be willing to serve in a future multi-jurisdictional task force that would seize weapons from Americans. Incredibly, they asked a number of soldiers if they would be willing to shoot their fellow Americans if they resisted surrendering their weapons. Another soldier told me that a similar written questionnaire was handed out to soldiers at a military base in the South.

The Plan to Disarm America

The people who plan to bring America into the coming world government know that the existence of a strong U.S. military represents one of the greatest practical threats to their efforts. Their strategy has been to progressively weaken America's military while building up the standing army of the United Nations. As early as 1961, President John F. Kennedy ordered the State Department to produce a program entitled *Freedom from War: The U.S. Program for General and Complete Disarmament in a Peaceful World* (Dept. of State Publication 7277). This three-phased program proposes that, during Stage I, the United States would gradually decrease its army, air force, and naval forces. In Stage II, the present stage of the plan, "The U.N. peace force shall be established and progressively strengthened." Finally, "In Stage III, a progressive controlled disarmament would proceed to a point where no state (including the U.S.) would have the military power to challenge the progressively strengthened U.N. peace force."

Significantly, President Bush signed an executive order in November 1990, transferring one-third of America's strategic reserve aircraft from the active military over to the Financial Crimes Enforcement Network (FINCEN) for special operations at a cost of $12.8 billion—which will be paid by U.S. taxpayers. These aircraft were painted black without external markings and are now used by FINCEN and other special multiple-jurisdictional task forces like the one we witnessed in action during the tragic holocaust at Waco, Texas.

The Cooperation Between Russia and America

The world-renown Russian writer Alexander Solzhenitsyn has observed that "there also exists another alliance—at first glance a strange one, a surprising one—but if you think about it, one which is well grounded and easy to understand. This is the alliance between our communist leaders and your capitalists."[21] That may seem an unlikely union, but, in fact, the elite financial and business leaders believe that the key to bringing about their dream of a one-world government requires a gradual merging of the Russian and American systems. Working behind the scenes over the last seven decades, multinational companies have provided staggering amounts of technology and finances to keep the economically bankrupt Soviet system afloat. Most of the truck production within Russia over the last 70 years came from plants and machinery provided by Ford Motor Company. The communist government of Angola would have fallen before the democratic forces of the National Union for the Total Independence of Angola (UNITA) if tens of millions in financial and economic aid had not been provided by the Exxon Oil Company. Recent reports confirm that former U.S.S.R. President Mikhail Gorbachev received over $300 million from the Rockefeller and Mellon Foundations to establish his private foundation to prepare the way "for world peace."[22] Meanwhile, German Chancellor Helmut Kohl arranged to provide another $100 million in support for Gorbachev from German industrialists. Gorbachev most likely is being groomed for another key role in the future integration of the nations of Eastern Europe and Russia.

The United States and Russia recently signed agreements calling for increased military cooperation between our armed forces. Exchanges of officers who will train, observe, and command small units of the other nation's armies are part of this agreement. Joint seminars and intelligence exchanges are also included. Increasingly we are receiving reports of Russian weapons that have been seen on U.S. military bases together with reports of foreign troops, including soldiers from the Ukraine, Norway, and Finland, training on American soil. Recently, photos were taken of advanced Russian T-80 tanks being transported on flatbed trailers on a highway in the American southwest on April 24, 1994. In July 1993 a huge Russian Anatov 124 Condor transport plane, the largest cargo plane in the world, flew into the military section of Palm Beach International Airport in Florida. Photographs were taken of five American Apache military helicopters, with their advanced avionics and weapons systems, being loaded on the Russian cargo plane to fly back to Mother Russia. And newspapers have reported that hundreds of American troops were now operating inside Russia under the command of Russian officers.[23]

Welcome to the New World Order!

CHAPTER 6

Preparations for a One-World Government

I have just finished reading a provocative study that was published in July 1994, called "Renewing the United Nations System." This startling report was financed by the Ford Foundation and authored by two former U.N. officials, Sir Brian Urquhart and Erskine Childers. The study concluded that massive changes are needed to streamline U.N. operations. With improved efficiency and control in mind, the authors recommended that the United Nations General Assembly, the Security Council, the International Monetary Fund, the World Health Organization, and the International Labor Organization be transferred to one central location—possibly Bonn or New York. Interestingly, the authors also suggested that the present voting system used by the International Monetary Fund be abolished and

replaced with a radical new system that will allow
impoverished Third World nations to dictate where
and when loans would be made from rich countries
to poorer ones.

This far-reaching proposal obviously has as its
goal the laying of a foundation that will ultimately
result in a one-world government. Consider this
quote: "While there is no question, at present, of the
transformation of the U.N. system into a suprana-
tional authority, the organization is in a transitional
phase, basically shaped and constrained by national
sovereignty, but sometimes acting outside and beyond it." Notice the phrase "at present." Repeatedly,
the document used terms such as "gradual limita-
tion of sovereignty"; "notable abridgments of national sovereignty"; "chipping away at the edges of
traditional sovereignty"; and "small steps towards
an eventual trans-sovereign society." Throughout
this extensive document the authors discuss their
strategy for progressively stripping our nations of
their cherished sovereignty. Their plan is to proceed
quietly step by step to avoid creating a political backlash from the citizens of the western democracies
who will be forced to surrender their freedom and
sovereignty.

One example of the shift away from national sovereignty to the coming one-world government is found in
the 1991 General Assembly resolution on humanitarian emergency assistance. Discussing the "emergency-
driven temporary cessation of sovereignty," the
document notes that for the first time "consent"

appeared instead of "request," and "country" instead of "government." The full statement thus reads: "Humanitarian assistance should be provided with the consent of the affected country and in principle on the basis of an appeal by the affected country." In other words, the United Nations no longer feels it is necessary to obtain a request from the leadership of a national government to intervene inside a nation's borders. As long as the United Nations believes the country's population will consent to the intervention, then it feels it is justified in intervening. This is a revolutionary change from the original founding principle of non-intervention that governed the actions of the United Nations for the last 50 years. Secretary General Boutros-Ghali's 1992 report, "An Agenda for Peace," contained a significant indication of his thinking: "The time of absolute and exclusive sovereignty, however, has passed, its theory was never matched by reality."

Some of the U.N. report's recommendations, if enacted, would make us take some very significant steps toward world government. Throughout the document the authors talk about interim actions that must be taken "until the world is ready for world government." The authors suggest that the United Nations should raise funds for its own budget by assessing a global surcharge tax on "all arms sales," on "all transnational movement of currencies," on "all international trade: or on the production of such specific materials as petroleum," or "a United Nations levy on international air and sea travel." Other recommendations include assessing a "one day" income tax on all people of the planet every year. The United Nations group has also called for a one-time global tax to be used to reduce government deficits and stimulate economic activity. Proposals to have the United Nations apply a global tax on the citizens of the world are one more indication of the gradual shift from an international consultative body to the beginnings of a one-world superstate.

Back in 1945 the British Foreign Secretary, Ernest Bevin, called for the creation of a United Nations Assembly that would be directly elected by all citizens worldwide. This radical proposal was rejected by the founding nations in favor of our present U.N. representational system, where each government and nation has a vote. It is significant that there are now serious calls for creating a directly elected Parliament of the World as an interim step to establishing a world government. The 1994 study, "Renewing the United Nations System," lays out the necessary steps to establish a powerful new world parliament. This is obviously a key step to building public support for replacing the sovereignty of our individual nations with a newly enhanced United Nations that will ultimately become the nucleus of a powerful world government. There is an enormous difference between the present U.N. system of an assembly of representatives of national governments and the proposed plan that would have parliamentarians directly elected by all citizens throughout the planet. Using the example of the directly elected European Parliament representing the citizens of the European Union, many are now calling for a "world people's assembly."

Unfortunately, for people who truly love democracy, the European Parliament example is not promising. Despite the trappings of democracy, the European Parliament does not have the democratic power to choose leaders, set laws, or establish taxes. All real power in the European Union remains in the hands of the 21-member Executive Commission. The directly elected European Parliament, then, remains nothing more than a showpiece "debating society" with no real power or substantive influence. The pattern of all international institutions is that power is exercised by the members of the elite from behind locked boardroom doors. Then their decisions are sold to the public through highly orchestrated public relations efforts and media manipulation.

History suggests that real democracy can function practically only at the local or national level. Once we move to the arena of international politics between nation-states, true democratic government is replaced by sophisticated tradeoffs negotiated behind the scenes between the power brokers of these international organizations. The current arrangement in the European Union is a preview of where the true power will lie in a future world government. In such a setup, a powerful individual could easily arise and seize full control of the future world government.

Abolishing the Nation-State

The elite groups that are planning a one-world government have embarked on a program to subvert
and diminish the sovereignty of nation-states, including America and Canada. President Clinton appointed Strobe Talbott (CFR) as deputy secretary of
state at the State Department. In Talbott's article,
"The Birth of the Global Nation," reported in *Time*
magazine (July 20, 1992), he wrote:

> All countries are basically social arrangements. . . . No matter
> how permanent and even sacred they may seem at any one
> time, in fact they are all artificial and temporary. . . . Perhaps
> national sovereignty wasn't such a great idea after all. . . . But
> it has taken the events in our own wondrous and terrible cen-
> tury to clinch the case.

How do you feel knowing that some of the most
powerful leaders ruling the country believe that
America, patriotism, and even the Constitution
weren't "such a great idea after all"?

In 1939, socialist author H.G. Wells wrote *The
New World Order*, claiming there must be a synthe-
sis in the future between western capitalism and
eastern communism into a world socialism. In his
Experiment in Autobiography (1934), Wells stated:

> The organization of this that I call the Open Conspiracy . . . an
> adequately implemented Liberal Socialism, which will ulti-
> mately supply teaching, coercive and directive public services
> to the whole world, is the immediate task. . . . I believe this idea

of a planned world-state . . . will happen very quickly. . . . Only after a huge cultural struggle can we hope to see the world-state coming into being.

The globalist expressions such as "rule of law," "world law," "collective security," "world order," and the "new world order" are code words that these elitists use in the media when referring to their plans for a one-world government.

Henry Morgenthau (CFR), a former treasury secretary for President Roosevelt, declared,

> We can hardly expect the nation-state to make itself superfluous, at least not overnight. Rather, what we must aim for is recognition in the minds of all responsible statesmen that they are really nothing more than caretakers of a bankrupt international machine which will have to be transformed slowly into a new one.[1]

The key ingredient to this formula is their plan to "financially bankrupt the international machine." Nations will be forced to turn to the International Monetary Fund (IMF) and World Bank for a financial bailout, but under the condition that borrowers abandon their national sovereignty to the United Nations. It is quite ominous that the IMF and the World Bank, the very institutions that can trigger a worldwide financial collapse, also admit that the key event that would allow them to seize control of the nations is an international financial collapse. It is not a coincidence that Mexico's currency crisis, with a 40 percent devaluation of the peso, occurred within one year of Mexico joining the North American Free Trade Agreement.

There is a continuous struggle for ethnic survival, religious rights, and national sovereignty at the forefront of international affairs today. Wherever these rights or interests are threatened by conflict there is a call for the United Nations to intervene. This follows a planned strategy that was developed in the last century by German philosopher Georg Hegel. The Hegelian Dialectic theorizes that "conflict brings change, and controlled conflict brings controlled change." Therefore, if you have an agenda to institute massive political change you must be in a position to trigger major conflicts and crises. These manufactured crises are designed to create turmoil and focus everyone on the "problem." This will then allow the globalist elite to propose their "solution" to the crises that their actions have secretly triggered.

Consider carefully how several recent international crises have developed in Somalia, Rwanda, Haiti, and Bosnia. Ask yourself: Why did the United Nations Security Council wait until these crises escalated to the point where human disaster affected millions? Is it possible that some of these situations were allowed to develop into total catastrophes to provide an excuse for the elite groups to move us closer to a world government? As the existing governments in these Third World trouble spots disintegrated into total anarchy, the United Nations moved in with their advisors to create a kind of trustee-ship—the 1990s version of colonialism. In a 1993 article in the CFR journal *Foreign Affairs*, Boutros Boutros-Ghali, the secretary general of the United Nations, declared that he felt the need to "rethink the question of sovereignty."[2]

A Growing Power

There is a growing perception that the United Nations is gaining in power at the same time the United States is losing respect around the world due to its weakened military and constantly changing foreign policy under both Presidents Bush and Clinton. Peter Tarnoff (CFR), the number-three man in the State Department, gave a speech in May 1993 indicating the tragic disarray in President Clinton's foreign policy, which was characterized by a loss of confidence and vision. In explaining why he felt that America could no longer set its foreign policy solely on the basis of its own national interest, Tarnoff stated, "We simply don't have the leverage, we don't have the influence, we don't have the inclination to use force and we certainly don't have the money."

For 70 years, other nations have depended on America to provide firm leadership based on principle and its own national self-interest. Today, however, no nation knows what to expect next from the United States' foreign policy. Clinton's mishandled foreign policy has been characterized by broken promises, changed directions, and numerous empty threats that were not backed by firm action. The disarray and vacuum of leadership in foreign policy was so obvious that former President Jimmy Carter seized the opportunity to inject himself into various diplomatic trouble spots in North Korea, Haiti, and Bosnia, with or without President Clinton's blessing.

British Foreign Secretary Douglas Hurd claimed in an interview that the United Nations needs to prepare itself to take on an "imperial role." He stated that the United Nations must usurp national sovereignty and take control as the occupying power when governments collapse, as in Somalia and Cambodia. During an interview held at the United Nations in New York, Secretary Hurd drew attention to what he called "a new phase in the world's history." He said that there is a need for the United Nations to intervene in crisis situations earlier to "prevent things getting to the stage where countries are run by corrupt warlords, as in Somalia."

Hurd also warned that since the breakup of the former Soviet Union—leaving three or four "crisis areas"—the United States was the lone superpower and it had no wish to become the "policeman of the world." The United States is calling for a more unified and efficient structure at the United Nations, arguing that there is an urgent need to better organize the world body to deal with global hot spots like Yugoslavia and Haiti. This is part of a trend of powerful elite groups encouraging a new variation of neo-colonialism. They propose that the United Nations establish some kind of "trusteeship" over nations that have found their governments in disarray due to famine or civil war, such as occurred recently in Somalia and Rwanda. These tragic situations are ready-made for those who have a desire to establish the United Nations as the nucleus of the coming world government.

One of the key goals of the globalists is to create a permanent standing army of significant size that would allow the Security Council to enforce the will of the world body against any nation or group of nations that opposes its agenda. In the last four years alone, the United Nations has engaged in more peacekeeping operations than it did in its first 40 years. Since 1987 the United Nations' peacekeeping budget has increased over 1,000 percent with a staggering 7,000-percent increase in military personnel in U.N. police operations. In addition, 100 times as many civilian personnel are now involved in U.N. peacekeeping operations. Since the election of Secretary General Boutros-Ghali, the U.N. Security Council has deployed troops in 19 countries around the globe at an annual cost of over $3 billion. The number of U.N. soldiers serving in operations increased 400 percent in 1993 with over 100,000 "blue beret" troops now deployed in peacekeeping operations from Yugoslavia to Haiti.

A Permanent Army

Despite Washington's growing reluctance to risk the lives of American soldiers in wars in far-off places, the United States cannot avoid the wars of the future. For the next few years, America will remain the only nation with huge transport planes, a sealift capacity, spy satellites, and technical intelligence facilities that make global interventions possible and relatively safe. During the last three years America provided a significant level of support to the U.N. peacekeeping force in Cambodia. In Bosnia, with NATO's coordination, America provided logistical air and sealift support while the French, British, and other nations supplied troops on the ground. However, NATO is unwilling to act outside of Europe and the Mediterranean basin.

Meanwhile, the United Nations has a worldwide membership and the authority to order interventions. Significantly, a September 26, 1994 article in *Newsweek* called for the creation of a standing army for the New World Order—an army that can respond to future crises anywhere in the world. "The United Nations needs its own army, accountable not to national governments but to the United Nations itself. The rich nations would have to donate equipment to such an army; real live soldiers would be recruited from volunteers. Some would be trained mercenaries, like the Nepalese Gurkhas; others would be units from the armies of the western world."

Recent articles have also appeared in *The New York Times*, *Time* magazine, and *Economist* magazine calling for the creation of a permanent standing army for the United Nations under the control of the U.N. Security Council. The August 1994 issue of the respected *Economist* magazine observed that in Somalia and Rwanda, the U.N. tried and failed to create a professional army assembled from the disparate units of dozens of military forces provided by its member states. Among the problems were ammunition that did not match the weapons, troops who were not trained for the equipment they had to use, and soldiers who were commanded by foreign officers who did not speak the languages of the troops they led.

As the tragedy of Rwanda unfolded, the United Nations saw disaster coming but found itself paralyzed into inactivity by competing political agendas and general indifference. The United Nations finally began to move into action after the horrible pictures of genocide filled our television screens, but it was a case of "too little, too late."

As one commentator noted:

Never has intervention been needed more quickly than in Rwanda; never has it materialized more slowly. A prompt response when the slaughter began in April could not have saved all the victims, but it might have saved a great many. . . . Their foot-dragging over Rwanda is the best argument yet for the United Nations to have a small flexible peacekeeping force of its own.

The *Economist* argued,

A standing force would respond to emergencies only when the Security Council told it to . . . it would be ready to try at once, not after U.N. officials had gone cap in hand to umpteen governments. The idea bristles with tricky questions: command, recruitment, training, pay, nationality, transport, supply, and support back-up. But it should be possible to create a brigade-sized force of this kind. And it is what the United Nations needs if it is to be a peacekeeper worthy of its name.

On October 6, 1994, Canada and Russia jointly announced their agreement on a common agenda for reforming and strengthening the United Nations. Significantly, their report calls for "devising a rapid-response capability" to dispatch military forces to trouble spots when peace negotiations fail. *Southam News* reported on October 7, 1994, that Canadian Foreign Affairs Minister Andre Ouellet announced its launching of a major effort to establish a "permanent U.N. army of standby forces from various countries." Although two members of the U.N. Security Council, Britain and the United States, are unhappy with the plan, France, Russia, and possibly China are supporters. The creation of a permanent U.N. armed force will be one of the key milestones on the road to a world government.

Secretary General Boutros-Ghali has repeatedly called for the creation of a special U.N. rapid-deployment military force of sufficient size to defeat any potential opponent. He wants member states to provide trained soldiers, equipment, and funding on a permanent basis. He is committed wholeheartedly to the concept of the coming new world order that plans to replace national sovereignty with a world government led by the United Nations.

The Exploding World Population

Since World War II the world has been politically and militarily divided between East and West. Today, however, a new global division has arisen between the North and the South, based on the enormous disparity in wealth and resources. Recognizing this division is fundamental to our understanding the massive forces that have begun to reshape our planet. The key problem facing the political elite is the overwhelming imbalance in wealth, resources, and population between the First World of the Western nations and the Third World of the impoverished nations of Asia, Africa, and South America. This disparity will produce massive immigration pressures, legal and illegal, in the coming years.

It took thousands of years, until 1800, for the world to reach a population of one billion. But it took only a little over a century, until 1930, for it to reach two billion souls. By 1960, only 30 years later, another billion was added. By 1974, in only 14 more years, we added another billion. The earth reached a total of five billion citizens in 1988 and will reach a staggering six billion in the next few years.

During the nineteenth century the largest increase in population was in Western nations. But in recent years, population growth within North America and Europe has slowed considerably due to smaller family units. At the same time, the population in Third World countries has dramatically increased, not just because more children are being born but also because fewer people are dying at an early age. The introduction of antibiotics, improved sanitation, and modern drugs has massively improved the mortality rate in these nations. As a result, with far fewer people dying at younger ages, the world's population is growing at an unprecedented rate of 1.7 percent every year. Ninety-five percent of that growth is taking place in the Third World, with more than a hundred million people added to the earth's population every year. For example, in the 25-year period from 1950 to 1975, the population of China almost doubled from 554 million to 933 million. And from 1948 until 1995, the population of Kenya grew from five million to a staggering 26 million. The world's population is growing relentlessly like a tidal wave that inexorably advances, destroying everything in its path.

A recent study by *Worldwatch*, *The State of the World*, reveals that at the same time that the world population is exploding, the world's food supply is rapidly dwindling.[3] The recent devastation of Canada's fisheries are cited as only one example of what we can expect in the future. The Reuters press organization reported on January 15, 1995 that

> the swelling human population is on course to surpass the world's ability to provide food within a few decades or sooner. The impending shift would lead to a future so different from the recent past that it is difficult to even imagine. The world food economy is in danger of being converted from a buyers' market to a sellers' market.[4]

The study also reported the conclusions of the president of Worldwatch, Lester Brown, who said in his interview that there are ample signs of a coming disaster. "The wake-up call will come from China, in the form of massive imports of grain."[5] Significantly, in 1994, China imported massive quantities of wheat and bought corn for the first time in years. In the fall of 1994, China's leaders responded to their food crisis by banning any exports of its own corn. According to *Worldwatch*, the major famine problems in the past were not caused by lack of world food production but rather by poor distribution. The *Worldwatch* study indicated that food shortages could switch countries from stability to instability almost overnight.

The Threat from Illegal Immigration

The disparity in population growth rates worldwide is best expressed by considering the differences between southern Europe and its close neighbor, North Africa. In Spain, France, Portugal, Italy, and Greece the combined populations will increase by only 4.5 million in the next 35 years. However, during the same period the population in Morocco, Algeria, Tunisia, Libya, and Egypt will increase by 20 times, adding more than 100 million new citizens. The vast majority of these Third World countries are populated by young people below the age of 25. In Kenya, 52 percent of the population is under age 15.

Another problem is that in most of the developing nations, unemployment rates exceed 70 percent among the young. These rising populations will produce enormous pressures on the West as more and more of these people seek to escape their desperate fate. They will try to immigrate to the promising future they believe exists only in the Western nations. Their hopes are fueled by western television and its images of opportunities, wealth, and welfare awaiting them if they succeed in immigrating.

Despite its sophisticated security technology, America has been unable to stem the overwhelming invasion of one-and-a-half million illegal immigrants crossing its borders every year. And in the Third World there is a massive move from the countryside into the cities. The Third World citizens who have the resources to do so are often encouraged to attempt an escape to the vastly improved opportunities offered to the few who can successfully immigrate to the West.

A provocative and frightening novel called *The Camp of the Saints* was published in France in the early 1970s. It warned of the coming invasion of the West by millions of impoverished citizens from the Third World. Author Jean Raspail prophetically describes how, following a devastating famine in India, an Indian Messianic figure arises and demands that the poverty-stricken citizens of the Third World invade the "paradise" in the Western nations. As a result, millions of desperate Indians seize and board ships that they then sail toward the shores of Europe.

"The nations are rising from the four corners of the earth and their number is like the sand of the sea. They will march up over the broad earth and surround the camp of the saints and the beloved city."

In response, the nations of the West are stunned. They are unable to devise an appropriate solution to stem this overwhelming tide of humanity sailing into the open harbors of Europe. Despite their orders, the soldiers of NATO retreat and refuse to fire upon the defenseless masses.

Although Raspail's concluding scenario is unlikely, the problem faced by the West is real and will not go away. Illegal immigrants from China, Haiti, Mexico, and South America continue to pour into America, Canada, and Europe despite all of our border guards and security defenses. Recently, an article in *The Washington Times* warned of this continuing onslaught. Samuel Francis warned about the dangers from illegal immigration: "Not since Genghis Khan rode out of the Asian steppes has the West—both Europeans as well as the United States—encountered such an alien invasion."

To the south of a prosperous European Union lies a huge population in North Africa that feels excluded from the benefits of the modern world economy. The European Commissioner from Portugal, Joao de Deus Pinheiro, warns of the dangerous demographic changes occurring in North Africa. In Algeria, Morocco, Tunisia, and Libya a huge and growing population of extremist Muslims are clamoring for improvements in their lifestyle—improvements that

their governments cannot deliver. Pinheiro warns of
the danger in Algeria, which is destroying itself in an
Islamic civil war. "Because the birth rate is higher
than the growth rate, people are getting poorer every
year. With satellite television they see every day images of affluent western society. They are in hell but
see images of paradise." The phenomenon of worldwide satellite television, which allows over a billion
people in the impoverished Third World to witness
world events and the prosperity of the West, will
have profound consequences beyond anything we
have ever imagined.

After decades of accepting immigrants from
many countries, France and Germany have begun to
seal their borders against the onslaught from poor
nations. In an astonishing reversal of two centuries
of open immigration, the new hard-line interior
security minister of France, Charles Pasqua, has
launched draconian police actions against the growing numbers of illegal Algerian immigrants from
North Africa. When my wife Kaye and I were in
Paris one recent summer we watched the French police stop and interrogate individuals from Algeria
and North Africa. In a 24 hour period, the interior
ministry interrogated over 17,000 North African
Muslims throughout France. Pasqua said, "When
we have sent home several planeloads, even boat-
loads and trainloads, the world will get the message.
We will close our frontiers."[6]

Even in America, the nation that happily accepted
immigrants for the last 200 years, the doors are

beginning to close. Proposition 187 was passed in California, denying services to those who cannot prove they or their parents are here legally. While it is perfectly understandable that the American population will resist massive illegal immigration, the pressures from the Third World will increase inexorably in the years ahead. One past example of such pressure took place when thousands of Albanians fled in desperation from the tyranny of their dictatorship by seizing ships and fleeing toward Italian ports that represented freedom and opportunity. Similarly, in June 1933, a freighter steamship from Thailand arrived off the coast of New York City with almost 300 Chinese people who had sailed for thousands of miles to reach the shore of the "golden city." Recently, a study of the people who are entering Spain illegally indicated that many of them had come thousands of miles from southern Africa and Asia.

Japan, Europe, and Australia are among those that are closing their doors to immigrants. This only increases the pressures on Canada and the United States. This, in turn, will encourage the elite that lead our societies to develop new global policies that will usher in the New World Order they desire. Their solution is to transfer enormous amounts of wealth from the North to the impoverished nations of the South in the vain hope that this will encourage the potential immigrants to remain at home despite the often brutal conditions they face.

Leo Tindemans, the former prime minister of Belgium, was one of the founders of the European

Union. Despite his earlier optimism that democracy would flourish in a new United States of Europe, he is now warning of the danger of the rise of nationalism and fascism as Europe struggles with its growing problems, which includes illegal immigration. The U.S. ambassador to NATO, Robert Hunter, also warned that if the European Union fails to incorporate the nations of Eastern Europe that have been set adrift, "then the demagogues there will prevail." The old optimism that fascism and a new Hitler could never arise again in Europe is now giving way to a profound pessimism. The dark forces of "fire and blood" from the past days of nationalistic madness could rise to drench the world in blood once again. These fears could easily play into the hands of a future dictator in Europe.

The Antichrist—the Coming Dictator

In his prophecy about the great metallic image, Daniel confirmed that the Antichrist will arise out of the ten-nation revived Roman Empire. In addition, the prophet warned in Daniel 9:26 that "the people of the prince who is to come shall destroy the city and the sanctuary." This prophecy was specifically fulfilled when the legions of Rome burned the city of Jerusalem and destroyed the Temple on the ninth day of Av, A.D. 70. But it's important to note that there is a prophecy within a prophecy in Daniel 9:26. The "prince who is to come" will come out of the "the people" who "shall destroy the city." History records that it was the Roman Empire and its armies that destroyed Jerusalem and the Temple in A.D. 70. Therefore, the "prince who is to come" must come out of the Roman Empire.

The final world emperor who will become the Antichrist will rule the ten-nation Roman confederacy based in Europe. Daniel declared that "his power shall be mighty, but not by his own power" (Daniel 8:24). That is, he will receive supernatural power from Satan, which will enable him to achieve spectacular results in politics, economics, and war. The Bible tells us that this man will come forth "in the latter time of their kingdom" and that "when the transgressors have reached their fullness, a king shall arise, having fierce features, who understands sinister schemes" (Daniel 8:23). This tyrant will be satanically possessed and deeply involved with the occult. Daniel also said that he "shall prosper and thrive"—he will initially produce economic prosperity to gain favor in his rapid rise to power. His brilliant economic policies will produce massive wealth; "through his cunning he shall cause deceit to prosper under his hand" (Daniel 8:25).

"Come now, you rich, weep and howl for your miseries that are coming upon you! Your riches are corrupted, and your garments are moth-eaten. Your gold and silver are corroded and their corrosion will be a witness against you and will eat your flesh like fire. You have reaped up treasure in the last days" (James 5:1-3). In light of the prophecy in James 5:4 and the reference to worldwide famine in Revelation 6 (which would result from the economic collapse in the last days), it is possible that the coming financial crisis will provide an opportunity for the Antichrist to appear on the scene with a brilliant plan for a new economy.

As a result of his initial successes, the satanically empowered Antichrist will proudly "magnify himself in his heart" (Daniel 8:25) and blaspheme against God. Daniel declared that "by peace [he] shall destroy many" (Daniel 8:25 KJV) indicating he will subtly use false peace treaties to conquer many nations. The Antichrist will make a seven-year treaty with Israel as part of his satanic strategy to "destroy the mighty, and also the holy people" (Daniel 8:24). He will hate the Jewish people because they bear God's holy name and they remain His chosen people. Despite his satanic powers, he will be totally destroyed when he attacks the armies of heaven at the return of Jesus Christ at the Battle of Armageddon. When he is defeated by Christ, both the Antichrist and the False Prophet will be cast into the lake of fire forever. My book *Prince of Darkness* explores the many biblical prophecies about the fascinating career of the Antichrist and his ultimate destruction in the final years of this age.

CHAPTER 7

Russia's Role in the Last Days

The Russians continue to build up their powerful military forces while the West is rapidly reducing its armed forces and military preparedness. Despite constant media propaganda that Russia is no longer a military threat, the huge Red Army remains the greatest military machine on earth in manpower and weaponry. Many commentators have pointed to the ineffectiveness of the Russian attack on Chechnya as evidence that the Red Army is no longer a threat. However, the confusion was caused by the ongoing internal battle for control of the Red Army and Russia itself. Such struggles, as well as the current economic and political problems within Russia, will not prevent the nation from invading the Middle East as the prophet Ezekiel predicted thousands of years ago.

History reveals that Russia often attacked her neighbors during times of internal crisis as a means of uniting the nations against external enemies. There are indications of growing imperialism in the Russian military, the intelligence agencies, and among those who are ruling the nations from behind the scenes. The recent brutal invasion and wholesale bombing of thousands of civilians in Chechnya, a southern province of Russia that wants to become independent, is just one indication that the leaders in Moscow are reverting to their historic totalitarian and imperialistic methods.

Russia's Secret Plan

During the 1930s, Dimitri Manuilski, a political instructor at the Lenin School for Political Warfare and teacher of Mikhail Gorbachev, taught the necessity of deceiving the West prior to launching an all-out military assault on the Western nations:

War to the hilt between communism and capitalism is inevitable. Today of course, we are not strong enough to attack. Our time will come in 30 to 40 years. To win, we shall need the element of surprise. The bourgeoisie . . . will have to be put to sleep. So we shall begin by launching the most spectacular peace movement on record. There will be electrifying overtures and unheard of concessions. The capitalist countries, stupid and decadent, will rejoice to cooperate in their own destruction. They will leap at another chance to be friends. As soon as their guard is down, we will smash them with our clenched fist.[1]

This documented communist strategy is significant if we wish to understand the true meaning of the events transpiring within Russia today. The communist leaders realized long ago that they could never surpass the West economically. They saw that they needed to develop a long-range strategy of deception that would motivate elite leaders in the West to assist them. From the beginning of the 1917 Russian Revolution, communist leader Vladimir Lenin openly admitted the basic strategy of deception that governed Russian behavior: "We advance through retreat."[2] In other words, they would publicly pretend that Russia's situation was much more desperate than it was in order to motivate western leaders to provide massive amounts of advanced technology and billions of dollars in credits while allowing western military defenses to disintegrate.

By 1921, only four years after the 1917 Russian Revolution, communist economic principles had brought Russia to the edge of economic collapse. Realizing Russia's desperate need for western credits, technological assistance, and a more diligent workforce, Lenin introduced limited capitalism under his New Economic Policy. Five years later, after the Russian economy had stabilized, Lenin ordered the businessmen and farmers who had prospered during the five years to be thrown into concentration camps. That was one of six separate "glasnosts" the communists have used to deceive the West about their plans to destroy us. Each time, as they are doing today, western leaders have rushed in to "save Russia" from the disastrous consequences of communism.

Today, the secret elite ruling the Western nations believe they can move Russia and America towards a historic partnership to achieve a one-world government. However, dedicated communists are still ruling Russia and the Commonwealth of Independent States through their continuing control of the military, state industries, the renamed KGB, and the renamed communist party controlling the Russian parliament. These Russian forces believe they can double-cross their allies, the naive western elitists, by launching a devastating attack on the vital and strategic oil fields of the Middle East and by joining with their Arab allies in an all-out invasion of Israel.

Sir William Stephenson, who was the head of Combined Allied Intelligence Operations during World War II revealed that Soviet President Mikhail Gorbachev, in a speech to the Soviet Politburo in November 1987, laid out Russia's deceptive strategy. Gorbachev told his communist associates,

> Comrades, do not be concerned about all you hear about glasnost and perestroika and democracy in the coming years. These are primarily for outward consumption. There will be no significant internal change within the Soviet Union other than for cosmetic purposes. Our purpose is to disarm the Americans and let them fall asleep. We want to accomplish three things: One, we want the Americans to withdraw conventional forces from Europe. Two, we want them to withdraw nuclear forces from Europe. Three, we want the Americans to stop proceeding with Strategic Defense Initiative.[3]

If you compare the startling geopolitical events of the last decade with the secret communist agenda laid out by Mikhail Gorbachev, you will conclude that their strategy has succeeded brilliantly: 1) America has withdrawn several hundred thousand of its troops from Europe, leaving only a token force. 2) President Bush ordered the withdrawal of all nuclear missiles from Europe. In addition, Bush withdrew all nuclear weapons from American Navy ships and eliminated the Fail Safe system of B-52 bombers on constant alert that protected North America for 50 years. 3) Finally, the Americans stopped their development and deployment of its brilliantly conceived Strategic Defense Initiative, which would have protected the West in the event of an attack from a significant number of incoming enemy ballistic missiles.

So while Russia continues the most massive armaments buildup in history, Western leaders continue to disarm because they believe the lie that Russia is both harmless and truly democratic.

Russia's imperialistic goals cannot be realized unless the western nations can be defeated without triggering a mutually suicidal thermonuclear war. Their objective is to win the final battle with the West without fighting a cataclysmic war. The only practical way to do that is to seize the supplies that allow our western economies to prosper—the strategic minerals of South Africa that are essential for our advanced technologies, and the enormous oil reserves of the Middle East that provide the fuel needed by western industry. With less than 100 days' worth of oil reserves, Japan and Europe could easily be forced to capitulate to Russia if their vital oil supplies were cut off. If Russia can obtain control of these mineral and oil deposits, then she can force both Europe and the Pacific Rim countries to submit to Russian domination without conducting an invasion that could trigger a nuclear war.

Significantly, Soviet Secretary-General Leonid Brezhnev articulated the above strategy in "Brezhnev Doctrine" in 1973: "We will take the two great treasure chests upon which the West depends: the strategic oil reserves in the Middle East and the strategic minerals in Southern Africa, and then we will dictate the terms of surrender to the United States and to the West."[4] After decades of American State Department promotion of economic sanctions and political pressure against South Africa's government, the communist-led African National Congress of Nelson Mandela took over the government.

South Africa and Russia are the only sources on earth for 12 different minerals that are essential for the production of advanced technologies and missile defenses. A U.S. Joint Chiefs of Staff study found that America could not sustain its defense production in the event of a cutoff of these vital strategic minerals from South Africa. Significantly, western intelligence agencies recently reported that Joe Slobo (a KGB agent), Mandela's top communist aide, recently held meetings with his counterparts in Russia to discuss plans to limit the export of strategic minerals to the West.

The Arms Buildup

Even liberal commentators admit that the massive American arms buildup by President Reagan's administrations finally brought Communist Russians to the point where they realized they could not keep up with America's advanced economy and weapon technology. However, the greatly enhanced military force that Reagan built is now being dismantled as rapidly as possible by the Clinton administration. Dick Cheney, President Bush's former defense secretary, severely criticized Clinton for "squandering the legacy" of Desert Storm's warriors. Representative Jack Kemp recently reported that the United States is "cutting 15,000 personnel, one ship, 37 primary aircraft and one combat battalion each month."

The Russian military still contains over 4.5 million troops, including 350,000 secret police, interior ministry troops, and Spetsnaz special-forces commandos. Despite its obvious economic problems, Russia still maintains an enormous military force in comparison to less than two million American soldiers. And we must keep in mind that only 500,000 of America's troops are combat-ready soldiers. The Russian navy remains four times larger than the U.S. Navy. The Russians have 450 submarines compared to only 138 American subs. They have ten times more tanks and armored vehicles than America. In the event of war, the Russian army can field over 70,000 battle tanks compared to little more than 22,000 American tanks. Meanwhile, Russia is building 3,500 new tanks every year while America has stopped production of M-1 tanks.

A Future Invasion?

The Russian arms buildup is not confined to Russia. Seven of Russia's largest military bases are located in the Middle East. Russia maintains 14 major air bases in Libya alone with more than 550 Russian combat aircraft. To put this situation in perspective, Russia now has more air force jets in Libya than the total combined air forces of England, West Germany, and France. In addition, Russia has prepositioned a staggering 16,000 tanks and armored cars in Libya. This means that Russia has a tank force in Libya greater than the combined tank forces of France, Britain and Germany.

It's important to note that Libya has only three million citizens and no significant enemies. Why would Libya's Colonel Qaddafi require a larger military force than the major powers of Western Europe combined? Obviously, Libya has neither the intention nor the capability to utilize such a vast military force. This enormous buildup in Libya and other Middle Eastern countries will most likely be used by Russia and her allies in a future war against Israel and the strategic oil interest in the Middle East.

Despite all of the peace talks and negotiations over the last few years, the Middle East remains the most likely area in the world for the next great war to occur. During the last five years Russia has supplied over $21 billion in new advanced weapons to

Syria without any hope of repayment of billions of dollars owed for past arms sales. In one 18-month period, both Afghanistan and Iraq received a staggering $20 billion each in sophisticated weapons while billions of dollars in arms were sent to Yemen to threaten Saudi Arabia.

The *Sunday Times* of London reported that a former KGB general officer, General Oleg Kalugin, has revealed that Russian military officers developed plans to trigger a nuclear "seismic bomb" that would induce huge earthquakes throughout America.[5] Secret records were discovered last year at the Soviet Academy of Sciences that describe how the earth's tectonic plates could be disturbed by a massive nuclear bomb that would trigger huge earthquakes. While this was reported in European newspapers, it was ignored by U.S. newspapers.

The Dangers of Rising Russian Imperialism

In *Foreign Affairs*, Canadian journalist Stephen Handelman wrote:

> Russian policy makers committed a fundamental mistake. They tried to develop a free market before constructing a civil society in which such a market could safely operate. As a result, businessmen, politicians, and law enforcement agencies suffer. . . . Many activities that are required for a market economy to function remain illegal or unprotected by legislation; other activities that are considered unlawful according to Western norms, such as organized crime, are not specifically prohibited.[6]

The danger is that the collapse of political control in both the former USSR and now within Russia will not lead to democracy and a capitalist free-market economy. The political disarray and staggering growth of organized crime has created a bizarre alliance between the old communists, the military, the renamed KGB intelligence agencies, and numerous powerful criminal gangs. A large segment of organized crime in Russia is involved in the smuggling of military equipment, strategic minerals, and nuclear weapons.

Meanwhile, there is a growing danger that the West is relying solely on President Yeltsin, who has lost the respect of most Russians. If he wants to stay in power, Yeltsin will be forced to make secret alliances with the military of the new Russian "Mafia." The real danger will arise as Yeltsin or the ultranationalist who replaces him as president in 1996 attempts to reestablish military control over portions of the former Soviet Union as well as rebellious parts of Russia, such as Chechnya. Thus Russia is a wounded but powerful bear that still poses a major threat to its neighbors.

U.S. intelligence leaders and the Clinton administration are now wondering how far they should intervene to protect the Russian nuclear arsenal. The problem is not a new one. American intelligence learned of the plotting against Gorbachev in the months leading up to the August 1991 "phony" coup. Once they recognized Gorbachev's political weakness, the U.S. administration established contact with Yeltsin as a possible replacement leader. During those months, U.S. intelligence agents were sent to assist President Yeltsin to establish his personal security and provide him with sophisticated communications security equipment. Incredibly, despite the strongest possible objections by the head of the U.S. National Security Agency (NSA), which intercepts top-secret enemy communications, President Bush ordered that the secret information obtained by NSA intercepts be given to Yeltsin to assist him against the coup leaders. This unprecedented transfer of intelligence to Russia, an acknowledged enemy, helped Yeltsin defeat the "so-called" coup led by hardline military and KGB leaders.

This transfer of secret NSA intelligence intercepts to the president of Russia was done with great stealth. Despite the fact that U.S. law clearly demands that the intelligence committees of the House of Representatives and Senate must be formally notified, President Bush kept this transfer of American intelligence a secret from Congress. The U.S. Administration offered this help because it believed that Yeltsin was more committed to western-style democracy and economic reform than Gorbachev.

Various media reports have claimed that Gorbachev received a number of warnings about the coming coup, including a telephone call by President Bush. However, as I have detailed in my book *Prince of Darkness*, this phony "coup" was actually planned by Gorbachev together with the coup "hardliners" including Vladimir Kryuchkov, KGB chairman, and Soviet Defense Minister Dmitri Yazov. The purpose of the false coup was to pretend to the West that the hardliners had tried and failed to stop the democratic reforms. This bit of Russian political theater succeeded in convincing western leaders that the West could safely disarm because the so-called democratic leaders Gorbachev and Yeltsin were believed to be in control of Russia's military. However all eight coup leaders have been released and pardoned. During interviews with the *Toronto Star*, Canada's leading newspaper, each of the eight coup leaders admitted that Gorbachev planned the coup with them for three weeks prior to his phony "arrest."

As the "coup" commenced, NSA intercepts of Kryuchkov's and Yazov's messages to the Soviet military commanders were secretly transmitted to Yeltsin. The top American intelligence communications specialist was secretly sent from the Moscow embassy to work with Yeltsin at the Russian White House. He made sure that Yeltsin's telephone communications were secure when he called the generals to advise them to reject the hardliners' appeals and refuse their calls. Although the Soviet defense minister and the head of the KGB used Russia's highest security communications to reach the commanders of the key army divisions, everything they said was intercepted by sophisticated American surveillance technology. Within minutes of their calls, Yeltsin knew what his opponents were up to. Unfortunately, President Bush's decision to provide this top-secret intelligence to Yeltsin revealed to the Russians that America had penetrated every one of their secret technologies and advanced codes. The secret communication interception technologies that might have prevented a future disaster upon America were compromised by revealing to the Russians that we had the capability to listen in on everything they said. Following the phony coup, the new leaders of Russia have greatly enhanced their ability to protect their sensitive military communications from American technology because they know exactly what had been penetrated in the past.

The president's decision to provide this extremely top-secret intelligence to Yeltsin, overruling his intelligence chiefs, is even more astonishing in light of the law he signed on August 14, 1991, only four days before the coup. President Bush signed that day a congressional amendment to the 1947 National Security Act—an amendment that made it illegal for the president to refuse to fully inform Congress about covert intelligence actions, including the provision of secret intelligence communications to the Russian president.

The Identity of "Gog and Magog"

The names "Gog and Magog" are famous in biblical prophetic literature and rabbinical writings because of their role in the great War of Gog and Magog as predicted by the prophet Ezekiel (chapters 38–39). The book of Revelation (chapter 20) also records that millions will once again join with the nations represented by "Gog and Magog," led by Satan, in a final attack against the beloved city and camp of the saints at the end of the Millennium. This final war will be the last battle in human history.

Prophecy indicates that three enormous wars will convulse the planet during the apocalyptic period known as "the last days." The first war, as described by Ezekiel, is that of Gog and Magog, the coming Russian-Arab invasion against Israel. The second battle, seven or so years later, is described in Joel, Zechariah, and the book of Revelation (16:16). This second war is known as the Battle of Armageddon. This cataclysmic conflict will involve the armies of the entire world pitted against each other and finally, against Jesus Christ. Revelation 20:8 tells us about a third war, a final battle that will occur 1,000 years later at the end of the Millennium. A large number of people born during the Millennium to those who survive the tribulation period will choose to join Satan in his attack against the City of God, once more led by Gog and Magog—the nation of Russia and other nations to the extreme north of the Holy Land.

Bible students who wish to clearly understand end-time prophecies know that properly identifying the nation of Magog is important. "Magog" is a real nation occupying a territory that was known to Ezekiel and his Jewish readers in the fifth century before Christ. I believe that evidence supports the con-

clusion that Magog refers to the ancient territory of
Scythia, which is currently occupied by Russia and
several of the southern republics of the Commonwealth of Independent States (formerly the USSR).

Most prophecy teachers believe that "Magog"
refers to the ancient tribal groups that once occupied
the area that now comprises Russia. However, a
number of liberal Christian scholars have challenged
this identification. Some scholars suggest that Magog
was connected with some small tribal groups in ancient Mesopotamia in today's Iran. Others suggest
Magog was connected with the tribes led by Gyges in
the area of Turkey, known to the ancients as Lydia, to
the south of Russia.

In addition to rejecting Magog as Russia, many
liberal scholars reject any literal interpretation of the
reference to Magog. They tend to interpret Ezekiel's
prophecy about the future war of Gog and Magog as
merely a symbolic, apocalyptic war between good
and evil.

If we want to understand God's prophetic message
regarding the events in the last days, we need to correctly identify Gog and Magog. Following is a summary of the information I have drawn together after
some years of researching this question.

Jewish Scholarship that Identifies
Magog with Russia

The passages in Ezekiel were studied in minute detail for thousands of years by Jewish sages. Therefore, their conclusions should throw some light on

the true meaning of the Hebrew words "Gog and Magog." Note that Genesis chapter 10 lists Magog as a literal grandson of Noah, who ultimately gave birth to a nation. This name, Magog, was well known to every Jew who studied this Genesis passage every year as part of their weekly Sabbath reading of the Torah. The prophet Ezekiel included the name Magog together with the names of other specific countries such as Libya, Persia, and Ethiopia in his prophecy about the yet-future war. This suggests that Ezekiel expected the name Magog would be understood by his Jewish readers as a real nation, not as an abstract symbol of evil.

A recent commentary on the book of Genesis, *Bereishis—Genesis: A New Translation with a Commentary Anthologised from Talmudic, Midrashic and Rabbinic Sources*, includes this comment about Genesis 10:2: "Magog is mentioned several times in Scripture, e.g., Ezekiel 38:2; 39:6 as the name of the land of Gog. *Kesses HaSofer* identifies them with the Mongols who lived near China, for in fact the very name Mongol is a corruption of Magog. He also cites Arab writers who refer to the Great Wall of China as the wall of Al Magog."[7] The 1961 commentary on the Torah by Dr. J.H. Hertz (the late Chief Rabbi of the British Empire), *The Pentateuch and Haftorahs*, comments as follows: "Magog—The Scythians, whose territory lay on the borders of the Caucasus."[8]

A brilliant Jewish commentary on *Ezekiel*, published in 1980 by The ArtScroll Tanach Series, comments on Magog in this statement:

The various traditions concerning the identity of Magog, who in Genesis 10:2 is listed among the sons of Noah's son Japheth, tend to place the land of Magog in what today is southwest Russia—The Caucasian region, which lies between the Black and Caspian Seas. . . . This is in agreement with *Yerushalmi Megillah* 3:9 which renders Magog as "the Goths," a group of nomadic tribes who destroyed the Scythians and made their homes in Scythian territory. . . . Our identification of Magog as Caucasia, which was at one time inhabited by the Goths, is based on the assumption that the land of Magog is named after Japheth's son.[9]

The *Ezekiel* commentary further noted,

Rabbi Chisdai Ibn Shaprut wrote to the kind of Khazaria (a Caucasian kingdom in southern Russia which converted to Judaism in the eighth century after Christ) in which he addresses the king as "prince, leader of Meshech and Tubal." This salutation, drawn from our verse indicates that the Gaonim had a tradition that these countries were indeed located in Russia.[10]

The highly acclaimed *Ezekiel* commentary concludes this section with a fascinating note: In this light one may understand an oral tradition passed down from the Vilna Gaon, that when the Russian navy passes through the Bosporus (that is, on the way to the Mediterranean through the Dardanelles) it will be time to put on Sabbath clothes (in anticipation of the coming of the Mashiach). Flavius Josephus, who lived at the time of Saint Paul, wrote a definitive history of the Jewish people called the *Antiquities of the Jews*. The historian Josephus identified Magog in these words. "Magog founded those that from him were named Magogites, but who are by the Greeks called Scythians" (pp. 30,31).[11]

Christian Scholarship that Identifies Magog as Russia

Young's Analytical Concordance of the Holy Bible, in dealing with Magog, speaks of ancient Scythia or Tartary, a name used to describe southern Russia in past centuries. Dr. R. Young said that the name Gog was derived from a phrase that meant a "high mountain" and that "Gog" in Ezekiel 38 referred to "A prince of Rosh, Mesheck, Tubal, and Tiras, in ancient Scythia or Tartary." Young also described "the descendants of Magog and their land, called Scythia, in the North of Asia and Europe."[12] The authoritative 1973 reference work, *Eerdman's Handbook to the Bible*, came to the same conclusion: "Magog, Meshech, Tubal and Gomer were all sons of Japheth (Noah's son). They gave their names to Indo-European peoples living in the Black Sea/Caucasus region, on the northern fringe of the then-known world."[13]

The Comprehensive Commentary of the Holy Bible, edited by Dr. William Jenks, provided some fascinating information regarding Magog. "The Jews of his day thought 'Magog to be the Scythian nations, vast and innumerable, who are beyond Mount Caucasus and the Palus Maeotis, and near the Caspian Sea, stretching even to India.'"[14] Dr. Jenks then quotes Bochart on the following information:

> The Koran, and a Christian poet of Syria (Ephraem the Syrian) before the Koran was published, both allude to a fable of Alexander's shutting up the barbarous and troublesome nations, Gog and Magog, near the Northern Pole by an iron and brasen wall. The mountain Scythians extended hence (from the river Araxes) to the Caucasus, and those of the plain to the Don, the Sea of Azof, and the Northern Ocean. It is credible, that from the Rosh and Meshech nations dwelling about the Araxes, are descended the Russians and Moscovites.[15]

Dr. John Gill, a major Calvinist theologian of the eighteenth century, wrote *A Commentary on the Old Testament* in 1748, including his fascinating comments on Magog's identification:

> The countries of Gog and Magog, according to the Arabic geographers [*Geography Arabic* par. 9. clim. 5. line 22], are surrounded by Mount Caucasus, which Bochart [*Pha'eg.* l.3.c.13.col.187] conjectures has its name from thence . . . Gog-hasan, or Gog's fortress. This land of Magog is the same with Cathaia or Scythia . . . Gog is further described as the chief prince of Meshec and Tubal: some render it, prince of Rosh, Meshec, and Tubal taking Rosh, as the rest, for the name of a place, a part of Scythia, from whence the Russians came, and had their name. So it is rendered by the Septuagint, Symmachus and Theodotion; and some later Greek writers [Zonaras, Cedrenus] make mention of a country called Ros, which they say, is a Scythian nation, situated between the

Euxine Pontus (Black Sea) and the whole maritime coast to
the north of Taurus, a people fierce and wild.[16]

Dr. Dwight C. Pentecost is the author of an
excellent study of the major themes of Bible
prophecy entitled *Things to Come*. During the last
few years I have had the opportunity to discuss a
number of prophetic issues with Dr. Pentecost, and I
have a great appreciation for his superb book. In his
book he quoted the scholar Professor Bauman on the
identification of Magog as follows:

Magog's land was located in, what is called today, the Caucasus and the adjoining steppes. And the three, Rosh, Meshech
and Tubal were called by the ancients, Scythians. They
roamed as nomads in the country around and north of the
Black and the Caspian seas, and were known as the wildest
barbarians. . . .[17]

One of the most important scholarly tools em-
ployed in the exegesis of Scripture is *Gesenius' Hebrew and Chaldee Lexicon*. For many years this
book has been referred to by numerous scholars as a
major authority on the precise meaning of Hebrew
and Chaldee words found in the original manuscripts
of the Old Testament. Regarding Magog, he wrote:

Magog - PR. N. of a son of Japheth, Genesis 10:2; also of a
region, and a great and powerful people of the same name,
inhabiting the recesses of the north, who are at some time to

invade the Holy Land, Ezekiel 38, 39. We are to understand just the same nations as the Greeks comprised, under the name of Scythian (Josephus *Antiquites of the Jews* 1.6.1).[18]

In addition, Gesenius' comment on the name "Gog" described him as a "prince of the land of Magog . . . also of Rossi, Moschi, and Tibareni, who are to come with great forces from the extreme north (38:15; 39:2), after the Exile (38:8,12) to invade the holy land, and to perish there, as prophesied by Ezekiel."[19] Gesenius identified the Revelation 20:8 passage as a reference to a final war involving "Gog and Magog" at the end of the Millennium. However, he indicates this final war is a totally different event: "Gog and Magog in the Apocalypse belong to a different time to those spoken of in Ezekiel, so it is in vain to point out a discrepancy."[20]

The literal interpretation of "Magog" by Gesenius stands in stark contrast to the allegorical interpretation of modern scholars who treats Ezekiel 38, 39 as "apocalyptic literature" referring only to a symbolic war between good and evil. Gesenius identified Magog as a real country, to the extreme north of the Holy Land, that will invade Israel in the future. He identified the land with the "same nations as the Greeks comprised under the name of Scythians."

In light of the numerous Jewish and Christian scholars who identify Magog with Scythia, we must answer these critical questions: Who were the Scythians, and what territory did they occupy?

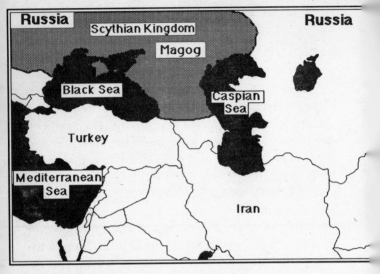

The Location of Scythia and Magog

Professor G. Rawlinson wrote a definite study of the ancient tribes and empires that ruled the Middle East, called *Five Great Monarchies*. His section dealing with Assyria (chapter 9) included this footnote: "The Scythians proper of Herodotus and Hippocrates extended from the Danube and the Carpathians on the one side, to the Tanais or Don upon the other."[21] The areas described by Professor Rawlinson as being ruled by the Scythians are located in the south of Russia and in the southern republics of the commonwealth of Independent States (the former USSR). I have included a map that illustrates the geographic area where the ancient Scythians ruled.

The Coming Russian-Arab Assault

The prophecies of Ezekiel 38 and 39 tell us that Russia (Magog) will lead a confederacy of nations in an all-out military invasion of Israel in the last days. The miraculous defeat of Magog at the hand of God will set the stage for the final rise of the one-world government of the Antichrist. In fact, the defeat of Russia and its allies through the supernatural intervention of God will prepare the way for the rise of Antichrist over the ten nations that will arise within the confines of the ancient Roman Empire. Ezekiel's prophecies described an enormous military power to the extreme far north of Israel—a power that will lead a huge alliance of Russian, Arab, North African, and Middle Eastern nations in an overwhelming assault on Israel in an attempt to destroy the chosen people.

Ezekiel prophesied to "Gog," the leader of Russia, as follows:

> On that day when My people Israel dwell safely, will you not know it? Then you will come from your place out of the far north, you and many peoples with you, all of them riding on horses, a great company and a mighty army. You will come up against My people Israel like a cloud, to cover the land. It will be in the latter days that I will bring you against My land, so that the nations may know Me, when I am hallowed in you, O Gog, before their eyes (Ezekiel 38:14-16).

Despite the incredible military strength of the coming Russian-Arab assault, Israel will be victorious because the Lord will intervene in a supernatural manner to save His chosen people. After moving their troops into the nations surrounding Israel, the Russian and Arab armies will prepare to invade the Holy Land. However, Ezekiel warns us that the Lord will unleash the greatest earthquake in history to destroy these invaders:

> Surely in that day there shall be a great earthquake in the land of Israel. . . . And I will bring him to judgment with pestilence and bloodshed; I will rain down on him, on his troops, and on the many peoples who are with him, flooding rain, great hailstones, fire, and brimstone (Ezekiel 38:19,22).

The soldiers of Gog and Magog will be destroyed by earthquake, plague, hailstones, fire, and brimstone sent from God. In addition, the Lord will afflict the Russian-Arab armies with a madness that will cause each soldier to attack his brother soldier until finally 85 percent of the invading army will be left dead on the mountains surrounding Israel (*see* Ezekiel 39:2,11-16). The number of dead soldiers will be so many that the prophet tells us that it will take seven months to bury them.

This War of Gog and Magog will eliminate the great military superpower of Russia and its plans to defeat the Western democracies. When Russia joins with the Arab nations to attack Israel, their motive will be to conquer the strategic Middle East and seize its enormously valuable oil reserves. Yet the miraculous defeat of Russia and her Arab allies will drastically alter the geopolitical balance of power. When Russia is defeated, the newly united European Union will emerge as the greatest economic, political, and military power on the planet. These pivotal events will set the stage for the rise of the new European superstate and the emergence of the new leader who will ultimately assume the role of the Antichrist, the final world dictator.

CHAPTER 8

Israel's Role in the Coming World Government

The Middle East is of immense strategic value to any superpower that wishes to dominate the world. This area contains 65 percent of the world's exportable oil reserves and its location dominates both the Suez Canal and the Straits of Hormuz, controlling the vital shipping lanes. Therefore, any aspiring global superpower will seek to conquer the Middle East and acquire the oil reserves that fuel the industrial societies of the West and the Pacific Rim by first conquering Israel.

Israel is the key to the military control of the Middle East because it occupies the vital land bridge linking Africa, Europe, and Asia. With its well-motivated and superbly trained army, its magnificent air force and sophisticated military tactics, Israel has withstood the enormous Arab military armies that attacked her during four recent wars. This geopolitical reality is obvious to every military planner and political strategist in Europe, Russia, and the Far East. According to the ancient prophecies, the super-powers will marshal their huge armies in two great invasions of the Holy Land in the end times. Scripture tells us, however, that these huge armies will be destroyed by the hand of God.

The prophet Ezekiel foretold that Russia and the Arab nations will first attack Israel without warning in the War of Gog and Magog. After God's super-natural destruction of these invaders, Israel will sign a seven-year treaty with the new ten-nation confederacy, the rising superpower in Europe. Rather than trust in the power of the Lord that saved her from the Russian-Arab armies, Israel's wicked leaders will trust in a piece of paper promising the protection of the revived Roman Empire and its new leader, the Antichrist.

The Old Testament prophets and the book of Revelation foretold that the cataclysmic Battle of Armageddon will occur at the end of this seven-year-treaty period. The massive military forces of both East and West will gather their armies into northern Israel for this final battle. The supernatural defeat of these armies at the return of the Messiah as the King of kings will set the stage for the establishment of His Messianic kingdom.

The Arab-Israel Peace Talks

The nation of Israel is now approaching an abyss that many friends of the Jews believe will place the nation in danger of total defeat and annihilation in its next war against the Arab nations. Israel now faces its greatest moment of danger in its modern history. As the Jewish state approaches its greatest crisis she is led by men who have lost the hardened and realistic military approach that characterized her past leaders. Today's Israeli leadership is desperate for a final comprehensive peace treaty that will demonstrate the Arab's acceptance of the legal right of the Jewish state to exist in the Middle East. At a time when Israel needs a resolute King David to lead them, the nation is led by men who are no longer able to refuse relentless Arab demand for concessions.

Sidney Hook, in his book *The Hero in History*, records Emperor Napoleon's sage observation on the supreme value of leadership in determining the outcome of a war: "An army of rabbits commanded by a lion is better than an army of lions commanded by a rabbit."[1] Unfortunately, the Arab nations realize that Israel's current leaders are desperate and intend to capitalize on Israel's weakening resolve to face the long struggle which lies ahead. The Palestine Liberation Organization (PLO) clearly reveals the Arab perspective: "Promise them anything and deliver nothing."

The history of "peace negotiations" has been marked by a long trail of Arab demands and Jewish concessions—and no change whatsoever in the Arab's unrelenting hatred and continuing terrorism. Meanwhile, the Arab states continue a staggering military arms buildup in preparation for the final Jihad, an Arab "holy war" that will stop at nothing to annihilate the Jewish state.

The "peace at any price" attitude on the part of Israel's current Labor Party was starkly illustrated in January 1995 when Mahmoud Abbas, head of the PLO negotiating team that secretly met in Oslo, Norway, released his fascinating new book called *The Road to Oslo.* His book contained a staggering revelation that has produced a major political scandal in Israel. Mahmoud Abbas has alleged that, during the months prior to the 1992 Israeli elections when the right wing Likud party was defeated, leading members of the opposition Labor Party illegally met numerous times with PLO negotiators. Mahmoud Abbas claimed that, during these illegal and secret meetings, opposition Labor Party officials encouraged the PLO leadership to reject the Likud-led Israeli government's peace offers. Their alleged joint conspiracy was intended to influence the approaching election by motivating Jewish voters to support the Labor Party in the hopes that they could produce the peace agreement that had eluded the Likud Party. If subsequent investigation proves the allegation is correct, it will likely lead to the collapse of the Labor government and possible treason trials for the Israeli politicians involved in the affair.

The prospects for a lasting peace in the Middle East are grim. The problem is that even Israel's total surrender of the West Bank, Gaza, and the Golan Heights will not satisfy the true ultimate goals of the Arab nations nor the PLO. Since the Arab's true stated goal is the annihilation of Israel, these surrenders of land will not bring a lasting peace. Instead, they will simply alter the strategic situation massively and irreversibly in favor of the Arabs without removing the underlying causes that have motivated the last four wars against Israel.

We should remember that the Arab nations tried to annihilate the Jewish state in three wars—1948, 1956, and 1967—long before the Jews had occupied the West Bank, Gaza, and the Golan Heights. Obviously, Arab motivation for war against the Jews will never be satisfied by the surrender of occupied territories to the PLO and Syria. These surrenders will simply allow the Arabs to be in a much improved strategic position to launch a final war against Israel.

Despite the current peace euphoria, Israel's Arab neighbors will continue to harbor strong reasons to launch a war against the Jewish state long after the peace talks have concluded. Despite negotiations with the White House, Israel will not be able to rely on the West for its security in the future.

The Secret Israeli-Vatican Agreement

An incredible allegation was made recently by *Inside Israel*, an Israeli news magazine. In July 1994 they reported that government sources have privately revealed that Shimon Peres, Israel's foreign minister, offered Pope John Paul II and the Vatican the control of the Holy City. During an interview with the weekly Israeli newspaper *Shishi*, Mark Halter, a French writer, revealed that he delivered a letter from his friend Peres to the Pope in May 1994—a letter that laid out Israel's offer. Halter stated, "Peres offered to

hand over sovereignty of Jerusalem's Old City to the
Vatican. . . Jerusalem will stay the capital of Israel but
the Old City will be administered by the Vatican. The
city will have an Israeli mayor and a Palestinian
mayor, both under orders from the Holy See. The program was originally submitted to the Vatican by Peres
two years ago, just before the Oslo talks began."

According to Israeli and Vatican sources this plan
was also discussed with the PLO. Apparently, Yasser
Arafat has provisionally agreed to the plan. In effect,
the plan calls for the legal extraterritoriality of the
Old City in the same sense that an embassy in a foreign capital has legal extraterritoriality. In addition,
the airport at Aterot will fall under the same legal
status and may become a major meeting place in the
Middle East. The idea is that the only way to assure peace in the Holy City is to allow a "neutral"
power, the Vatican, to guarantee the protection of
the religious sites of the three major religions by
using troops from the mercenary Swiss Guards that
presently guard the Vatican in Rome. The motivation for this astonishing agreement is the enormous
difficulty in getting either Israel or the PLO to relinquish their demand for control over the politically
and religiously vital area of the walled Old City and
the Temple Mount.

The Italian newspaper *La Stampa*, an authoritative
source on Vatican affairs, on September 10, 1993,
confirmed this startling plan a few days before Arafat
and Rabin signed their historic agreement on the
White House lawn. Naturally, the Israeli Foreign

Ministry has publicly denied the plan's existence. However, Israeli government officials privately admit that the plan does exist and it is the true political position of the Labor government. Remember, too, that Yitzhak Rabin first denied the existence of an earlier secret letter of agreement with the PLO. Later, when Arafat publicly revealed the letter, Rabin was forced to admit he had signed the agreement. Similarly, despite its initial public denials, the Labor government has entered into an astonishing agreement with the Vatican regarding the control of the most sacred land in Israel. Keep in mind that the Vatican has shown nothing but hatred and contempt for the Jews for centuries. This same Vatican, desiring to curry favor with the Arabs, has refused for over 45 years to recognize Israel as a nation.

Incredibly, this plan calls for the Old City of Jerusalem to become a second "Vatican" with the holy sites of the three major religions within the Old City to be placed under the ultimate protection and authority of the Pope. The plan calls for a Palestinian state to develop in a confederation with the kingdom of Jordan. Of course, the likeliest outcome of such a plan is that the PLO will ultimately overthrow the forces of King Hussein to rule the enlarged state of Palestine-Jordan.

Significantly, in connection with this plan, Faisal El Husseini, the PLO's chief negotiator concerning Jerusalem, revealed that Rabin had secretly agreed that there would be a freeze on Jewish housing construction within Jerusalem. Despite denials from the government, very little new Jewish neighborhood construction has been permitted recently. The ultimate goal of the plan is for the walled Old City to become the religious capital of the new Palestinian state. However, the administrative and political capital of Palestine would be located in Nablus in the West Bank. The sources providing these details state that Yasser Arafat will be freely permitted to visit the Temple Mount whenever he wants. Apparently Arafat was promised that the Temple Mount will become independent of Israeli control.

There is no question, then, that the current Labor government is the most antireligious government in Israel's modern history. Their cynical contempt for God's promise of the Holy Land to Abraham's posterity has motivated them to secretly agree to hand over the Golan Heights, Gaza, and the West Bank. New polls indicate that over 70 percent of the Jewish citizens of Israel have lost confidence in their present government leaders and the state of the current peace talks.

The Balance of Power

After surrendering the West Bank, Gaza, and the Golan Heights to its enemies over the next two years, Israel's security will depend on the relative balance of military power between the Arabs and the Jewish state. A fascinating and disturbing report called "Israel's Nuclear Imperative" by the *Islamic Affairs Analyst* in April 1994 provided an excellent summary of

the balance between the forces available to the Arab
nations and the nation of Israel. In addition the study
examined the growing danger of all-out war in the
Middle East.

Here are the comparisons: the key front-line Arab
states surrounding Israel's borders are Egypt, Syria,
Lebanon, and Jordan. Israel is a very small nation
about the same size as the state of Rhode Island with
only five million citizens. It is surrounded by 21 Arab
nations with a land area over 500 times larger than Israel. The Arab nations are populated by 200 million
Arabs and they own 65 percent of the world's exportable oil. Israel has 172,000 soldiers in its standing
army with another 430,000 civilian reservists who
can be mobilized within 48 hours. The total available
military manpower of Israel adds up to 602,000 men
and women. The International Institute for Strategic
Studies (IISS) report for 1994/95 calculates that Israel
can mobilize 3,895 tanks and 478 combat aircraft in
the event of war.

Meanwhile, according to the IISS report, the front-
line Arab states of Syria, Lebanon, Egypt, and Jordan
have 1,679,900 soldiers (including reservists), 9,175
tanks, and 1,247 combat aircraft. When we add a second ring of surrounding Arab states—Saudi Arabia,
Iraq, Yemen, and Libya—Israel faces an additional
1,454,000 soldiers, 6,460 tanks, and 1,124 combat
aircraft. Then we must add another 1,019,750 soldiers, 2,389 tanks, and 659 aircraft from the six Gulf
states, the three Moslem nations of East Africa and
the four Arab states of North Africa.

When Israel's military strategists add up the total Arab forces facing Israel they number 4,153,650 armed Arab soldiers, 18,024 main battle tanks, and 3,030 combat aircraft. In addition, Israel faces a determined enemy in Iran. The Iranian army has 863,000 soldiers, 1,245 tanks, and 295 planes.

Obviously, a future invasion would not involve the complete armies of every Arab nation. However, Israel must take into account the awesome strategic and tactical disadvantage she faces in any future conflict. Also, during an Arab-Israeli war, any attempt by the West to resupply Israel with arms or men would face the daunting threat of the enormous Arab armies. In past wars all of the Arab allies of the West and many European NATO nations refused to allow America to refuel her supply planes or fly over their territory in the effort to resupply weapons and ammunition to the Jewish state.

History reveals that the most certain indication of an adversary's future threat comes from an objective analysis of that nation's military capability. Israel's generals must carefully consider the true motive behind the massive armaments buildup of the Arab states at the same time they talk of peace. For example, Egypt signed the Camp David peace treaty with Israel in 1979. Meanwhile, despite its staggering poverty during the last 16 years since the Camp David treaty, Egypt has doubled the number of its battle tanks from 1,600 to 3,300. Egypt also dramatically increased the quality of its air force through its conversion to advanced American and French fighter aircraft. The Egyptian army has also purchased 2,400 antitank guided weapons.

This huge upgrade in Egypt's military capability since the Camp David agreement was paid for by $30 billion in American civil and military aid. What's especially interesting is that Egypt has no credible enemy other than Israel. Why would Egypt spend massively on its military forces if it truly wanted peace with Israel? The answer is clear. Egypt and its Arab allies are preparing for a war of annihilation against Israel while taking advantage of every opportunity to reduce Israel's strategic depth during the peace talks.

Syria has increased its armed forces as well—to more than 800,000 troops, 4,500 battle tanks, and 591 fighter planes and bombers. Recently, Yeltsin wrote off over $10 billion in past armaments debts to Russia, and its military is now rapidly upgrading Syria's air defenses. Saudi Arabia has spent a staggering $250 billion in the last decade on high-technology weapons. While Iran is far from Israel, its Islamic leaders are absolutely determined to wipe the Jewish state from the map. With more than 850,000 soldiers, 1,200 tanks, and 295 aircraft, Iran will play a key role in any future conflict.

The Threats to Israel

Ballistic Missiles

Not only do the Arab nations have a staggering array of conventional weapons and massive armies, they also have used their massive oil earning to purchase enormous numbers of deadly ballistic missiles—missiles like the ones used by Iraq during the Persian Gulf War. The news media claimed that the American Patriot antimissile missile successfully shot down most of Iraq's SCUD missiles, but the truth is that very few of the incoming missiles were totally deflected from causing damage. There is no truly effective antimissile defense today against incoming ballistic missiles. Some very promising "Star Wars" technologies were developed in American defense laboratories in the 1980s. However, these advanced missile defenses were never produced because the U.S. Congress decided not to fund President Reagan's Strategic Defense Initiative.

All of Israel's neighbors have now acquired ballistic missiles that can rain deadly destruction on Israel's military bases and its unprotected cities. Iraq's new Tammus I missile has a range of over 1,200 miles, allowing it to hit any area of Israel at will. The devastating effect on Israel's civilian morale during the Gulf War attack by only 39 Iraqi SCUD missiles demonstrated to Israel's enemies that these ballistic missiles are the weapons of choice during the next war. Syria has acquired hundreds of accurate SS-21 missiles and new SCUD-C missiles capable of carrying conventional, chemical, or biological warheads. Iran was forced to the bargaining table during the Iran-Iraq War as its cities suffered a continuous assault by ballistic missiles from Iraq in "the War of the Cities." Having learned a bitter lesson, Iran has spent staggering sums during the last five years to purchase new SCUD-C and Nodong-1 missiles from North Korea. In addition, Iraq, Libya, and Egypt have all acquired numerous ballistic missiles in the last five years.

Chemical and Biological Weapons

Egypt, Syria, Iraq, Iran, and Libya have developed advanced chemical and biological weapons that could devastate Israel's population. According to Israeli and Western intelligence agencies, most of the present Arab chemical weapons are variations of mustard gas and nerve gas. Some of these weapons can kill in only seconds.

Most of Iraq's military chemical weapons inventory was destroyed by U.N. inspectors following the Gulf War. Despite the fact that Iraq had successfully hidden its total chemical-biological weapons program from the Western intelligence services prior to the war, the inspectors discovered more than 50,000 shells and warheads filled with chemical weapons ready to fire. In addition to 50 chemical warheads loaded on SCUD missiles, the inspectors destroyed over 12,000 155-mm artillery shells filled with mustard gas and 10,000 rocket warheads filled with deadly sarin nerve gas, which kills in seconds. A staggering 300 tons of Iraqi mustard gas and sarin nerve gas were ready to place in additional warheads at the time the Gulf War ended.

While the U.N. inspectors destroyed a large percentage of Iraq's chemical weapons, recent Iraqi defectors confirm that massive numbers of new chemical and biological weapons have been produced. Libya is rushing ahead with its production of chemical and biological weapons at new plants in Tarhuna, near Tripoli, and at Sheba, far to the south. Meanwhile, Syria, Israel's deadliest enemy, has stockpiled tens of thousands of chemical and biological weapons including mustard gas, anthrax, and sarin nerve gas bombs for its MIG-23 bombers. Syria now produces hundreds of tons of nerve gas every year.

According to international treaty, chemical and biological weapons are now illegal. However, intelligence sources confirm that the Arab states are developing sophisticated biological weapons that modify existing micro-organisms and diseases to make them even more deadly. In a 1970 study, the World Health Organization revealed that an attack on a typical city of five million in the West with an anthrax biological weapon would kill more than 100,000 victims, with an additional 150,000 citizens incapacitated. The report warned that an attack that used botulism to infect the water supply of a small city of 50,000 would kill over 60 percent of the population.

Thermonuclear War

Israel's military strategists must now face the growing certainty that some of its Arab enemies will soon acquire nuclear weapons. Intelligence reports from Germany confirm that Iran purchased four nuclear weapons from Islamic Kazakhstan in 1992. Iranian intelligence agents acquired two Russian-produced 40-kiloton nuclear warheads that were designed to be used with ballistic missiles. In addition, Iranian agents purchased a nuclear bomb designed to be dropped from a bomber and a nuclear artillery shell. With the help of several German high-tech companies, Iran has now successfully modified these nuclear warheads to allow them to be launched against Israel's cities using her new longer range SCUD-C ballistic missiles. New advanced long-range missiles have also recently been added to the arsenals of Iraq and Libya.

Israeli intelligence reports tell us that Iraq was within six months of producing her own nuclear weapon when the Gulf War disrupted their sophisticated plans. However, Iraq still has more than 70,000 well-trained nuclear scientists and remains determined to develop its own nuclear bomb.

A recent report in the *Islamic Affairs Analyst* revealed that Iraqi intelligence agents had acquired more than 60,000 nuclear-weapons-related scientific documents from the West prior to the 1991 Gulf War. Incredibly, a former Saudi Arabian diplomat, Mohammed al-Khilewi, revealed in a July 1994 report that his country had provided almost $10 billion to both Pakistan and Iraq to assist their nuclear weapons programs. The plan was that Saudi Arabia would receive several nuclear weapons from her allies once they successfully produced a certain quantity of warheads. In addition, Arab intelligence services are now trying to purchase some of the more than 45,000 nuclear weapons produced by the former Soviet Union.

A False Sense of Security

As Israel negotiates a retreat to its pre-1967 borders, she is surrendering the most important military advantage she possesses in her long-term life and death struggle with the surrounding Arab states. In light of the Arabs' huge conventional armies and many chemical, biological, and nuclear weapons, Israel desperately needs to retain the strategic depth provided by its military control of the Golan Heights and the West Bank. As I shared in my book *Messiah— The War in the Middle East*, the high mountain ranges of the West Bank and the biblical territory of Judea and Samaria are a great military obstacle facing the attacking Arab armies. Today, the invading armies of Iran, Iraq, Syria, and Jordan must cross the exposed Jordan River valley, the lowest place on earth, before they can begin to climb through the mountains of the West Bank on their way to Tel Aviv. There are only five passes through these mountains that would allow Arab tanks and infantry to attack the Jewish population centers along the Mediterranean coast. Over 80 percent of the population of Israel lives in the coastal plain surrounding Tel Aviv.

Once Israel surrenders the West Bank to the PLO, the remaining Israel territory will be only nine miles wide at the center. That leaves no room for Israel's army and tank divisions to maneuver. In addition, there are no natural defenses along the flat coastland. If Arab armies ever pour through the mountain passes of the West Bank, the Jewish population of Israel would be annihilated within days or hours. In such a scenario, the only remaining option for Israel's military commanders would be to unleash a devastating nuclear attack on both the invading Arab armies and their capitals. Though such a counterattack

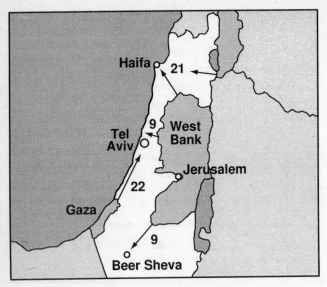

*Israel's Military Risk after surrendering the
West Bank, Gaza and the Golon Heights.*

would destroy a great number of Arabs, it would not
save Israel's population from a final holocaust, as the
Arabs would then launch a devastating rain of missiles continuing chemical and biological warheads. By
the time the Western nations reacted, it would be too
late. The terrifying situation would resemble Rwanda
or Dunkirk with Western ships trying to evacuate the
surviving refugees while the majority of the Jewish
population would already have been slaughtered.

The same strategic situation prevails in northern
Israel as the Israeli government prepares to surrender
the strategically vital Golan Heights to Syria. Today,
Israel's tanks sit on the Golan Heights only 20 miles

from the Syrian capital of Damascus. Any Syrian attack can now be easily repelled and Israeli tanks can threaten Damascus with immediate retaliation. In addition, Israel's present surveillance outposts on Mount Hermon in the Golan Heights allows them to observe any suspicious Syrian military activity taking place. However, Israel's Labor government is now planning to surrender this strategic corridor to its Syrian enemy despite the fact that Syria has used the Golan Heights to attack the Jewish state three times in the last four decades.

Syria is a Moslem state ruled by a brutal military dictatorship that has broken virtually every agreement it has ever negotiated. Its Islamic population and army are absolutely committed to the destruction of Israel. The surrender of the Golan Heights will not eliminate Syria's fundamental motive to destroy Israel. It will simply encourage Syria to believe that it can use the tremendous military advantage of a Syrian-controlled Golan Heights to launch a successful final attack on Israel.

The false sense of contentment and the belief that peace has finally arrived has caused Israel's present leaders to experience unwarranted feelings of safety. Meanwhile Israel's military security continues to deteriorate month by month. As the Israeli army retreats from Gaza and the West Bank, its security forces are unable to effectively pursue Arab terrorists. Nor can they intercept terrorist threats from within Palestinian-controlled areas. Meanwhile, the new Palestinian "police forces," composed of former terrorists, are unable and unwilling to deter new terrorist attacks on Israeli targets. Although the Oslo peace agreement has authorized only 14,000 Palestinian police workers, Yasser Arafat has created a police force of more than 30,000 "former" terrorists to enforce his dictatorial rule.

Israel's Terrible Dilemma

The major military threats from Syria, Iraq, Egypt, and Iran arise from their massive armies, huge sophisticated air forces, new ballistic missile capabilities, chemical and biological weapons, and now, nuclear weapons. In addition, these states are active sponsors of continuing terrorism in Lebanon, Israel, and Palestine. When the West Bank (Judea-Samaria) becomes the independent Arab state of Palestine during the next two years, Israel may find that it will be virtually compelled to strike pre-emptively with its nuclear weapons during the next military buildup to war. If Israel's generals conclude that an Arab attack is imminent, they will have to decide whether or not to move ahead with a nuclear attack. They will have some difficult decisions to make: When should Israel use her nuclear weapons of last resort? Should they wait until the Arabs launch their massive array of chemical, biological and possibly nuclear weapons on Tel Aviv and other Jewish cities? Should they wait until the Arab armies are pouring through the streets of Jerusalem and Tel Aviv and slaughtering Jewish women and children? Or should Israel launch her nuclear weapons at the moment her intelligence agencies confirm that the Arab states are about to attack?

Ideally, the deterrence theory suggests that Israel's nuclear weapons should prevent the Arabs from launching an attack on her. However that is theory, and the reality in the Middle East is quite different. The Arabs have recently attacked Israel twice, once in the Six-Day War in 1967 and again in the 1973 War of Atonement. These attacks came despite the fact that the Arabs knew the Jewish state possessed nuclear weapons. Another sobering concern for Israel's strategic planners is that the Islamic Arabs have a fatalistic religious philosophy that promises that adherents of Islam will go to Paradise if they destroy the Jews and infidels, even if they trigger the destruction of their own nation. We witness this fatalistic attitude in the actions of the Islamic Hamas suicide bombers who blow up themselves and innocent Jewish victims.

If Israel concludes that the Arabs are prepared to launch an all-out attack with chemical, biological, or nuclear weapons despite the certainty of Israel's devastating nuclear counterstrikes, then her plan of nuclear deterrence will have failed. Tragically, following the deadly logic of war in the Middle East, when Israel's generals conclude that the Arab nations are going to attack, an immediate pre-emptive nuclear attack on the Arab armies and weapons armories would become necessary.

At that point the only remaining questions will revolve around the timing and targeting of these weapons. Israel's initial strike would include the use of low-yield nuclear weapons targeted against Arab military bases. Israel has produced hundreds of sophisticated nuclear warheads with small yields. These micro-nukes have a yield equivalent to ten tons of TNT and are designed to destroy a military target without devastating the surrounding civilian population. There are also somewhat larger warheads called mini-nukes with a yield of about 100 tons of TNT as well as tiny-nukes with a yield equal to 1,000 tons of TNT. Israel can deliver a micro-nuke blast as an earth-penetrating missile warhead (EPW) to destroy enemy underground command bunkers. Such micro-nukes delivered by bombers or missiles can also destroy an enemy airfield.

Israeli scientists are also developing high-speed Arrow anti-tactical ballistic missiles with mini-nuke warheads that can, hopefully, destroy incoming ballistic warheads in flight. The present American Patriot missile simply deflects an incoming ballistic SCUD missile so that it goes off-target. However, if the warhead is chemical, biological, or nuclear, diverting it will not provide the desired protection. Incoming nuclear, biological, or chemical missile warheads must be destroyed in the air as far from their targets as possible.

The Israeli army can use tiny-nuke warheads with 1,000-ton TNT yields against Arab armored, artillery, and infantry units. These small nuclear warheads are true battlefield weapons (as opposed to the nuclear weapons from the superpowers, which are designed to destroy cities). These tiny-nukes would be used in precision missile attacks against enemy army units with a lethal radius of 500 yards. These tactical warheads can be fired at an invading army division that is only one mile away—and your own troops would survive. When these tactical weapons are exploded in the air almost no radioactive fallout is produced.

Israel has also developed the most sophisticated neutron bombs in the world—bombs that can kill all living creatures within a mile or two but leave buildings intact. They are especially designed to attack tank formations or hit the Arab military headquarters that are often hidden deep beneath the civilian areas of their capital cities. A neutron bomb can kill a soldier with intense gamma rays that cause his body to glow and reveal his skeleton through his flesh for a second before his flesh literally melts as he stands transfixed by the invisible blast of the rays. This may be what the prophet Zechariah described when he told of the effects of God's wrath against the Antichrist's armies when Jesus Christ returns following the Battle of Armageddon: "This shall be the plague with which the LORD will strike all the people who fought against Jerusalem: Their flesh shall dissolve while they stand on their feet, their eyes shall dissolve in their sockets, and their tongues shall dissolve in their mouths" (Zechariah 14:12).

The tragic history of 4,000 years of continuing warfare in the Middle East suggests that no enduring peace is likely until the Messiah comes to change the hearts of men forever. The fascinating report "Israel's Nuclear Imperative" in the *Islamic Affairs Analyst* warned that Israel "must abandon the illusion that the Third Temple is forever and that genocide is a phenomenon of the past."[2] Speaking about the role of Israel's nuclear weapons, the report said,

> Their essential purpose is to protect Israel from attack by credible deterrence and, when necessary, by pre-emption and war fighting capability. "In a dark time," says the poet Theodore Roethke, "the eye begins to see." Embedded in this ironic observation is a vital lesson for Israel: Do not be lulled into complacency by promises of regional cooperation and peace. . . . Rather, take courage and counsel from the prospect of protracted conflict, from the dreary "darkness" which is certainly more difficult to live with but illuminates Israel's only reasonable path towards real security.[3]

The Russia-Arab Invasion

In Ezekiel's prophecy (chapter 38) we read that the northern invasion of Israel will come at a moment when the Jews will be expecting peace. For almost 50 years the Jewish state has lived as an armed camp surrounded by implacable enemies with armies ready to attack at any moment. But the Bible foretells of a time when Israel will be lulled into thinking that peace has finally come. "In the latter years you will come into the land of those brought back from the sword and gathered from many people on the mountains of Israel, which had long been desolate; they were brought out of the nations, and now all of them dwell safely" (Ezekiel 38:8). The prophet's words confirm the peaceful expectations of Israel when the sudden invasion will occur. Then the prophet addresses the leader of the Russian-Arab force: "You will say, 'I will go up against a land of unwalled villages; I will go to a peaceful people, who dwell safely, all of them dwelling without walls, and having neither bars nor gates'" (Ezekiel 38:11).

God's Miraculous Intervention

The coming invasion of Israel will be short-lived; God will intervene at the point when Israel faces total disaster. " 'It will come to pass at the same time, when Gog comes against the land of Israel,' says the Lord GOD, 'that My fury will show in My face. For in My jealousy and in the fire of My wrath I have spoken: "Surely in that day there shall be a great earthquake in the land of Israel" (Ezekiel 38:18,19).

Why will the Lord intervene to destroy the Russian and Arab armies? For over seven decades, since 1917, Russia has killed millions of Christians and Jews in concentration camps, forced famines, firing squads, and planned genocide. Estimates run as high as 20 million Christians and up to five million Jews who perished in Russia during this century. There is coming a day when the Lord will finally exact His vengeance on those who killed His children.

However the most important reason God will intervene as never before is found in these words of Ezekiel: "Thus I will magnify Myself and sanctify Myself, and I will be known in the eyes of many nations. Then they shall know that I am the LORD" (Ezekiel 38:23). The Lord will demonstrate His overwhelming power as He saves Israel, proving to everyone on the planet that He is the God of Israel. This miraculous demonstration will prepare the hearts and minds of

many for the incredible struggle to come between
Christ and Antichrist. In addition to revealing His
awesome power to the Gentile nations, the Lord will
also reveal Himself to His chosen people Israel: "So I
will make My holy name known in the midst of My
people Israel, and I will not let them profane My holy
name anymore. Then the Nations shall know that I
am the LORD, the Holy One in Israel" (Ezekiel 39:7).

The Palestine National Covenant

The Palestine Liberation Organization created the
Palestine National Covenant in 1974 to define its official position and goals. As part of the secret Oslo,
Norway, peace negotiations Yasser Arafat and the
Palestinian negotiators agreed in writing that they
would immediately convene the Palestinian National Assembly and remove the clauses in the PLO
covenant that called for the destruction of Israel and
unending war with the Jews. This commitment by
the PLO was fundamental to the peace accord because it would be insane for Israel to negotiate with a
group that officially demanded her destruction.
However, despite the passage of many months since
the signing of the initial agreement, the PLO and
Yasser Arafat now categorically refuse to change the
Palestine National Covenant.

To understand the significance of their refusal, we
need to understand the actual text of the document
that governs the Palestinian organization. While
many Christians have heard of the covenant, most of

them have never read the actual wording. More than 50 percent of the 33 clauses in the covenant either declare or imply that Israel has no right to exist as a nation. Other clauses call for continuation of the armed struggle. Significantly, the covenant only recognizes those Jews who lived in Palestine before the so-called "1948 Zionist invasion" as legitimate co-inhabitants who have a right to share the land. The covenant demands that all other Jews leave Palestine or be killed.

Article 2 of the covenant defines Palestine as an indivisible territorial unit including all of Israel, the West Bank, Gaza, and Jordan—within the original 1948 frontiers of the British Mandate. This means that the Palestinians do not believe any "Jewish" state has a right to exist on a single mile of territory side-by-side with an Arab-Palestinian state. It is simply an all-or-nothing proposition.

Article 3 guarantees the Palestinian-Arab people legitimate rights to the land but does not provide any such rights for the Jews. In Article 7 the covenant declares that it is essential that every Palestinian be provided with a revolutionary Arab upbringing to prepare him for the armed struggle with the Jews. All Arab educational institutions are called to work toward this goal. Furthermore, the covenant demands that every Arab must sacrifice his material possessions and his very life until the final liberation of Palestine from the Jew is achieved.

The PLO covenant declares in Article 9 that armed struggle is the only way to liberate Palestine. Armed struggle is thus declared to be "strategic, not tactical." Article 10 demands that terrorist actions must be escalated and expanded until final success is attained. The framers of the covenant declared in Article 13 that Arab unity will lead inevitably to the final liberation of Palestine while the liberation of Palestine will support the cause of Arab unity. They are deemed to be inseparable.

Article 14 states that the destiny of the Arab world depends on the success of the Palestinians, while Article 15 calls on all Arabs to take up the duty to repel the Zionist "imperialist" invasion. In addition, the charter calls on all Arabs to join the struggle to "liquidate the Zionist presence in Palestine." Finally, Article 19 rejects the 1947 partition of Palestine as fundamentally illegal, while Article 20 states that the 1917 Balfour Declaration, the Mandate Instrument, and all their political and legal consequences are void.

The PLO covenant literally defines who is and who is not a Jew. It states that Judaism is a revealed religion and denies that Jews are a separate nationality. Fundamentally, the covenant rejects the reality that Jews are an individual race with a separate identity. Instead, it declares that Jews are only citizens of their respective countries of America, Britain, Russia, and so on. The covenant rejects the Jewish claim of ancient historical and spiritual links between the Jews and the land of Palestine.

In addition, the covenant denies that the Jews have any right to settle in any part of Palestine and create a Jewish state and homeland. Article 21 reiterates that the Palestinian Arab people, expressing themselves through the Palestinian armed revolution, reject any other alternatives to the total liberation of Palestine.

Meanwhile, Article 22 states that the Zionist movement is "fanatical and racist" and says that its methods are those of "fascists and Nazis." The covenant claims that the nation of Israel serves in the role of a manpower base for world imperialism and that the Jewish state is a constant threat to true peace in the Middle East.

All of the declarations I've just detailed are taken directly from the PLO covenant that was adopted in Cairo on July 17, 1968, by the Fourth Palestine National Assembly. This document remains today as the unchanged and unmodified ideological statement of the Palestine Liberation Organization. In the months that have followed the signing of the peace treaty with Israel, the PLO still offers feeble excuses to justify their refusal to change the wording of this document. Their excuses include "technical problems" in convening a special session of the National Council of the PLO, the only body authorized to change the covenant if they can muster a 66 percent majority for the vote.

The hard truth is that this PLO covenant still represents the original and the present objectives and goals of the Arab leadership and the Palestine Liberation Organization. It is a tragedy of biblical proportions for Israel to surrender the West Bank, Gaza, the Golan Heights and half of Jerusalem to Arabs who openly demand that the Jews must be destroyed. Israel's leadership is now fulfilling the prophecy of Isaiah 28, which predicted over 25 centuries ago that the leaders of the Jewish state would make lies their "refuge" and would make a "covenant with death" and an agreement with hell in the closing years of this age.

The Redemption of Israel

There is a lot of discussion in the Jewish community today about the coming of the Messiah. One evidence of this is found in a recent article by Rabbi Sholom Klass in the *Jewish Press* (Aug. 5, 1994), called "The Wars of Gog and Magog and the Messiah." The author reviewed the signs of the Messiah's return as found in the Talmud as well as in the Midrash, Rambam, and the Gaonim, which were written in the era following the writing of the Talmud.

In the trying times of persecution during the Middle Ages, the Jews held to the hope that their Messiah would bring about their redemption through a miraculous deliverance. Saadia Gaon (tenth century) taught that the Messiah will bring the Jews back to the Promised Land. The Midrash points to the appearance of the prophet Elijah three days earlier for the purpose of announcing the arrival of the Messiah. Moses Maimonides declared the necessity of belief in the coming Messiah, but maintained that the Messiah will eventually die and his son will arise to succeed him as king.

The writing known as the *Chasam Sofer* suggests that the Messiah may be living among us today, waiting for the sign from God to announce his mission. In the book of Kabbala, known as the *Zohar*, we find a different interpretation of the Messiah. The preexistence of the Messiah is acknowledged in this book and it declares that he is now waiting in Paradise. From there he will descend to earth in a pillar of fire. It is fascinating to read in this work the many references to the suffering that the Messiah endures to bring about the atonement of Israel's sins.

The rabbis have regarded the growing speculations about the coming Messiah with fear because of past misfortunes which came about from a series of false messiahs who arose during the Middle Ages. The worst disaster was produced by the exploits of the false messiah Shabbetai Zvi (A.D. 1666) followed by another impostor, Jacob Frank (eighteenth century). While the Jewish rabbis have encouraged their followers to hope for the Messiah's deliverance, at the same time they have actively discouraged any speculative calculations about the time of his coming because of the dangers from extravagant hopes and the disappointments that inevitably follow.

When the political movement known as Zionism arose at the end of the nineteenth century, many religious Jews were opposed to a return to the Holy Land. They believed they should wait for the Messiah to appear and lead them home to Jerusalem. However, Rabbi Zvi Hirsch Kalischer and Rabbi Shmuel Mohilever taught that the redemption of Israel would come through the Jews returning to the Holy Land. They taught that the Messiah would appear and the predicted miracles will occur when the Jewish people begin to build their homes once more in the Holy Land, rebuilding Jerusalem and the Temple. They believed that Jews returning to live in Eretz Yisrael and rebuilding its ruins were acting in obedience to God's command. One of their key arguments was that many of the commandments of the Torah could only be fulfilled when the Jews once again lived on Israel's sacred soil. The great Jewish Rabbi Moses Maimonides declared, "The beginning of the redemption will be through the consent of other nations. The ingathering of Jews will begin and then G-d will gather them from amongst all the nations" (*Mishneh Torah*).

The Rebuilding of the Temple

Scripture clearly predicts that Israel will rebuild its Temple and resume animal sacrifice in the final years leading to the return of the Messiah. The prophet Daniel tells us that the Antichrist will initially befriend Israel by signing a seven-year treaty with the Jewish nation (Daniel 9:27). Then, after three-and-a-half years, this tyrant will break his covenant and defile the Temple. The prophecy declares, "He shall confirm a covenant with many for one week; but in the middle of the week He shall bring an end to sacrifice and offering" (Daniel 9:27).

For almost 2,000 years, many Jewish people and rabbis have felt that the Temple belonged to their past. The vast majority of rabbis reject the concept of a future rebuilt Temple, a renewed Levitical priesthood, and animal sacrifice. However, there are a number of groups in Israel that are now making preparations for the building of the Third Temple. More than 500 young Jewish men from the tribe of Levi are now trained in the elaborate, ancient Temple rituals described in the Scriptures. The Temple Institute in Jerusalem has recreated at least 75 of the required Temple worship utensils, including the breastplate of the high priest, the blue dye required for the robes of the high priest, and the seven-branched candelabra. Levite musicians are being trained in the use of ancient musical instruments, including the silver trumpets that will be blown to announce the Day of Jubilee. And finally, sophisticated archaeological and engineering studies have been undertaken to determine the proper location of the ancient Temple so that it can be determined where the Third Temple should be built.

While there are many different viewpoints about the correct location of the Temple, the burden of evidence still leans toward the northern platform position that I and numerous others such as Dr. Asher Kaufman have written about. We have concluded that the original Temple was located in the wide open area to the north of the Dome of the Rock. The Holy of Holies must have been located where the Moslem Dome of the Tablets is now found. This suggested location would place the Temple directly in a line opposite the sealed Eastern Gate.

The strongest reason that convinces me that this northern position is correct is the location of the Eastern Gate. The Bible, the Mishneh, Josephus, the Mishneh Torah, and the Talmud all agree that the five Temple gates lined up in a straight line opposite the Eastern Gate. The Mishneh Torah, for example, declared that the priest would sacrifice the red heifer on the Mount of Olives directly opposite

the Eastern Gate. He could look above the Eastern
Gate and through the five gates of the Temple and
see the veil of the Holy of Holies. For him to do that
would be impossible unless the Temple was located
directly opposite the Eastern Gate.

All of the ancient documents available to us describe the Temple Mount as having only one gate on
the entire eastern side with the Temple opposite this
gate. Several years ago, James Flemming, a Christian
researcher, was examining and filming the Eastern
Gate from a position several yards in front of the gate
near some old Arab graves. The ground suddenly
collapsed and he landed in a pit 15 feet below, surrounded by bones. When he came to, Flemming was
amazed to see the top of an arched gate directly in
front of him. He had inadvertently discovered the remains of the original Eastern Gate built by King
Solomon 3,000 years earlier. The original gate was
located directly below and slightly in front of the
present Eastern Gate that was built by King Herod
2,000 years ago.

In a similar manner, archaeologists discovered
years ago that the original Damascus Gate was buried
in the ancient past and later rebuilt in the same location at a higher level. Despite a century and a half of
archaeological investigation concerning the Temple,
no one has ever found the slightest evidence that
there was a second gate on the eastern wall of the
Temple Mount anywhere to the south of the present
sealed Eastern Gate. Until someone finds conclusive
proof that there is another gate on the eastern wall of
the Temple Mount opposite the Dome of the Rock or

some other location south of the present Eastern Gate, I remain convinced that the original Temple was located in the open area to the north of the Dome of the Rock. This is important because this location is the only possible position that would allow Israel to rebuild its Temple without violating and destroying the Moslem Dome of the Rock.

The Coming of the Messiah

The Jewish sage Moses Maimonides, known as the Rambam, declared that in the future the Messiah would appear to reestablish the glory of King David. He would build the Holy Temple and would gather all the exiles from all over the world. On the other hand, in the *Talmud Yerushalmi* (Maaser Sheini, chap. 5:2), we find the statement: "Rabbi Acha said: 'The Beit Hamikdash (holy Temple) will be built first, before the advent of the Kingdom of David'" (the coming of Messiah). In confirmation of this position, which I and many prophecy teachers hold, the *Pnei Moshe* states that first the land will be settled, then the people will become prosperous, after which they will build the Temple and, finally, the Messiah will come. In the *Mar'eh Panim*, the Gaon Moshe Margolis wrote that when Jacob predicted the future of Judah (Genesis 49) he first foretold that the Temple will be rebuilt first and then Messiah would come.

CHAPTER 9

The Ecumenical
World Church

Revelation chapter 17 warns about the pagan apostate church that will arise after the true followers of Christ are taken to heaven in the rapture:

> I saw a woman sitting on a scarlet beast which was full of names of blasphemy, having seven heads and ten horns. The woman was arrayed in purple and scarlet, and adorned with gold and precious stones and pearls, having in her hand a golden cup full of abominations and the filthiness of her fornication. And on her forehead a name was written: Mystery, Babylon the Great, the mother of harlots and of the abominations of the earth (verses 3-5).

During the rapture, hundreds of millions of true Christians from Protestant, Catholic, and Orthodox churches will be instantaneously translated to the New Jerusalem. However, among these churches are hundreds of millions more people who will remain on earth during the tribulation period because they had never truly repented of their sins and trusted completely in Jesus Christ as their Lord and Savior. Jesus warned, "Not everyone who says to Me, 'Lord, Lord,' shall enter the kingdom of heaven, but he who does the will of My Father in heaven" (Matthew 7:21).

In the book of Revelation, one of the angels spoke to the prophet John as follows: "Come, I will show you the judgment of the great harlot who sits on many waters, with whom the kings of the earth committed fornication, and the inhabitants of the earth were made drunk with the wine of her fornication" (Revelation 17:1,2). This key verse indicates the universal, worldwide nature of the pagan apostate church that will be allied to the rising power of the Antichrist during the first three-and-a-half years of the tribulation period. This ecumenical church will provide propaganda support for the consolidation of the Antichrist's New World Order. During her period of great power this church will ruthlessly persecute anyone who refuses to join her pagan worship rituals. John described his vision of this coming inquisition by Mystery Babylon against those new Jewish and Gentile believers who will become martyrs during the tribulation period: "I saw the woman, drunk with the blood of the saints and with the blood of the martyrs of Jesus" (Revelation 17:6).

Obviously, Mystery Babylon, the apostate pagan church of the last days, will not develop overnight. Such a massive ecumenical organization, involving many diverse religious groups, will require years of development through being created by negotiation and conferences leading up to the beginning of the seven-year tribulation period. It is therefore quite probable that we will witness the initial steps toward this one-world church of the last days before the rapture takes the Christians home to heaven.

The Center of the Apostate Church

I realize that there are many born-again Catholics who are grieved in their spirit when a Bible teacher comments on the prophecies that reveal Rome as the headquarters of the Mystery Babylon religion of the last days. The only thing I can say is that I do not feel any animosity towards Catholics as individuals. However, I do feel strongly about the nonbiblical heresies that, over the last 1,500 years, have led hundreds of millions of people to endanger their eternal souls.

While it is true that there are many born-again Catholics, we cannot ignore the vast gulf that exists between the teaching of the Roman Catholic Church and the teaching of Jesus Christ as found in the Bible. The most fundamental difference is the ultimate source of spiritual truth. As the Roman Catholic Council of Trent declared in 1564 (it has never been rescinded), Rome believes that the truth concerning salvation, etc., is determined solely by the popes and church councils, not by the Bible as the Word of God. In contrast, as a Protestant Christian, I recognize that the only authoritative source of divine knowledge about salvation, etc., is the inspired Word of

God. In addition, while Rome declares that men can-not be saved apart from membership in the Roman Catholic Church, the sacraments, the confessional, and the last rites, the Bible assures us that we are saved solely based on our faith and trust in Jesus Christ's completed atonement for our sins—paid for us on the cross 2,000 years ago.

The Roman Catholic Cardinal D'Allen stated that the Protestant focus on the Bible's authority was an obstacle to the ecumenical union of churches world-wide. Cardinal D'Allen declared, "The Reformation was a Protestant revolt disrupting the unity of the church. Union will take place when the rebels accept the authority of the Pope and abandon the authority of Scripture. Rome can accept nothing short of this."

What is the proper identity of this mysterious symbol of religious persecution, Babylon the Great, the Mother of Harlots? In Revelation 17:7,9 an angel tells the prophet John, "I will tell you the mystery of the woman and of the beast that carries her, which has the seven heads and the ten horns . . . Here is the mind which has wisdom: The seven heads are seven mountains on which the woman sits." This inspired statement that the woman sits on seven mountains or hills is the clearest possible declaration we have that the final apostate church will be based in Rome. While the apostate Babylonian church of the tribula-tion period will involve all religions joined together, Revelation 17:7,9 indicates clearly that this world-wide church will have its headquarters in Rome.

What evidence do we have for this conclusion? One is that coins issued by the Roman government during the first century of the Christian era carried the motto "the city on seven hills" in reference to the capital of the Roman Empire. And virtually every one of the classical Roman writers and poets, including Virgil, Horace, and Ovid, referred to Rome as the city of seven hills. Interestingly, some of these writers referred to Rome as *Septiceps*, the seven-headed city, a term that is virtually identical to the phrase used by the prophet John.

It is also fascinating to note in Revelation 17 that the angel, describing the apostate church, said, "On her forehead a name was written: MYSTERY, BABYLON THE GREAT" (Revelation 17:5). Roman writer Marcus Seneca tells us in his book *Controversia* (Chapter V.i) that the harlots of ancient Rome used to identify themselves to their customers by wearing their names on a label on their foreheads.

A Roman Catholic commentary on the prophecies of Revelation, *The Book of Destiny* (published in 1956 by Bernard F. Leonard), also identified this city as Rome. There are few Catholic commentaries on Revelation, and it is intriguing to note that *The Book of Destiny* was approved by the Roman Catholic censor with the words *Nihil Obstat* and contained the imprimatur of the bishop of Sioux City, Iowa.

Leonard writes,

This great harlot is a city whose apostasy from the true faith is a monstrous thing. This may point to Rome. Rome is the Holy City of Christ, the center of His eternal kingdom. . . . And the apostasy of this city, and her becoming the head of an empire that would lead all possible nations and peoples into Antichrist-worship would indeed merit for her the title of THE GREAT HARLOT. The apostles called ancient Rome 'Babylon' (1 Peter V:13). So the conclusion is near that the great harlot of the future shall be Rome.[1]

This book is still sold today in many Roman Catholic bookstores.

Pope John Paul II and the Last Days

Karol Wojtyla of Poland was elected pope in October 1978. While he is a strong supporter of world government he is not the first pope to promote this idea. His predecessor Pope Paul VI wrote a papal encyclical that called on the nations to abandon sovereignty to form a world government.

Karol, now known as Pope John Paul II, is constantly calling for the nations to abandon their opposition to world government. Malachi Martin, a Jesuit writer who is very close to the pope and has excellent sources in the Vatican, wrote in his book *The Keys of This Blood* about the pope's plans for a one-world government. Martin says that the pope "has plans and is working for a genuinely geopolitical structure: a One World Government that is both viable and humanly acceptable."[2] John Paul II believes that "the establishment of an order based on justice and peace is vitally needed today as a moral imperative valid for all peoples and regimes . . . this is the only path possible."[3]

The Fatima Vision

A curious bit of information was recently revealed about the thinking and motivation of Pope John Paul II. Several books, including Malachi Martin's *The Keys of This Blood*, indicate that the political and religious agenda of the pope is strongly influenced by various predictions regarding the future of the papacy. One of these is the so-called "Vision of Fatima." When he became pope in 1978, John Paul II was given access to the secret message of Fatima, which Catholics believe was entrusted to the Church through a series of visions granted to several children in Fatima, Portugal, beginning on May 13, 1917. Supposedly, a vision of Mary appeared to three peasant children at six different times over a five-month period in 1917. They claimed she gave them three secret messages.

Let me interject here that I do not believe the Fatima vision is a genuine prophecy from God. Regardless of the apparent sincerity of the witnesses, the vision's message is in absolute opposition to the Bible. Fundamentally, this vision elevates Mary and demands that the world (and Russia especially) "must be consecrated to Mary." There is not a single passage in the Bible that supports such a demand. On the contrary, we are commanded to worship God alone. In addition God warns us in Isaiah 42:8, "I am the LORD, that is My name; and My glory I will not give to another." The significance of the Fatima vision and the Malachi vision (which will be discussed later) is that they give us an insight into the thinking and motivation of John Paul II, who is one of the key individuals moving us toward the one-world government prophesied in the Scriptures.

The first two secret messages of Fatima were revealed during the decades following 1917. The first vision supposedly warned that mankind as a whole was proceeding down a path of sinful rebellion that would lead millions to eternity in hell. Then during the 1930s, the second message was gradually released to the public, warning about the beginning of World War II and the growing physical and spiritual danger to the West from the godless Communist state of Russia.

The third vision was held in total secrecy until 1944. At that time the sole survivor of the children who witnessed the apparition was still living. She was commanded by her bishop to write the secret message on a piece of paper, seal it in an envelope, and deliver it to the Vatican. This witness, a woman named Lucia, claimed that Mary demanded that the third message remain secret until 1960. Then whoever was the pope at that time was to open the message and act on its instructions. This third vision, known as the Third Secret of Fatima, is believed to concern the military and political dangers that would afflict the West in the closing year of the millennium. While the actual wording of the Third Secret remains known to a very few people, the general outline of its message has become known through the papacy of John Paul II.

This last vision of Fatima apparently has three parts. First, if the Vatican neglects to take the actions demanded, physical catastrophes—wars, earthquakes, floods, and so on—will supposedly destroy the nations and peoples as punishment for rejecting God's laws. Second, a refusal to comply with the message's demands would trigger a growth of atheism and massive worldwide apostasy from the Catholic Church. In addition, Russia's godless ideology would sweep throughout the world, causing millions to lose their faith. This would conclude with a devastating world war that would bring mankind to the very edge of extinction. However, a remnant was to survive the holocaust and gradually revive in the next millennium.

The third part of the Fatima message supposedly promised that this devastating war, followed by spiritual catastrophe, could be averted if, first, the pope and his bishops published the warnings of Fatima in 1960, and second, the pope and cardinals "consecrated" Russia to the Virgin Mary. (This continued focus on Mary rather than the Bible's command to focus on Jesus Christ convinces me that the Fatima vision is not of God but rather a deception launched by Satan.)

The pope in 1960, John XXIII, allegedly read the Fatima message but rejected its authority and refused to carry out the instructions. According to Malachi Martin, Pope John XXIII explained his refusal to his papal successors by saying, "These [predictions] do not concern our times."[4] The next pope, Paul VI, also refused to comply with the demand of the vision. When Pope John Paul II was questioned about the actions of these previous popes, he told the interviewer, "Given the seriousness of its contents, my predecessors in the

Petrine Office diplomatically preferred to postpone publication [of the vision] so as not to encourage the world power of Communism to make certain moves."[5] Apparently these popes believed the West was vulnerable and that Russia's dictators would have accelerated their plans to attack the Western nations if they had known the precise words of the Fatima warning. This fear was made evident in 1957 when Cardinal Ottaviani, a politically astute churchman, told Malachi Martin that the dangerous "secret" must be buried "in the most hidden, the deepest, the most obscure and inaccessible place on earth."[6]

During a papal audience in Saint Peter's Square on May 13, 1981, the pope noticed a little girl wearing a picture of Mary at Fatima. At that exact moment the Turkish assassin Mehmet Ali Agca fired two bullets at John Paul's head. He missed his target by several inches because the pope had bent his head to greet the child. The next two bullets hit John Paul's body, disabling him for many months.

During his painful convalescence following the attempt on his life, John Paul II spent hours studying the secret Fatima message. He tried to obey the command of the Fatima vision by holding a special service in Fatima, Portugal, on May 13, 1982, one year to the day after the assassination attempt. In the ceremony he "consecrated" the world to Mary with "a special mention of Russia."

Pope John Paul II is unusual among the popes of this century in his earnest devotion to Mary. His personal motto is *Totus Tuius* (Entirely Yours). He publicly attributes his motivation and the direction of his life to Mary. John Paul II has stated that he consecrated and dedicated himself as "priest, as bishop, and as cardinal to Mary."

There is no question that Mary was truly blessed by God when she was granted the privilege of becoming the birth mother of Jesus Christ. All Christians of all denominations rightly consider Mary as one of the most blessed persons in the Bible and in history. Her admirable character and spiritual life stimulate sincere admiration among all those who love Jesus Christ as their personal Savior and Lord. However, the Bible, which is the only infallible source of God's commands to Christians, has never commanded or permitted the worship of anyone other than God Himself.

The Bible tells us through the words of the apostle Paul, that "there is one God and one Mediator between God and men, the Man Christ Jesus, who gave Himself a ransom for all, to be testified in due time" (1 Timothy 2:5,6). It is significant that none of the apostles mentioned Mary during the decades following Christ's ministry. Through God's grace, every Christian can approach God's throne directly because Christ shed His blood for us on Calvary. We do not need anyone to intercede on our behalf. Jesus Christ, as Almighty God, loves each of us so much that He came to this earth to die on the cross and bear the punishment for our sins so that, once we repent and turn from our sinful path to follow Him as our Lord, we might enter into a complete and joyful relationship with Him forever.

As I mentioned earlier, during his time in recovery, the pope began to seriously consider the Fatima vision and its meaning for his mission and the Roman Catholic Church. John Paul II believes his personal destiny is to rule over the Catholic Church during the crisis described in the Third Secret of Fatima. According to Malachi Martin, John Paul II is waiting for a miraculous intervention from heaven that will stun the world with its display of supernatural power. In *The Keys of This Blood*, Martin wrote about the pope's belief, based on the Fatima visions, in a future appearance of Mary in connection with a spectacular astronomical event involving the sun:

He is waiting, rather, for an event that will fission human history, splitting the immediate past from the oncoming future. It will be an event on public view in the skies, in the oceans, and on the continental landmasses of this planet. It will particularly involve our human sun, which every day lights up and shines upon the valleys, the mountains and the plains of this earth for our eyes. But on the day of this event, it will not appear merely as the master star of our so-called solar system. Rather, it will be seen as the circumambient glory of the Woman whom the apostle described as "clothed with the sun" and giving birth to "a child who will rule the nations with a scepter of iron." Fissioning it will be as an event, in John Paul's conviction of faith, for it will immediately nullify all the grand designs the nations are now forming and will introduce the Grand Design of man's Maker. John Paul's waiting and watching time will then be over. His ministry as the Servant of the Grand Design will then begin. His strength of will to hold on and continue, and then, when the fissioning event occurs, to assume that ministry, derives directly from the Petrine authority entrusted solely to him the day he became Pope, in October of 1978. That authority, that strength, is symbolized in the Keys of Peter, washed in the human blood of the God-Man, Jesus Christ. John Paul is and will be the sole possessor of the Keys of this Blood on that day."[7]

Apparently John Paul believes this global apparition will astonish the population of earth. It is alleged by Martin that the pope thinks this phenomenon will give him the authority to create a new religious renaissance and rule over a new church-state world government. Various catholic organizations such as Opus Dei, the Catholic Campaign, and others are now working behind the scenes to abolish the separation of church and state. Interestingly, *Time* magazine, on December 9, 1991, carried an article questioning the historic separation of church and state.

The Saint Malachi Predictions

It appears that another series of curious predictions from a Saint Malachi in A.D. 1148 has also convinced Pope John Paul II that he is presiding over the last days of his church. On several occasions, John Paul has indicated that he believes he is the last pope who will follow the teachings of Christ and truly believe in Jesus Christ as the Lord God Almighty. It is an open secret in Italy and Europe that many of the present priests, cardinals, and bishops are no longer true believers in the inspiration of the Scriptures and the historical credibility of the gospel of Christ. These modern Catholic leaders have rejected the fundaments of New Testament faith, such as the virgin birth and the resurrection of Jesus Christ. Pope John Paul II fears that, following his death, the conclave of cardinals who will choose the next pope will elect someone who will not uphold historic Christianity. Apparently his fear is based on his belief in an 800-year-old prediction from Saint Malachi.

Maol-Maodhog O'Morgair, later known as Saint Malachi, was born in Armauth, Ireland, in A.D. 1094. After a life of faithful service he was appointed Metropolitan Bishop of Ireland in 1133. He later died in A.D. 1148. Many people in the Irish church and some in the Vatican today believe he authored an unusual prophecy that foretold the future of the Roman Catholic Church for the next 850 years. The prophecy supposedly described all of the popes from Pope Celestine II, who ruled in A.D. 1143, until the last pope, who would rule during the final destruction of the Catholic Church almost 1,000 years later during the Battle of Armageddon. This curious prophecy of Saint Malachi consists of a series of poetic stanzas in Latin that purport to describe 111 future Roman popes who would rule the Vatican. According to Saint Malachi's prediction, there would be 111 popes in the Catholic Church following Pope Celestine who died in A.D. 1146. Some researchers have suggested that the descriptions of the future popes were quite accurate, but it is very hard to verify this.

Let me reaffirm that I do not place any faith or confidence in any prophecy or prediction except those found in the inspired pages of Holy Scripture. All other predictions are simply human speculations.

However, since Pope John Paul II apparently believes
in the Fatima vision and the poetic vision of Saint
Malachi and looks to them for guidance it is vital
that we explore these visions to understand the motivations and thinking of those who will play major
roles in the events of the last days.

Below is Saint Malachi's list of the last ten popes
to rule the Roman Catholic Church:

Number	Poetic Description	Name	Years of Rule
106	Pastor Angelus	Pope Pius XII	1939 – 1958
107	Pastor et nauta	Pope John XXIII	1958 – 1963
108	Flos florum	Pope Paul VI	1963 – 1978
109	De medietate Lunoe	Pope John Paul I — 1978	
110	De labore solis	Pope John Paul II	1978 – present

The papal leadership still to come is described as:

111	Glorioe Olivoe	Pope Peter	The Final years of this age

The ancient prophecy of Saint Malachi concluded
with a prediction that the last pope of the Roman
Catholic Church will rule following the death of the
present pontiff, Pope John Paul II, who is pope number 110. Furthermore this curious prediction suggests that the last pope will be the first pontiff in
2,000 years who will dare to assume the name of
Peter, choosing the name Peter II of Rome. In a poetic manner, the prophecy purports to describe the
details of the final pope's destiny.

After detailing his visions, Saint Malachi wrote the following Latin words to describe the last pope: "*In persecutione Extrema Sanctae Romanae Ecclesiae sedebit Petrus Romanus qui pascet oves in multis tribulationibus, quibus transactis, certus septi collis dirurtur et pie ex tremendis predicabit populum suum.*" Translated into English, this reads as follows: "In the last persecution of the Roman Church, Peter the Roman will rule. He will have great tribulation which will end with the destruction of the city on seven hills."[8]

According to Malachi's vision, the final pope of the Roman Catholic Church will be from Italy. The prediction suggests he will take the name Peter II and will come to power in the Vatican in the final days of this century during the tribulation when the world is overcome by military and political catastrophes as described in the book of Revelation. The important point is that Malachi believed his prophecy would conclude the final days of the millennium. Based on these extrabiblical predictions, Pope John Paul II believes that he will lead the world during the political, religious, and military crisis that will lead to the appearance of the Antichrist.

The Beginning of the Apostate Church

Pope John Paul II has an agenda to create a universal church involving all of the world's religions. Following ecumenical discussions between the Archbishop of Canterbury (representing the Church of England) and John Paul II (as reported in *Time* in October

1989), the archbishop commented on a beautiful ring the pope had given to him. He stated that it was not a wedding ring, but it could be considered an engagement ring symbolizing the coming reunion between their two churches.

Three years earlier, in 1986, John Paul II met with the Dalai Lama, the head of Tibetan Buddhism, and other false religionists at Assisi, Italy. In this historic meeting, the pope joined in a circle to pray and meditate with snake handlers from Togo, shamans and witch doctors from Africa, Hindu gurus from India, Buddhist monks from Thailand, and liberal protestant clergymen from Great Britain. Many Catholics were stunned to hear the pope declare, at this inter-religious meeting, that there are many paths to God.

During his February 1993 visit to Benin, Africa, the pope preached a message of unification with false satanic religion. He held meetings with a number of voodoo practitioners and sorcerers. Voodoo worshipers believe in many deities and use snake rituals. The Associated Press gave an account of the pope's visit with the following headline, "Pope Meets with Voodoo Believers." The newspaper reported, "Pope John Paul II on Thursday sought common ground with the believers in voodoo, suggesting they would not betray their traditional faith by converting to Christianity."[9] In other words, they could retain their voodoo while joining the Catholic Church. Pope John Paul also explained to the voodoo witch doctors that in the same way that they worshiped their ancestors, so also did Christians revere their "ancestors in the faith, from the apostles to the missionaries."[10]

According to the Associated Press account, voodoo priests warmly welcomed the pope. "'I have never seen God, but today when I have seen the pope, I recognize that I have seen the good God, who prays for all the voduns,' said Sossa Guedehoungue, head of Benin's vodun community."[11]

Catholic Apostasy

Pope John Paul II has noted with alarm that during the last few decades the Roman Catholic Church has experienced massive defections from the faith by bishops, priests, nuns, and laymen. In addition, many churches in Western Europe and North America have abandoned traditional Catholic doctrines and minister to few attendees. Many parishes have no priest because so few young men join the priesthood. Some parishes are forced to hire priests from South America because none are available from North America.

John Paul II also confided to associates that his attempts to reform the moral atmosphere in the Vatican were thwarted by a large network of actively homosexual priests and higher church leaders who resisted every attempt at moral reform. Evidently these problems were not new, for Malachi Martin reported that a number of wicked and immoral priests and bishops had infiltrated the highest levels of the Vatican during the reign of Pope Paul VI in 1963. Ominously, Pope Paul VI warned about "the smoke of Satan which has entered the Sanctuary,"[12] referring to incidents of satanic ceremonies and pagan initiation rituals in the Vatican—rituals that defiled the holy name of Jesus Christ. European newspapers have reported numerous cases of satanic pedophilia involving priests, nuns, and bishops in Turin, Italy, and various cities in America.[13] These evil rituals involve the sexual defilement of innocent children by satanic priests who openly worship Satan.

Researchers who investigated the sudden mysterious death of Pope John Paul I in 1978 revealed that this genuine and humble Christian leader, who preceded the present Pope John Paul II, was appalled at his discovery of the lack of spirituality and true faith among those who rule the Vatican. During the 30 days in which he ruled the papacy, John Paul I discovered that more than 100 members of the secret occult group, the Freemasons, had infiltrated high positions within the Vatican, including its powerful financial institutions. According to Roman Catholic law, it is illegal for a priest or bishop to belong to the Freemasons or any other secret occult group. It is significant to note that the list of secret Masons within the Vatican, selected by John Paul I for immediate dismissal, was found in his papal apartment when his body was discovered by his servants. Although the evidence strongly indicated that he had been poisoned, there was no serious investigation and his body was immediately cremated (as required by Italian law) to prevent an autopsy from being performed.

Afterward, investigations by the Italian government revealed that a large and powerful fascist and Freemason intelligence organization called Propaganda Due (P2) existed within the highest levels of Italian society and the government. Propaganda Due is an anticommunist, fascist organization that was founded in the early 1960s with Licio Gelli as its Grand Master. P2 has its headquarters in Rome with branches in France, Switzerland, the United States, and South America. It is a private intelligence organization created by the Masonic Lodge that receives funds from the CIA and the Vatican. P2 was used to secretly transfer over $100 million to the Solidarity labor organization in Poland. The Italian Parliamentary Commission that investigated P2 concluded that it was controlled by secret sources "beyond the frontiers of Italy."

In 1979, a man named Mino Percorelli defected from P2 and claimed that the CIA was behind it. Two months later, he was murdered. It was found that members of P2 included Michelle Sindona and Bishop Paul Marcinkus, high officials of the Vatican Bank, who were later charged with massive bank fraud. Other key P2 members included the former prime minister of Italy, Giulio Andreotti, the Vatican secretary of state Cardinal Villot, and Agostino Casoroli, the Vatican foreign minister. Investigators also found thousands of secret members of P2 in the judiciary, the police, and the military. Judicial authorities determined that P2 had plans to overthrow the existing democratic government of Italy. Unfortunately, after the election of John Paul II the individuals implicated in Freemasonry and illegal financial dealings of the Vatican Bank were never prosecuted and still remain in their powerful positions.

Opus Dei, which means "God's Work," was created as a secret organization under the direct control of the pope by a Catholic priest named Jose Maria Escriva de Balaguery in Spain in 1928. Escriva was succeeded in 1975 by Alvaro del Portillio. Pope John Paul II made Portillio a bishop. At one time, Opus Dei was funded by William Donovan, the World War II director of the Office of Strategic Services, which later became the Central Intelligence Agency. The membership of Opus Dei includes 1,500 priests and 75,000 lay members. This organization has a goal to achieve "a practical union of church and state." Another secret Vatican organization, Pro Deo, meaning "For God," is in reality the Vatican's secret intelligence agency. It was created during World War II in Lisbon, Portugal, but was moved to the Vatican after the war.

Protestant Apostasy

First Timothy 4:1,2 tells us, "The Spirit expressly says that in latter times some will depart from the faith, giving heed to deceiving spirits and doctrines of demons." The Bible further warns that growing worldwide apostasy would characterize the church during the last generation leading to the return of Christ: "For the time will come when they will not endure sound doctrine, but according to their own desires, because they have itching ears, they will heap up for themselves teachers and they will turn their ears away from the truth, and be turned aside to fables" (2 Timothy 4:3,4).

We should not be surprised at the progressive abandonment of the authority of Scripture among churches today; the prophets warned this would happen. This growing apostasy is leaving many new believers in great spiritual danger due to the lack of truly biblical teaching in our churches. A confidential survey in 1982 by sociologist Jeffrey Hadden asked about the private religious convictions of Protestant pastors and found that a majority of these mainline ministers have lost their faith.

When asked if they still believed that Jesus Christ was God, over 45 percent of the ministers said no. An astonishing 80 percent of the ministers rejected both the claim that the Bible is the inspired Word of God and that Jesus is the Son of God. Thirty-six percent of these pastors do not believe that Jesus Christ actually rose from the dead. Anyone considering these horrifying results will realize why the mainline churches have lost their moral and spiritual influence in society.

Ministers who have abandoned the fundamentals of the Christian faith should be honest enough to leave the church and admit they no longer hold the historic faith of the fathers. This rejection of the fundamental doctrines of the Christian faith explains why these religious leaders are willing to abandon the theological differences that have separated the Protestant and Catholic churches over the years to join in the powerful ecumenical one-world church of the last days. The apostate church of the end times will be a church with the lowest common denominator faith that holds almost no fundamental doctrines other than secular humanism and a pagan, idolatrous worship of "the god within."

God's command to those who will repent of their sin and follow Him is that we must base our life, our teaching, and our eternal hope solely on the truth revealed by the unchanging Word of God:

> As for you, continue in the things which you have learned and been assured of, knowing from whom you have learned them, and that from childhood you have known the Holy Scriptures, which are able to make you wise for salvation through faith which is in Christ Jesus. All Scripture is given by inspiration of God, and is profitable for doctrine, for reproof, for correction, for instruction in righteousness, that the man of God may be complete, thoroughly equipped for every good work (2 Timothy 3:14-17).

Catholic-Protestant Unity

Throughout South America and many other countries, Catholics are abandoning the Mass in record numbers to accept Jesus Christ as their only Savior and to worship with fellow Christians in both pentecostal and evangelical churches. Those who are working behind the scenes to produce an ecumenical world-church recognize that these evangelism efforts are proving very effective among both Catholics and mainline Protestants.

In response to this problem for the Catholic Church, a group of 40 prominent Protestant and Catholic scholars met on March 29, 1994, to sign a historic and astonishing compromise to ban evangelism efforts directed at each other's members. Entitled *Evangelicals and Catholics Together: The*

Christian Mission in the Third Millennium, this unprecedented agreement commits these leaders to reject the command of Christ to go into all the world and preach the gospel to every creature. According to this covenant, these Protestant leaders agreed that "Christians must stop aggressive proselytizing of one another's flocks and work together more closely."

A Catholic priest, Richard Neuhaus, stated that this was the first time since the Protestant Reformation that Protestants and Catholics "joined in a declaration so clear in respect to their common faith and common responsibility." Significantly, although the document is not an official agreement between the denominations, Neuhaus told the *National and International Religion Report*, April 4, 1994, that he had received strong encouragement from "appropriate parties at the Holy See" in the Vatican at Rome. These Catholic theologians would love to put an end to Protestant evangelical missions in Catholic countries because the evangelism efforts are winning great numbers of Catholics to faith in Christ. This agreement to cease proselytizing, then, is one-sided because it will only serve to prevent Catholics from leaving Catholicism.

In this same ecumenical theme, the Archbishop of Canterbury, Dr. Carey, who presides over the Church of England, has severely criticized Anglican pastors who have persevered in evangelical efforts to preach the gospel of Jesus Christ to Hindus, Jews, Buddhists, and other non-Christian groups. Archbishop Carey has instructed his ministers that nonbelievers in Jesus Christ are just "fellow travelers"

on the road to spiritual enlightenment and, therefore, they must not be evangelized. In addition, the
archbishop declared that he plans a trip to Rome in
the near future to discuss how to remove obstacles to
ecumenical unification. All that serves as evidence
that the Church of England is spiritually bankrupt.

New Age Neopaganism

During the Presbyterian Church's Reimagining 1993
Conference, the leaders led participants in an unprecedented neopagan New Age religious service
that evoked the ancient pagan religions. The speaker
is reported to have said, "Sophia, Creator God, Let
your milk and honey flow. Sophia, Creator God,
Shower us with your love."[14]

A celebration of the "Lady's Supper" was reported
on by a traditional conservative church magazine, the
Presbyterian Layman, in its January/February 1994
issue. The magazine article stated, "The conference
glorified lesbianism and . . . some conference speak-
ers advocated adding books to the Bible to justify
feminist and homosexual activism." In an astonishing statement given at the Presbyterian conference,
another feminist speaker declared, "I don't think we
need a theory of atonement at all. . . . Atonement has
to do so much with death . . . I don't think we need
folks hanging on crosses and blood dripping and
weird stuff. . . . We just need to listen to the god
within."[15]

This infiltration of New Age philosophy continues to grow among a number of older mainline

denominations. Our Lord prophesied that this kind of apostasy would occur in the last days.

The World Council of Churches

For people who still doubt that the religious elite are planning to create an ecumenical one-world church, they should carefully consider the following.

The World Council of Churches (WCC) was funded in 1948 as a Christian organization dedicated to bringing about a universal cooperation among Christian churches worldwide. However, over the last 47 years, liberal and socialist theologians have taken control of the WCC until today the organization is barely Christian in any sense that would be recognized by Christians in the early church. Universalism and secular humanism has replaced biblical Christianity and its emphasis on teaching a lost humanity about the need for personal repentance. We are witnessing the creation of embryonic organizations that will ultimately produce the Mystery Babylon church of the last days.

Several years ago Archbishop Ramsey, president of the World Council of Churches, addressed a public meeting at the Roman Catholic Saint Patrick's Cathedral in New York. The meeting was attended by Archbishop Lakovas of the Greek Orthodox Church and Cardinal Cook of the Catholic Church. Incredibly, the president of the WCC declared, "I can foresee the day when all Christians might accept the Pope as Bishop of a World Church."

An article in the April 5, 1993, edition of *Christianity Today* by Tokunboh Adeyemo indicated the direction that the World Council of Churches is now pursuing. Significantly, the WCC Life and Work Slogan is "Doctrine Divides—Service Unites." This indicates the rejection of biblical doctrine as divisive in the interests of achieving a common consensus on the basis of the lowest common denominator theology. The WCC Secretary for Evangelism Raymond Fung indicated that evangelism encompassed every effort to improve the human condition whether it was made by Christians or non-Christians. He declared that Christians have no monopoly on evangelism.

The Bible teaches that evangelism is the proclamation of the good news of salvation in Christ for the express purpose of conversion. The WCC, however, teaches an implicit universalism and believes that the best of the non-Christian pagan religions is equal in value to (if not better than) the best of Christianity. As a result, the WCC believes dialogue and cross-fertilization are their highest goals. In contrast the historic teaching of Christianity is that all non-Christian religions are products of fallen human cultures.

Dr. David Gill, a WCC representative based in Geneva, Switzerland, announced to a radio audience during a 1974 British Broadcasting Corporation interview that the most important goal of the WCC is to "de-protestanize the churches" to prepare them to join the coming world church. That stands in stark contrast to the true priority of the church, which is to evangelize the world and create churches everywhere for teaching, fellowship, and the worship of Jesus Christ. The WCC disagrees, however, and has declared that cross-cultural evangelism is wrong and presumptuous. The WCC now demands that western Christian churches declare a "moratorium" on "evangelism" so that non-Christian cultures will not be offended by the claims of the gospel of Christ. Obviously, the leaders of the WCC assume a universalism where everyone will be saved in the end whether or not they respond to the gospel of Christ.

The 1973 Conference on World Mission in Bangkok articulated a new Christian world mission. This new WCC view taught that salvation should be replaced by a dedication to socio-political-economic well-being. The historic Christian focus on the need of sinners for reconciliation to God, spiritual growth via sanctification, and the hope of heaven were replaced by a radical secular humanism that focused solely on improving the social, political, and practical conditions of life. Incredibly, the leadership of the WCC declared at the Bangkok conference that this was "the close of the era of missions and the beginning of the era of mission."

The Good News!

One of the final prophetic signs that Jesus Christ is about to return is His prophecy that "this gospel of the kingdom will be preached in all the world as a witness to all the nations, and then the end will come" (Matthew 24:14). Despite all of the bad news around us, the gospel is truly being preached in all the world in the last days. The true growth of the church these days is astonishing! Starting with only one million Christians in China in 1949 when the

Communists took over, researchers estimate that since that time over 80 million Chinese have accepted Jesus Christ as their Lord and Savior despite the terrible religious persecution. One estimate suggests that over 25,000 thousand Chinese are dedicating their lives to Jesus Christ every day.

In the Muslim nation of Indonesia more than 20 percent of the population has accepted Christ. By 1900, only three percent of Africans had accepted Christ. However, in the last 90 years over 45 percent of the 500 million citizens in Africa have accepted Christ.

In Russia, the introduction of the gospel and the availability of Russian-language Bibles has led 100 million Russians to follow Christ. In South Korea the gospel was rejected for many years despite the valiant efforts of missionaries. However, as the winds of the Holy Spirit began to move throughout Asia following World War II, 30 percent of the population of Korea found faith in Christ.

Around the world, more than 85,000 people accept Christ as their Savior every single day. In the 2,000-year history of the church we have never seen such an astonishing move of God as we are witnessing today.

A Time of Spectacular Growth

A recent study by the Lausanne Statistics Task Force on the progress of evangelism concluded that the growth of the church is far greater than previously reported. In only 15 years from 1980 until now the number of born-again Christians has grown at a rate three times faster than the growth of the world's population. These historically verifiable records reveal this incredible growth in the number of Christians worldwide:

In 1430 Christians amounted to one in 99 of the world's population.

In 1790 Christians amounted to one in 49 of the world's population.

In 1940 Christians amounted to one in 32 of the world's population.

In 1970 Christians amounted to one in 19 of the world's population.

In 1980 Christians amounted to one in 16 of the world's population.

In 1983 Christians amounted to one in 13 of the world's population.

In 1986 Christians amounted to one in 11 of the world's population.

In 1994 Christians amounted to one in 10 of the world's population.

Consider these figures carefully. We are winning a significant remnant of the world's population during these last days! In only 60 years the number of Christians worldwide has grown by an astonishing 1,300 percent from only 40 million in 1934 to 540 million today. During that same time span, the world's population has grown by only 400 percent.

The broadcasting group World By 2000 tells us that Christian radio is now reaching almost half of the world's 360 "mega-languages," covering 78 percent of the earth's population. Evangelical broadcasters are now providing the gospel to every language group in the world.

The combination of evangelism efforts by mission organizations, hundreds of thousands of dedicated national pastors, and the word of Christian broadcasters is rapidly fulfilling the Great Commission. The accomplishments by the Wycliffe Translators and many others translating the Bible into the languages of millions who have not yet heard the gospel is one of the little-known miracles of the last days.

Despite the pessimistic analysis of any people that the population of the earth is growing faster than the church, the truth is that the gospel is being preached in all the world with astonishing success. A 1991 study by the National Council of Churches concluded that church membership is growing at twice the rate of the overall population throughout the world. Their study noted that the greatest growth was in evangelical churches.

PART 3

A World Headed Toward Final Judgment

CHAPTER 10

Living in
Perilous Times

The ancient prophets warned that the generation preceding the coming of the Messiah would witness the complete moral breakdown of society. We may very well be witnessing that breakdown today. For the last two millennia, western culture has reflected an almost universal acceptance of the fundamental values revealed in God's written revelation to mankind, the Bible. Even those who have rejected a personal faith in Jesus Christ still generally accepted the moral foundations based on the Ten Commandments and the teachings of Christ. However, all around us are signs that we live in a generation that has lost its moral anchor and spiritual compass, rejecting both Christian values and the guiding authority of the Word of God. In our present era alone, over 100 million people have died through devastating famine, plague, concentration camps, and world wars due to the evil acts of wicked leaders.

Having rejected Christ and the authority of Scripture, man is now set adrift without rules, without absolutes or a moral compass to direct his activities. Our schools and media have sown the wind of secular humanism and moral relativism, in which they teach there is no longer an absolute good or evil. As a result we are now caught in a whirlwind of corruption, pornography, sex crimes, and violence on our streets. Our society, as reflected in its media, schools, courts, and government, has progressively abandoned the moral teachings of Christianity. It is clear, then, that we are now fulfilling the prophecy that was written almost 2,000 years ago by the apostle Paul.

Paul accurately prophesied the attitude of modern men with corrupt minds. In his second epistle to Timothy, he warned about the perilous times of the last days:

> Know this, that in the last days perilous times will come: For men will be lovers of themselves, lovers of money, boasters, proud, blasphemers, disobedient to parents, unthankful, unholy, unloving, unforgiving, slanderers, without self-control, brutal, despisers of good, traitors, headstrong, haughty, lovers of pleasure rather than lovers of God, having a form of godliness but denying its power. And from such people turn away! (2 Timothy 3:1-5).

The Good News

We are indeed living in a time when men "resist the truth." The biggest offenders are the media, who not only resist the truth, but distort it. However, as we learned in the last chapter, more people than ever are turning to God through Jesus Christ. This tells us that positive things are happening in our country—contrary to what the media says. Two examples are the divorce rate in America and the attitude of young people about sex.

The Myth of America's Divorce Rate

After years of continuous media propaganda, most Americans have come to believe that 50 percent of marriages will end in divorce. However, the truth is that most marriages in America last a lifetime. The problem is that many reporters and editors do not understand statistics. For example, it was reported in 1981 that 50 percent of the marriages in America ended in divorce because the United States had 2,422,000 marriages and 1,213,000 divorces that year. At first glance it seemed to the media commentators that this proved that 50 percent of all marriages will end in divorce. The truth, however, is that this represents what happened only in that one year. Fully 90 percent of American marriages will survive without a divorce, according to the latest research. What's more, divorces actually declined by five percent from 1981 to 1987. A recent Louis Harris survey revealed that an incredible 85 percent of American husbands and wives said they would remarry their spouse if they could do it over again.

Despite the constant media message that sexual promiscuity is universal and that it is the key to happiness, the 1987 Louis Harris poll revealed that 80 percent of Americans say that "spousal sexual fidelity" is "a key to a good marriage." The respected Rand Corporation completed a study in 1991 which discovered that 96 percent of American adults claimed they were sexually faithful to their partner. The survey also showed that even those individuals who betrayed their spouses were usually unfaithful on only a single occasion. This picture of faithful, stable marriage totally contradicts the media's portrayal that constant infidelity and promiscuity are normal.

The American media also constantly suggest that most American children are living alone or with a single parent. However, the U.S. Census figures in 1990 revealed that over 72 percent of children under the age of 18 currently live with both parents. But it is true that those children who live in single-parent homes have much higher arrest rates and experience more discipline problems in school than children who live with both parents. The number of children between the ages of 14 and 17 who were arrested for violent crimes rose over 3,000 percent from 1950 to 1990. Significantly, studies of criminals in prison reveal that those kids who have no father in the home are twice as likely to drop out of school and three times as likely to abuse alcohol or drugs. In addition, when children are raised without a father's positive influence in their life, they are three times more likely to rape or murder as they become older teens.

The Lie About Teen Sexual Mores

Many teenagers look to their parents and teachers to help them establish moral boundaries to protect them from destroying their lives. Far from rejecting such moral teaching, many teens actually welcome caring intervention and moral guidance. In 1993, Emory University completed a fascinating study on the attitudes of more than 1,000 sexually active young teenage women. When asked what was the number-one thing they would like to learn about sexual activity, over 85 percent claimed they wanted to know "how to say no to a boy without hurting the other person's feelings."

While giving lip service to the promotion of abstinence for our teens, the Clinton administration has consistently shown that it does not believe that abstinence is a realistic and valid goal. The White House has turned down the funding of a number of programs in high schools that teach abstinence. The administration has chosen instead to continue spending $800,000 of taxpayer's dollars promoting "safe sex" with ads containing "dancing condoms." However, studies reveal that abstinence-training programs are powerful tools in the battle against teen pregnancies.

In 1993, Judge Frank Thaxton of Louisiana ruled that teaching abstinence to public school children is illegal. He claimed that teaching abstinence constituted "the establishment of religion" and was therefore forbidden by the U.S. Constitution. The attitude of the "safe sex" condom distributors is that teens will engage in sexual activity anyway, so we may as well protect them from the results of their activities—all while expecting the worst possible behavior from them. President Clinton appointed Dr. Joycelyn Elders, the so-called "condom queen," as Surgeon-General to oversee his administration's health programs. On one occasion, while promoting the use of condoms, she stated, "Abortion has an important and positive public-health benefit."[1] Incredibly, Elders also declared that the government should give drug-addicted prostitutes the drug Norplant, which prevents pregnancies, "so they could still use sex, if they must, to buy their drugs."[2]

According to an article in a *USA Weekend* magazine in November 1991, a study revealed that 54 percent of teens claimed they heard "too little" about how to say no to unwanted sexual activity during their sex education classes. A further 63 percent said they were troubled by the school's Safe Sex campaign theme that encouraged teen sexual activity with the use of condoms rather than teach them how to abstain from sexual activity until they were married. At the same time, teens are pressured by the media's constant message that immorality and promiscuity are normal and virginity is so rare that teenagers who reject sexual activity are odd.

The National Institute for Responsible Fatherhood in Cleveland developed an abstinence program to use with over 2,000 young adult men, the majority of whom had already fathered a child out of wedlock. As a result of this program, over 75 percent of these men have changed their behavior and not become teen fathers again. The Kenosha, Wisconsin, County Health Department achieved a major breakthrough in their program with teens, enabling many of them to reject a promiscuous lifestyle and avoid teen pregnancy. The basic philosophy of a successful abstinence program is an expectation that the teens can rise to a higher standard of responsibility for themselves and their actions while following a moral code.

The Signs of the Times

The U.S. Department of Health, under the leadership of Surgeon-General Joycelyn Elders, called on churches to adjust their teaching on homosexuality. Incredibly, a report from the Department of Health and Human Services warns against the dangers from a traditional Christian faith: "Religion presents another risk factor. . . . Many traditional fundamentalist faiths still portray homosexuality as morally wrong." The government report recommends: "Religion needs to reassess homosexuality in a positive context within their belief systems." If you've ever wondered whether the government was prepared to use its power to limit the churches' ability to preach the whole counsel of God, you now have your answer.

The American Bar Association (ABA) has declared war on Christianity. On May 5, 1989, the ABA held a seminar in San Francisco to teach lawyers about how they can effectively sue Christians and Christian

organizations for religious fraud and "the detrimen-
tal impact (emotional, financial, and civil-rights
wise) of religion and religious beliefs on American
society." These greedy lawyers are looking at the potential easy pickings available to their profession by
suing Christian organizations and churches that
they believe have "deep pockets." Christians aren't
alone in the battle to protect themselves from litiga-
tion-minded lawyers. The list of victims is long.

America is suffering from a plague of too many
lawyers who are destroying business and creating a
society in which the first response to any misfortune
is to look around for someone to sue. The United
States has 90 percent of the world's lawyers and suf-
fers from more court litigation than the rest of the
world put together. The cost of this legal morass is
staggering as it clogs the courts and causes many
small businesses to fold when they are sued. America now has 100 times as many lawyers as its greatest economic competitor, Japan. Meanwhile, Japan's
schools are producing 100 times as many engineers
as the United States. It does not take a genius to calculate where the economic growth will explode in
the years ahead.

One sign of the rising legal prejudice against our
faith in the courts can be found in the growing number of legal injunctions, heavy fines, and lengthy
prison sentences handed out to Christian protesters
who demonstrate against abortion clinics. In Georgia, for example, antiabortion, nonviolent Christian
protesters were sentenced to very long prison terms

and fines. Meanwhile, an Atlanta drug dealer was convicted in 1989 to only one year in jail for killing another drug dealer by shooting him 58 times.

Recently there have been some incidents where Christian protesters have killed abortion doctors. This is illegal and a sin against God. This battle for the soul of America will not be won through violent acts. If people adopt the carnal, violent techniques of this world, they will receive the judgment of God on their activities. We need to remember the instruction from God's Word that "the weapons of our warfare are not carnal," (2 Corinthians 10:4). This abortion battle is a spiritual fight for the hearts of men and women. At the same time, it is wrong for police and jail guards to deliberately use painful techniques when arresting protesters in order to punish them for exercising their constitutionally protected right to oppose the murder of defenseless unborn children.

The Convention on Children's Rights

Early in this century the communist leader Lenin laid out his strategy to attack the foundation of western culture: "Destroy the family and the society will collapse." Lenin correctly understood that our country will never be strong unless our families are strong.

One of the most insidious and evil attacks on the family today is the plan to eliminate the ability of parents to provide discipline to their children as a means of correcting their misbehavior. Bernie Sanders, an Independent congressman from the state of Vermont, recently introduced to Congress the United Nations Convention on the Rights of the Child. This treaty would make the act of spanking your child an illegal action punishable by law. In addition, the U.N. Convention would severely limit your ability as a parent to teach moral or spiritual guidelines to your child. Under this treaty, any application of physical punishment or discipline could result in your going to prison. Remember that this treaty would take legal precedence over any applicable U.S. state and federal laws. In the future, then, a liberal activist judge may find you guilty under this international law of taking your children to Sunday School against their wishes or for spanking your children to keep them away from some dangerous activity.

If you think I am exaggerating the risk posed to the family by this innocent-sounding treaty, then consider the many parents in Scandinavia who are already serving prison sentences for spanking their children. The December 1993 issue of the *McAlvany Intelligence Digest* reported that "in Finland it is illegal to spank your child. Kari Lappalainen was fined $100 for tugging the hair of the five-year-old child of his common-law wife. Anne Ekblom-Worlund, spokeswoman for the Finnish Supreme Court said, 'Parents are not allowed to use any physical force to discipline their children.'"

The Plague of Violence and Crime

The tidal wave of violent crime and dishonesty that is sweeping our globe is one of the key signs that we are rapidly approaching the final crisis of human history. The breakdown in morals that followed the abandonment of Christian values and prayers in our schools has produced a generation of young people who have lost respect for law, property, and human life. The situation in the inner cities has deteriorated to the point where bullets have become the leading cause of death for young black men.

Since 1960 the FBI reports that crime has increased by 560 percent while the U.S. population has increased only 41 percent in the same period. The Justice Department concluded that a staggering 80 percent of all Americans will become the victim of a violent crime at some point in their lives; 99 percent of these victims will be robbed at least once, while 87 percent will become the victims of property theft three or more times during their lifetime! This is almost unbelievable when you consider that most of us grew up in neighborhoods where few people ever locked their doors or feared personal violence.

The murder rate in America is now five times higher than in Europe and four times higher than in Canada. The epidemic of violent rape has grown to 700 percent higher than in Europe. More than five million Americans are victimized every year by violent criminals. During the tragic Vietnam War, 58,000 American soldiers lost their lives fighting for their country. However, during the last four years, 90,000 Americans were murdered on the streets of the nation almost twice as many as were killed in 13 years of fighting in Vietnam. This plague of violence amounts to nothing less than a war launched by criminals against peaceful citizens—a war in which evil men pursue their search for illegal drugs, gang warfare, and vengeance.

Crime and Punishment

The prison system in North America is in a mess. Consider the level of punishment that modern criminals receive for their crimes against other citizens in the unlikely event they are caught. A truly violent crime will usually earn less than 48 months in jail. Despite the widely publicized "war on crime," judges are now sentencing criminals found guilty of serious crimes with prison terms that are 60 percent shorter than those sentences handed out in 1954.

Our whole judicial system is in need of a major overhaul. Many prisons are dangerously over-crowded with two or three prisoners having to share one bed in rotation. There are also many reports of prisons that are "Club Feds" filled with outrageously expensive bodybuilding and recreational equipment. The *Reader's Digest* ran a disturbing article in their November 1994 issue that detailed some of the excesses in American prisons.[3] For example, the Mercer Regional Correctional Facility in Pennsylvania, with only 850 inmates, has a full-size basketball court, handball court, tennis courts, and volleyball area. Their well-equipped weightlifting area contains expensive electronic exercise bicycles and aerobics machines. There are three activity directors to plan the inmate's recreational time with five psychologists and ten counselors to care for their mental needs. The *Reader's Digest*'s survey concluded that

"Mercer is not an exceptional institution; it is, in fact typical." Their researchers concluded that expensive recreational equipment, theater and music groups, college courses and, of course, X-rated movies, are standard fare for those who have been convicted of crimes. This study concluded that "the overall cost of these prison amenities . . . takes up a huge portion of state correctional budgets, while thousands of violent criminals are released each year for lack of space."

Hundreds of millions are spent yearly on elaborate rehabilitation and therapy programs. However, after 30 years of these programs, the results are negligible. "When asked by *Reader's Digest* how many sex offenders he has rehabilitated in his years on the job, one New York State prison counselor bluntly responded, 'None.'" Prisoners convicted of sexual violence have now received approval from American courts to be allowed to possess in their cells brutally sadistic pornographic materials involving torture scenes. The moral system of our world has been turned upside down. Prisons like these cannot possibly represent a deterrent to the criminal predators among us.

Despite the increase of violence in North America, police statistics indicate that far less than one percent of the population is involved in violent crime. A small portion of these criminals are responsible for 40 percent of all the crimes. Less than ten percent of criminals commit 66 percent of the crimes. The average career criminal commits three crimes per week, amounting to a staggering 150 crimes every year of their lifetime in crime. Incredibly, over 93 percent are repeat offenders. However, of all those who are career criminals, less than seven percent commit violent crimes and less than one percent of these violent criminals commit the truly frightening crimes of sexual assault, brutal attacks, and murder.

If you asked experienced police officers to identify the truly violent criminals in their city who have committed the worst brutal crimes and who are likely to do so again in the future, they could immediately identify several hundred of these dangerous criminals in every community. If our legislators truly wanted to make our communities safe again, they could do it. They could pass laws that forced judges to sentence as habitual violent offenders those who have committed three or more truly violent crimes. These offenders should serve mandatory life sentences without parole. And those who take a life should forfeit their own life according to the law of God. This kind of judgment would prevent the worst violent offenders from continuing to inflict pain on other citizens. Of course, the laws would need to specify that the three crimes be real physical violence, not simple car theft or some other nonviolent crime. In addition, legislators should prohibit repeated violence offenders from being placed in "Club Fed" prisons. Instead, these criminals should be placed in austere prison camps in remote wilderness areas.

Modern criminologists, sociologists, and liberal politicians claim that the crime wave is caused by society, poverty, and poor career opportunities. This premise underlies the appallingly short prison sentences handed out to violent criminals. Rather than demanding that individuals take responsibility for their choices and actions, today's "authorities" blame social problems for criminal behavior.

Despite constant liberal propaganda to the contrary, murder rates have almost nothing to do with the level of unemployment. For example, during the Great Depression, the murder rate and property crimes throughout North America actually declined 40 percent. It is significant that in that era, people still taught moral values and the existence of an absolute good and evil.

A fascinating study by Professors Wilson and Herrnstein of Harvard University and the University of California discovered that crime rate is not related to economic and social causes as suggested by modern sociologists. Their study discovered that "during the 1960s, one neighborhood in San Francisco had the lowest income, the highest unemployment rate, the highest proportion of families with incomes under $4,000 a year, the least educational attainment, the highest tuberculosis rate, and the highest proportion of substandard housing. . . . That neighborhood was called Chinatown. Yet in 1965, there were only five persons of Chinese ancestry committed to prison in the entire state of California."

In a commentary on the twisted values that rule some of the leading members of the Clinton administration, consider the recent comments of former U.S. Surgeon-General Joycelyn Elders. Despite her testifying on his behalf, her son Kevin Elders was convicted and sentenced to ten years in prison for selling cocaine. Displaying the usual level of moral thinking that characterizes the Clinton administration, Joycelyn Elders excused her son's behavior in selling hard drugs. She explained, "I don't feel it was a crime." This is the same Elders that advocated legalization of all drugs, the distribution of condoms to elementary students, and attacked conservative Christian organizations that oppose abortion and promiscuity. Finally, Elders exceeded even President Clinton's minimal standards of decency by recommending that U.S. schools should teach children to masturbate as part of their sex education. Although Clinton had repeatedly praised Dr. Elders despite her outrageous statements, this was the final straw. The backlash forced him to fire her to avoid political repercussions in the new Congress with its Republican majority.

The AIDS Tragedy

The Bible warns that the generation living before the coming of Messiah will experience devastating plagues that will kill up to one-fourth of the planet's population. The dreaded plague known as AIDS may well be beginning the fulfillment of the prophecy of the fourth horseman of the apocalypse. The horseman prophecies describe the ultimate disaster, with one-quarter of humanity dying of famine and plague during the seven-year period known as the Tribulation. However, the nature of plagues is such that we would expect a worldwide epidemic to begin slowly and grow inexorably until it afflicts the whole earth. Jesus warned that there would be plagues in "various places" in the days leading to His return (Matthew 24:7).

Medical reports from around the world reveal that we are losing the battle against AIDS. After testing 13,000 pregnant women at prenatal clinics in South Africa, doctors were devastated to realize that a huge number of these women were infected with AIDS, yet they were unaware of the deadly virus they carried. At the rate of infection detected, the doctors estimated that over 500,000 South Africans now have the AIDS virus. A South African medical journal study in 1992 revealed that 47 percent of all those donating blood tested positive for AIDS. This study suggested that up to 50 percent of the whole population of South Africa will ultimately die of AIDS.

Tragically, the number of victims in Africa is now doubling every 13 months. Over 16 million people will be infected with AIDS in South Africa alone within the next five years. The CIA reported in 1992 to President Bush that up to 75 percent of the population of Africa south of the Sahara Desert will succumb to the AIDS virus and die during the next 10 to 12 years. This means over 375 million Africans will die of AIDS in the next dozen years. These figures are supported by a number of scientific reports from the Center for Disease Control in Atlanta, Georgia.

In Zaire, Zambia, and Uganda, the social structure of society is beginning to collapse as more than 20 percent of the population succumbs to AIDS. Recently, a medical study in Zambia concluded that virtually 100 percent of its army's soldiers are now infected with AIDS. This means that the armies and governments of Zambia, Tanzania, Uganda, and other central African countries will experience devastating collapse in the years ahead.

The Homosexual Agenda

Since the 1950s the media has constantly affirmed that up to ten percent of the population is gay or homosexual. Proven scientific findings, however, reveal that the number of homosexuals is only one to two percent of the population. However, homosexuals like to perpetuate the media's estimate rather than the scientific data. This is a significant part of their homosexual educational agenda to convince society that their perversion must be "normal" because of their false claim that one person in ten is gay. The homosexual community, though very small, is supported by powerful, elite leaders in government, law, and education worldwide.

An example of this campaign to make everyone believe that sexual perversion is "normal" appeared in my own city of Toronto, Canada. Recently, the extremely liberal Toronto Board of Education voted to support a board document called *"Sexual Orientation (Homosexuality, Lesbianism and Homophobia)."* Articles by George Jonas in the June 1 and June 27, 1992, issues of the *Toronto Sun* newspaper revealed details of this plan. The document demands that children in Toronto's secondary schools be indoctrinated in homosexual politics through an educational curriculum unit on sexual orientation. Incredibly, the document postulates that "there is a sickness or moral failing called heterosexism. It consists of the view that heterosexuality is the norm for all social and sexual relationships." This study says that heterosexism has caused gays and lesbians to be stigmatized as perverted, morally deviant, or mentally ill. This report claims that modern science has discovered that homosexuals are normal and healthy, but those who believe that sexual relations should occur only between a husband and wife "have mental health problems."

Incredibly, our local government voted to adopt this report, which demands that our children be told that the traditional view—that heterosexual relations between a man and woman is normal—should be rejected as false and outmoded. Further, the document states that "there is clear evidence that the traditional heterosexual nuclear family is a dangerous place for women and children—a place where the prevalence of physical and sexual abuse is disturbingly high." These morally outrageous statements are contradicted by studies that reveal that a home with a mother and father is the safest place to raise children.

The next stage in the homosexual political agenda is to instruct the next generation of children that their natural repugnance to homosexuality is actually a form of mental illness that needs to be treated. Wake up, Christians! There is a war going on for the souls of our children. We will lose this war unless we awaken to the real underlying issues. Christian citizens must begin to counterattack by demanding a return to the teaching of fundamental moral values in our schools, churches, and homes.

The Harvesting of Human Organs

Many people think that the idea of harvesting human organs is simply fiction, portrayed in Bram Stoker's novel *Frankenstein* and countless late-night movies that sought to depict the evil abuses of a "mad" doctor. In places like China, however, that is not the case. The respected human rights organization Human Rights Watch—Asia has interviewed many witnesses who confirmed that organs are harvested in China. Prisoners in Chinese concentration camps, who have been sentenced for execution, are oftentimes killed at a time, place, and in a manner to allow the profitable harvesting of their vital organs. These prisoners are shot in the head if there is a need for their hearts, lungs, or kidneys. If there is a need for a person's eyes, the prisoner will be shot in the heart.

Wealthy foreigners in need of an immediate transplant travel to a Hong Kong clinic or cross the border into mainland China to receive their "purchased" organ transplant. As soon as the wealthy patient arrives, a prisoner is brought to the medical laboratory, where he is executed by the doctors in a manner that preserves the value and use of his organs. These foreign patients are willing to pay up to $200,000 for the healthy heart of a young prisoner. Kidneys and lungs can fetch up to $80,000 on this macabre medical market of body parts. Reports have circulated about greedy doctors removing organs from prisoners the night before they were executed. The Human Rights Watch—Asia group confirmed that some executions have been deliberately "botched" to keep the prisoner alive as long as possible to improve the chances for a successful organ transplant.

Reports from South America and India confirm that some poor people have literally sold their vital organs to medical laboratories in return for desperately needed money. A judge in Brazil reported in 1992 that some of the young homeless street children who live in abandoned buildings and sewers have been kidnapped and taken to labs. Unspeakably evil medical practitioners operate on these kidnapped children to harvest whatever organs are needed by wealthy patients who fly in from Europe or the Middle East.

Amazingly, the American Medical Association's Council on Ethical and Judicial Affairs recently recommended that doctors be allowed to harvest organs from babies who suffer from a condition known as *anencephaly*. A baby with this tragic birth defect is born with part of its brain missing and will normally die within a few weeks. Although there is a real problem with a shortage of organ transplants for children under the age of two, this monstrous proposal is both illegal and immoral. The idea of transplanting an organ from a live donor to another patient represents a massive change from historical medical practice. This recommendation is one more step down the slippery ethical slope that is leading us toward the medical euthanasia that was practiced by Nazi doctors in the darkest days of World War II.

In those horrifying medical laboratories (located in concentration camps), Nazi doctors surgically removed the organs from live Jewish prisoners in diabolical experiments that resulted in the death of their patients. In addition, it was standard Nazi policy to medically segregate and execute thousands of people who suffered from birth defects, retardation, or were weak or senile.

Recent reports from Japan have confirmed that the Japanese Imperial Army, Unit 731, killed tens of thousands of Chinese and people of other nationalities in germ warfare and chemical warfare experiments. Many of these evil doctors occupy the highest positions in Japanese society today because they were never tried as war criminals.

The satanic Nazi philosophy was a radical departure from the Judeo-Christian perspective that has upheld Western civilization for 2,000 years. The Bible and teachings of Jesus Christ clearly hold that every single person is of infinite value because we are made in God's image. However, the Nazis rejected these Christian values and substituted them with a secular humanist view, which held that an individual had no inherent value except for his or her role in serving the Third Reich.

Tragically, the modern revival of neopaganism has turned our western moral values upside down. Today, respected doctors will calmly defend the most immoral and diabolical plans to kill a child to harvest his organs or to abort an unborn child under the justification that the pregnancy is economically "inconvenient" to the mother. These proabortionists declare that they believe that a 13-week-old unborn baby is simply part of the body of its mother and may be surgically removed in the same way we would remove a tumor. Part of the moral tragedy of our time is that millions in our nation have accepted this kind of reasoning. Two Nobel prize-winning scientists went so far as to suggest that a newborn infant should not be considered a human with legal rights until genetic testing determined that the baby was perfect. These scientists calmly suggested that if a defect was discovered, the child should be killed to keep imperfect children from polluting the race.

Incredibly, the media and other doctors have not reacted with condemnation to these kinds of suggestions. Such evil theories and actions are a grave threat to our moral order and a warning that it will not be long till the Antichrist appears.

Famine and Population

Since 1967, the earth's population has grown by two billion souls. Ninety percent of that population increase occurred in the Third World. During the last 30 days another ten million hungry humans arrived on earth.

Every month, another 5,000 animal and plant species become extinct as they succumb to the relentless population pressures on their precious and endangered habitats. Every month, another three billion tons of irreplaceable topsoil is lost forever. And every month, three million acres of Amazon rain forest are burned to provide logs and clear the land for farming. These forests, of course, are a major source of the oxygen we need for breathing.

Tragically, despite all of our new agricultural techniques, more people are facing famine today than at any other time in history. Indeed, Jesus warned that devastating famine would precede His second coming.

CHAPTER 11

The Media Attack on Christianity

A war is raging for the hearts and souls of your family. Writers and producers of movies, songs, talk shows, and other television productions have an agenda that is diametrically opposed to the moral and religious values of the average North American. The air waves are flooded with vile, profane, violent, and blasphemous programs that enter our homes through our TV sets. The truth is that there's an enemy in the camp.

Television's Influence

Researchers for a *Time*/CNN survey conducted in 1989 found that the average person now watches a staggering 30 hours of TV every week. When you consider that most people are awake for 16 hours a day, the 30 hours per week devoted to TV viewing adds up to almost 100 full days per year. This equals almost a third of people's waking lives. Over a normal 70-year lifetime, then, the average viewer will waste an astonishing 19 years in front of a television set.

While that amount of time is an issue, the real problem is the abysmal quality of the information and entertainment people are receiving. Instead of acquiring an at-home education through excellent university-level correspondence courses offered by the Learning or Discovery channels, most Americans and Canadians watch the mindless trash of daytime soap operas and violent, immoral action of evening programs. By age 18, the average student will have witnessed over 200,000 individual acts of television violence, including 16,000 murders.

In the past, most people acquired the information that shaped their philosophical world view from reading the Bible and other books. However, television programs, shaped by the minds of the media elite that are totally opposed to moral values, have now become the main source of information for over 65 percent of Americans. Michael Medved, one of the most insightful media critics in America, has written a powerful indictment of the media's all-out attack on the traditional and moral values of the average Christian viewer. I recommend that anyone who is interested in this issue should obtain Medved's excellent book *Hollywood vs. America*, published by Zondervan Publishing House in 1992.

A Media Agenda to Corrupt Morals

The media today display an overwhelming obsession with sexual immorality and perversion. Most Americans live in faithful monogamous relationships with their spouses, but movies and television portray immorality, fornication, and adultery as normal and common. According to the Harris Study completed in 1988, during the course of a single year, TV networks broadcast over 65,000 references to sexual activity during prime-time afternoon and evening television viewing hours. Incredibly, this amounts to 27 references to sexual activity every single hour of broadcasting. In one year the average TV viewer will view a total of 14,000 sexual depictions. During a recent sweeps week, when the networks showcased their best shows and tried to win the best ratings, they featured over 600 depictions of sexual activity. Significantly, 93 percent of the scenes were of immoral sex outside of marriage. This deluge of extramarital sex cannot help but weaken the moral fiber of the average viewer.

What is the public response to these media broadcasts and films? One poll discovered that 45 percent of past movie fans now refuse to attend theaters due to the pervasive violence, while more than 75 percent believe that the overall quality of movies has degenerated in the past two decades.

Michael Medved's book *Hollywood vs. America* revealed that the three major TV networks lost over a third of their audience, a total of 30 million regular viewers, who simply turned off the network television shows in disgust. As a result, the networks had zero profits in 1991. While they claim they are in the television and movie business to make money for their investors, most viewers reject these violent and pornographic films. However, the Hollywood elite continue to produce movies filled with violence and filth because their real motivation is to tear down fundamental Christian values that we treasure. There is a cultural war going on today for the souls of our nations.

According to an analysis by the *Rolling Stone Magazine*, during the 1991 opening television season, 26 new network shows portrayed crude sexual jokes or sexual activity. Married couples are quite rare on television today, with most new characters portrayed as single or divorced and involved in immoral sexual behavior. In contrast to the picture presented by current TV shows, over two-thirds of Americans over 18 are married. In fact, the 1982 Simenauer and Carroll survey found that 91 percent of Americans wanted to be married. The gulf between the Hollywood illusion and true American life is overwhelming. You would be hard-pressed to find a single female teen character on television or film that is not involved in immoral behavior. And it is not an accident that the rate of unwed teen mothers rose over 500 percent from 1960 to 1994. However, despite the media's unrelenting inducement to immorality, over 65 percent of female teens under 18 remain virgins.

Rock Videos and Records

Another example of the anti-Christian attitude is revealed by a video that was produced by the rock superstar Madonna. Her video, *Like a Prayer*, contains sacrilegious scenes displaying a statue of an African saint that weeps real tears and then comes to life. The video shows a partially naked Madonna kissing the feet of this icon. As he is gradually transformed into a real man, Madonna proceeds to make love to him. Finally, as the video closes, both of them display stigmata, the wounds on the hands and feet of Christ after He was crucified.

Parents are appallingly ignorant of the real nature of the rock music and videos their teenagers are listening to. This music contains a constant stream of messages about violence against women, torture, perversion, and murder. Many of the lyrics are simply unprintable. In a single record by 2 Live Crew entitled *As Nasty as They Want to Be*, teens will hear over 430 vulgar references to sexual activity, 80 references to human waste, and 163 degrading references to women.

"Roseanne" Attacks Christianity

The May 3, 1994, episode of ABC's "Roseanne" featured one of the most insidious attacks on Christianity that has appeared on prime-time television. Tragically, aside from an excellent critical article in the *AFA Journal* published in Tupelo, Mississippi, there was little, if any, reaction from the Christian public or churches. During this particular "Roseanne" episode, Dan and Roseanne express concern about where their 12-year-old son D.J. is spending his afternoons. They find out from their daughter Darlene that he has been secretly attending church services after classes in his search for moral values. Darlene reports to Roseanne, "It's worse than you thought. He's going to church!" After their son admits that he is attending church, Roseanne tells D.J. that he doesn't need to go to church because he can simply ask them anything he wants to know about God. "What religion are we?" asks the son. "I have no idea," Roseanne replies sarcastically.

The same program shows Roseanne lying about a new stove that she obtained dishonestly when a company mistakenly delivered two stoves instead of one. Rather than call on the company to return it, Roseanne tries to illegally sell the stove through a newspaper ad, where she tells the potential buyer that she won the stove in a game show. However, her son confronts his mom's dishonesty, saying, "You were never on any game show." She defends her lie by shouting at him, "I was too on a game show. And if you didn't spend all your time down at that da— church, you'd know that!" D.J. then asks Roseanne, "It's wrong to use swear words, right? Then how come you swear so much?" "Well," she replies, "because sometimes it's real hard not to. But, if I swore as much as I wanted to, I'd never say anything else! So you see, I'm using restraint and God loves that!" Later, D.J. asks why Roseanne always makes him lie about his age when they go to a theater. "More money to give to charity," she lies, although she despises charity.

When D.J. criticizes his sister for living with her boyfriend, he says, "I don't think Darlene and David should be having sex without being married." Roseanne and Dan refuse to answer. When Darlene asks about the stove, Roseanne insists that the company "gave" it to her. She defends her dishonesty by claiming that the theft is nothing to the "big company" who rips off "little people" like her all the time. Later, Roseanne sells the stove and divides the money with her partners. Confronted by her son as they divided the spoils, Roseanne screams at him, "Get off my back! Even God took a day off!"

This broadcast portrayed a young boy searching for some kind of moral anchor. However, when he raised questions about cheating, stealing, lying, and fornication, his parents ridiculed and attacked him for suggesting that there are standards of right and wrong that should govern our conduct. And in every episode, the program's many profanities and obscenities are accompanied by canned applause. The clear theme of this show and many others like it is total contempt for Christianity from the beginning to the last commercial. Perhaps what is worse is that this one broadcast received very few phone calls or letters of complaint.

This kind of attack on our faith is increasing throughout the media. Producers have seen that they can disparage our beliefs with impunity. Christians have become so accustomed to being ridiculed on television that they seldom react when their faith is denigrated. Consider what the reaction would be if "Roseanne" had chosen to make a mockery of Muslims or Judaism. Public demonstrations and lawsuits would have resulted if the producers had attacked any other major faith.

We Christians need to wake up and defend our beliefs when they are openly attacked. If not, we in America will witness a campaign against Christianity similar to the campaigns that the Nazi propaganda machine orchestrated against the Jews during the 1930s in their preparation for the Holocaust.

Recent Films that Attack Christianity

Dozens of anti-Christian films have appeared during the last few years. Consider this short list and you will see a clear trend in films that attack and denigrate the faith of millions of Christians. Most of these films have appeared on both television and in movie houses.

Poltergeist II. In this film, filled with New Age occult and satanic themes, a hymn-singing demonic preacher tries to destroy a child.

The Vision. This film shows Christians conspiring to use hypnotic technology on their TV show in an attempt to take control of the world.

Pass the Ammo. This film depicts an evil, conniving, immoral televangelist in a PTL-type scandal.

The Handmaiden's Tale. In this film, Christians have established a Christian fundamentalist totalitarian government

*Grant and Kaye Jeffrey filming on the
Mount of Olives opposite the Temple Mount.*

Map of Russian–Arab Invasion of Israel

The new MARC smart card with computer chip introduced by the U.S. military.

The proposed biometric Health Card could create a national identification system.

(Special thanks to Terry Cook for the photos)

Russian Tank on U.S. Interstate
April 21, 1994

*A photo showing a Russian T-80 tank
being transported on a flatbed truck in America.*

Russian Anatov 124 Condor Plane
Loading U.S. Apache Helicopters

*A photo showing Russians loading
American Apache helicopters at a base in Florida.*

*Grant standing in front of a burial cave
with the tombs of the early Christians.*

*Ossuaries (stone coffins)
of the early Christians
mentioned in the Gospels.*

complete with secret prostitution rings for the leaders, the burning of books, and the torturing of religious enemies.

The Rapture. This film attacks the hope of the resurrection. A deluded Christian woman, newly converted, takes her daughter into the desert to await the rapture. When it doesn't occur as she hoped, she shoots her daughter in the head while praying to God.

At Play in the Fields of the Lord. This film attacks missionary endeavors by presenting a group of unpleasant, crazy, and arrogant missionaries trying to force the natives in the Amazon rain forest to accept Christ. The Indians are presented as innocent and perfectly attuned to nature while the Catholic and Protestant missionaries are portrayed as evil, bigoted, psychotic, and mean-spirited.

Guilty As Charged. This absurd film presents a "scripture-quoting" religious nut as a murderous maniac who captures criminals who have been released by the courts on a legal technicality. This "Christian" then executes these criminals in his private basement execution chamber, which has crosses and Bible verses on the walls.

Star Trek V. This movie ends with Captain Kirk replying to a question by Dr. McCoy: "Is God really out there?" In what is clearly a New Age response, Kirk replies (pointing to his chest), "Maybe he's not out there, maybe he's right here. The human heart."

The Last Temptation of Christ. Despite the fact that over 25,000 Christians demonstrated against the film's release, the Hollywood studio that produced it totally ignored their heartfelt request to halt its release. The film contained 20 incredibly offensive scenes that totally perverted the historical truth about Jesus. For example, in one scene Jesus was shown as a voyeur watching Mary Magdalene having affairs with ten different men. Later in the film, the apostle Paul confessed that he never really believed in the resurrection. In the final dream sequence of the movie, Jesus is portrayed as making love to Mary Magdalene. Despite massive media approval and a huge advertising budget, the film bombed, costing the investors more than $10 million in losses.

Cape Fear. Martin Scorsese, who produced *The Last Temptation of Christ*, continued his campaign against Christian faith in *Cape Fear*, a remake of the 1940s thriller about an escaped convict who returns to attack his lawyer. However, in this remake, Scorsese reveals his true anti-Christian agenda by having the convict appear with crosses tattooed all over his back and Bible verses tattooed on his arms. The convict mutilates one victim while gratuitously claiming to be a pentecostal who is interested in saving people's souls. Later in the film, as he prepares to rape a woman, he asks her, "Are you born again? Soon you'll be talking in tongues." Between these despicable acts, the convict speaks in tongues. None of these anti-religious elements were in the original film. They were added by Martin Scorsese as his reply to those who dared to criticize his earlier film *The Last Temptation of Christ.*

The Hollywood elite are willing to go to abysmal depths in dredging the moral sewers to pander to the perverted tastes of their viewers. Incredibly, MGM paid $500,000 for the rights to a film script in which the president of the United States is portrayed having sex with a cow. In addition, the level of abusive and profane language in current Hollywood films is staggering. A recent study revealed that the R-rated films in 1991 averaged over 41 profane or vulgar references per film. Even children's films are not safe. Over 70 percent of the PG (Parental Guidance) films contained profane, sexual, and vulgar language.

In total disregard for realism, modern movies never show their characters praying to God for assistance or seeking spiritual guidance from their ministers or priests during a personal crisis. Have you ever seen a character on television or film search in the Bible for inspiration, as millions of people do every week in America? Despite impending death, sickness, or absolute disaster, no one ever prays to God or seeks spiritual help. I have not heard of any recent television show or movie that showed a character praying as he or she approached death. This is unrealistic, and it reveals a massive antagonism toward spiritual realities and the Christian faith.

In recent decades, writers, directors, and producers have demonstrated their hatred of the Christian faith by presenting numerous cinematic outrages that would have been unthinkable earlier in this century. The 1930 Production Code, which governed movies and television, set standards that forbade the open insults to Christianity that are common in today's movies. Until the mid-1970s, Hollywood complied with Article VII in this code, which declared: "(1) No film or episode may throw ridicule on any religious faith. (2) Ministers of religion in their character as ministers of religion should not be used as comic characters or as villains. (3) Ceremonies of any definite religion should be carefully and respectfully handled."

If this Production Code existed today, we would have been spared the despicable movies that, as of recent, have openly ridiculed the faith of millions of Christians. Moreover, while the media elite have mocked traditional Christianity, they have also displayed an uncritical acceptance of New Age, pagan, and occult religions. In the last several years Hollywood has produced 14 movies positively portraying the theme of reincarnation—a theme that is central in New Age and pagan religions.

Has the unrelenting focus on immorality, sexual license, and violence in movies attracted a larger American audience? No; attendance figures have dropped dramatically as Hollywood's movies have gotten worse. Consider these movie attendance figures: 1948—90 million; 1965—44 million; 1984—23 million; 1991—19 million. Despite millions of dollars spent on sophisticated advertising, films today are drawing 45 percent fewer moviegoers. As a result, movie ticket sales in the 1990s are the lowest they have been in the last 15 years.

Movie Violence and Violent Behavior

Despite denials from the Hollywood media elite, an analysis of nearly 200 studies on the relationship between watching television violence and actual incidents of physical violence concluded that some viewers are definitely influenced to behave more violently after observing such programs. Yet the amount of violence in movies today continues to increase. For example, the movie *Rambo III* depicted 106 violent deaths, while the movie *Die Hard 2* portrayed 264 people killed. Sixty-two percent of recent films included violent fight scenes and 39 percent featured graphic death scenes. According to the November 1991 report by the National Coalition on Television Violence, the wave of violence extends to music videos as well. An analysis of 750 recent music videos revealed over 20 acts of violence every hour.

How susceptible are viewers who watch media depictions of violence? It is important to realize that the majority of viewers do not respond to the programs by displaying violent behavior. However, careful studies, such as a 20-year study done at the University of Pennsylvania, reveal that up to 30 percent of viewers do become fearful or depressed as a result of watching violent shows. A further 11 percent tend to duplicate the violent acts they witnessed, and do so in some manner during the following years.

There is no question that the abysmal moral climate of eroding values and soulless characters that dominate modern films has influenced a great number of teens who seem to have lost any sense of purpose. One poll found that 67 percent of viewers felt that violence in television and the movies was "mainly to blame" for the raging epidemic in teen violence. Indeed, since 1951, the teen suicide rate has increased by over 400 percent. The Center for Disease Control reported in 1992 that more than one million teens tried to end their lives by suicide that year, with 276,000 of them sustaining injuries. And 8.3 percent of teens claimed in a recent survey that they had attempted suicide at least once. At a time when their lives should be filled with the joys of athletics, learning, and social activities, many teens find themselves in a search for meaning and fail to see that their life is of infinite value.

Today's epidemic of television violence also extends to children's cartoons. According to the respected study *The Violence Profile—1967–1989 Children's Programming*, which examined the prevalence of violence in children's cartoons, the average Saturday morning children's cartoon contains 25 acts of violence every hour. According to the National Coalition on Television Violence, in 1991–1992 over 72 percent of children's cartoons portrayed an average of ten acts of violence every hour. And the popular children's movie, *Teenage Mutant Ninja Turtles*, contained 194 acts of extreme violence.

Pat Buchanan, the political commentator and co-host of CNN's "Crossfire," wrote about the media elite's agenda to subvert the values and morals of the nation. "The arts crowd . . . is engaged in a cultural struggle to root out the old America of family, faith, and flag and recreate society in a pagan image."[1]

The Abuse of Artistic License

The federal government now supports the National Endowment for the Arts (NEA) with hundreds of millions of dollars each year to encourage the artistic community. Yet liberal and anti-Christian attitudes are common among those who are charged with administering these art grants. Consider some of their recent decisions: They refused a $10,000 grant to a group that wanted to teach young painters drawing skills. Their rationale was that this training "would stifle creativity." Later, these federally funded administrators decided to grant $70,000 to fund a gallery show of Shawn Eichman's "artistic" display of a jar containing her own blood and an aborted baby. The endowment also funded an exhibit showing an artist desecrating pictures of Jesus Christ. Then they gave a $20,000 grant to support an exhibit showing sexually explicit props covered with numerous Bibles. All of that was done using taxpayer's money.

This tendency to denigrate the spiritual values and religious feelings of the Christian taxpayers whose funds have supported these projects is quite selective. The NEA has targeted Christians but has wisely chosen to avoid attacking Jews or Muslims. An attack on Judaism would justly yield a massive anti-discrimination lawsuit from B'nai B'rith. If the NEA dared to insult the religious sensibilities of Muslims by defiling the Koran, they would likely pay for their "artistic license" with their lives. However, these liberal artistic administrators believe that it is safe to attack Christians because they correctly calculate that they can get away with it without any serious consequences. Christians need to use the full force of the new anti-discrimination and anti-hate laws to sue any group or individual who grossly, and hatefully, attacks the faith and beliefs of those who follow Christ.

The Attitudes of the Media Elite

What could possibly account for today's unrelenting attack on our moral values? Part of the answer is found in the results of a public opinion survey of 104 of the most influential television and media executives in America. These people are the key decision-makers who have chosen the films and programs that have received funding and promotion for the past few years. The respected Lichter/Rothman group study reveals a huge difference in the attitudes and moral values of media executives and the average American citizen. For example, an amazing 84 percent of these executives believe that adultery, divorce, and homosexuality are acceptable. Forty-five percent of these respondents claim to have no religious affiliation whatsoever. Ninety-three percent of them claim they never attend church or synagogue.

These media elite in Hollywood and New York live in a materialistic, secular, humanist world surrounded by people who share their immoral values. They wrongly assume that the rest of the nation shares their lifestyles, in which spiritual values are almost nonexistent. They are almost isolated from the mainstream world, in which a significant number of Americans and Canadians live in happy marriages and attend church fairly regularly.

To understand the vast gulf that separates the media elite from the average American, we should note that in contrast to the virtual absence of God from the lives of the media executives, 78 percent of Americans say that they pray at least once a week. In addition, 40 percent attend church or synagogue every week and admit that their belief in an absolute moral code from God is a major part of their life philosophy. A recent *Newsweek* poll found that

Americans are 500 percent more likely to attend church in a given week than they are likely to go to the movies.[2] A December, 1991, *Time*/CNN public opinion poll found that 78 percent of Americans believe that there should be prayer in school. Sixty percent claim they would not vote for a presidential candidate who declared he was an atheist.

Although the media likes to paint a bleak picture of what our world is like today, we should not despair. In December, 1991, a fascinating article in *U.S. News and World Report* revealed that an astonishing 56 percent of those polled claimed that a "closer relationship with God" was their greatest personal goal that year.[3] This is one of the most encouraging indications that many of our neighbors and friends are much more willing to allow us to share our faith in Christ than we have ever thought.

CHAPTER 12

The Attack on Privacy and Freedom

In 1994 the Clinton administration introduced massive Health Care Reform legislation that promised to provide universal health care for all citizens. Although the president's initial proposal was rejected, the White House and Congress are still planning to introduce universal health care in the future. However, buried deep within these proposed health care bills are provisions that will eliminate traditional patient/doctor privacy. It is not surprising that the president has failed to notify Americans of these threats to their privacy and freedom.

The New Health Security Card

The greatest threat is the new Health Security Card that President Clinton held in his hand when he introduced his plan on national television. While President Clinton stressed the importance of this card for our future health care, he failed to mention that the card would also introduce a national security identification card system that would enable a police state to control its citizens.

This card would be used along with a new nationwide computer system and would contain personal medical information about every single American citizen. This means that your most private medical tests and health records would be stored in a massive federal government computer database, and you would lose control over the most personal information you possess.

This Health Security Card is the opening wedge in the coming attack on our privacy and freedom. This attack that is now being planned will be worse than anything ever experienced in North American history. President Clinton's proposed National Health Board will establish "national, unique identifier numbers" for every American man, woman, and child—a number that will provide a positive identification from the moment we are born until the day we die. So every time you have a medical test or visit a doctor, pharmacy, or hospital, your private medical tests and personal information will be instantaneously transmitted to the federal government's health-record center. Your most intimate medical information will then go "on file" and become available thereafter for examination by any "authorized

individuals" or computer hackers who can break
into the federal health data bank.

The House of Representatives and Senate bills introduced by Hillary and Bill Clinton contain provisions that call for massive fines and heavy prison
sentences for any American who refuses to enroll in
their health plan. Obviously the real reason for these
severe penalties is to force every citizen to enroll in
this government health plan whether they want to
or not. If this plan or a similar scheme becomes law
in the future, the FBI and the police will achieve
their long-term goal of registering all American citizens in a national identification system. This, in
turn, will enable the government to monitor the actions of every citizen. Significantly, all dictatorships
require their citizens to carry their national identification card at all times. The proposed health card
will be a "smart card" with a computer chip containing unique biometric information that will absolutely identify that citizen and electronically
encode his personal health information. This en-
coded information may include your fingerprints,
your handprint, or your voice print—all of which can
provide positive identification to prevent the use of
counterfeit cards.

Eventually the pressure will grow to expand the
information that is contained in the national identification card. Ultimately, this could include your
Social Security number, immigration records, and
possibly your police files. Consider the many uses
today for the Social Security card, even though the
government originally promised that it would never

be used for identification purposes. Many leaders in Congress have also pressed for a national immigration "smart card" with a computer chip that provides absolute proof that an individual has the legal right to work in the United States.

Gun Control Regulations

Researchers estimate that there are over 200 million firearms in the United States, including almost 66 million handguns. The globalist elite who plan to dismantle the sovereignty of both America and Canada have a major goal. Their objective is to disarm civilians so there can be no credible opposition to the establishment of a new world order. The globalists know that many citizens will oppose the loss of their liberties and sovereignty, and that it would be virtually impossible to enslave people who still have their firearms. These New World Order elitists are aided by a growing number of liberals and leftists in the media who believe that no one except the police and the army should have access to firearms. These liberals tend to view firearms as a terrible social evil that must be eliminated.

Yet these liberals disregard the historical record that free men with access to firearms have been able to retain their liberties. History reveals also that people who surrender their firearms will ultimately find themselves at the mercy of both criminals and the military forces of a totalitarian regime. The necessity of disarming free men prior to enslaving them was recognized by Lenin, the communist revolutionary who destroyed freedom in Russia in 1917 and laid the foundation for the slaughter of over 60 million Russian citizens in this century. "One of the basic conditions for the victory of socialism is the arming of the workers and the disarming of the bourgeoisie" (the middle class; *Lenin's Collected Works*).

The political training of leaders in communist Russia included the "Rules of Revolution," which lay out several basic rules considered essential for overthrowing a free society. One of these fundamental rules is "register all firearms, under any pretext, as a prelude to confiscating them."

Back in 1787, Noah Webster, in his *an Examination into the Leading Principles of the Federal Constitution*, wrote this:

> Before a standing army can rule, the people must be disarmed, as they are in almost every kingdom in Europe. The Supreme power in America cannot enforce unjust laws by the sword, because the whole body of the people are armed, and constitute a force superior to any band of regular troops that can be, on any pretense, raised in the United States.

In other words, the fact that hundreds of millions of American and Canadian citizens have the legal right to possess arms and ammunition acts as a very real check on the tendency of elitist groups that wish to impose a totalitarian government on our nations. Those who want a one-world government want to deny citizens their constitutional right to legally possess firearms.

The introduction of gun control laws will accomplish two important objectives for the globalist elite. First, these new laws would make tens of millions of our citizens outlaws if they refuse to surrender their weapons. In addition, they will force over 100 million citizens to surrender their firearms to the government. This disarming of citizens will make the future introduction of a dictatorial government much easier.

James Madison wrote in *The Federalist Papers* that the possession of firearms by citizens prevented the illegal seizing of powers by a future government. "Americans need never fear their government because of the advantage of being armed, which the Americans possess over the people of almost every other nation." However, those in power today are working to eliminate this basic democratic right.

The *Wall Street Journal* recently described the potential disaster that would result if those who hate firearms achieve their goal of disarming honest, law-abiding citizens.

What will happen if severe restrictions on semi-automatic rifles pass Congress or the state legislatures today? Millions of citizens who still believe in the Constitution will not forfeit or register their firearms; squads of federal and state agents will snoop; massive no-knock warrants will be issued; and both citizens and police will die in raids. While previously law-abiding citizens (now felons) and police battle each other, the drug lords will continue their nefarious trafficking. Adding firearms prohibition to drug prohibition means war on

the innocent (and perhaps a police state), and by diverting police resources, will give armed pushers even more free reign.

The Russian writer Alexander Solzhenitsyn
warned in his excellent book *Gulag Archipelago*
about the dangers if free men surrender their
firearms to their government. He wrote his book on
the horrors of the communist system while he was
imprisoned in Soviet concentration camps. There,
Solzhenitsyn interviewed many men who had been
arrested by the KGB without any practical possibility of resistance because they had previously surrendered their firearms. Solzhenitsyn wrote,

> At what exact point then should one resist the commu-
> nists? . . . How we burned in the prison camps later thinking:
> what would things have been like if every security operative,
> when he went out at night to make an arrest, had been uncer-
> tain whether he would return alive and had to say good-bye to
> his family? Or if during periods of mass arrests people had not
> simply sat there in their lairs, paling with terror at every step
> on the staircase, but had understood they had nothing to lose
> and had boldly set up in the downstairs hall an ambush of
> half a dozen people with axes, hammers, pokers, or whether
> else was at hand. . . . The Organs [police] would very quickly
> have suffered a shortage of officers . . . and notwithstanding
> all of Stalin's thirst, the cursed machine would have ground
> to a halt.

All men and women who treasure their freedom
should carefully consider Solzhenitsyn's warning

against gun control laws. Those who are planning to eliminate our freedoms and our sovereignty are working behind the scenes to prevent any possibility of serious resistance by disarming citizens step by step before they openly attack our liberties.

During the last few years a number of laws have been passed in the United States and Canada to restrict the ability of citizens to own firearms. Although the U.S. Constitution and the laws of Canada clearly provide for the legal possession of firearms, there are many in the government and the liberal media today who are totally opposed to the public ownership of firearms. For example, the U.S. Congress recently banned a number of semi-automatic firearms. As an example of what is to come and of the true intentions of these politicians, consider several of the numerous bills that will attempt to regulate or totally ban citizens from possessing firearms or ammunition. There are hundreds of such proposed laws pending in both Canada and the United States.

- House of Representatives Bill 1501 by Rep. Yates (D-IL) would ban all handguns.
- House of Representatives Bill 1616 by Rep. Collins (D-IL) would require the registration of all handguns.
- House of Representatives Bill 3132 by Rep. Owens (D-NY) would ban handguns and ammunition.
- Senate Bill 892 proposed by Senator Chafee (R-RI) would ban the possession of all handguns.

- Senate Bill 109 by Senator Patrick Moynihan (D-NY) would require a written record of every round of ammo used.

Incredibly, Senator Moynihan has also proposed a bill known as S-179, which would place a 1,000 percent tax on .25, .32, and 9 mm ammunition. Such a bill is designed to make it virtually impossible for the average citizen to purchase ammunition.

History reveals that gun registration almost inevitably leads to gun confiscation. This pattern has occurred in this century in Russia, China, Cuba, Germany, Italy, Greece, Lithuania, Poland, Georgia, Romania, and now in New York City. The history of gun restrictions in New York City and Washington, D.C. shows that, when the government is given the right to license gun ownership, very few citizens will be allowed to have a license.

The people who strongly support gun control laws claim that the laws are designed to help reduce incidents of violence. However, even they admit that criminals will never obey these laws. A recent study concluded that only seven percent of the weapons used by criminals were purchased legally. This means that 93 percent of criminals are using illegal weapons today. Consequently, it's mostly honest, law-abiding citizens who will lose the right to possess a firearm for hunting, target shooting, or personal protection.

The unfortunate truth is that criminals will always have access to guns, even if all firearms were made illegal. Incredibly, the United States Supreme Court ruled in the *Haynes vs. U.S.* case in 1968 that criminals cannot be compelled to register their weapons because this would be a violation of their Fifth Amendment protection against self-incrimination! As a result, the city of New York modified its gun registration law to *exempt from gun registration convicted felons, mental incompetents, and social misfits!* The gun laws of New York City require only honest, law-abiding citizens to register their guns; criminals are exempt.

Many people who are unfamiliar with guns wonder why another citizen would want to own a firearm. In addition to the pleasures of target shooting, gun collecting, and game hunting, a firearm can help you protect your family from the wave of crime afflicting the nation. The reality is that every year a million average citizens use firearms to defend themselves against criminals. Interestingly, in only two percent of the one million annual cases where a citizen defends himself does the citizen actually shoot the criminal. The vast majority of the time the gun owner simply threatens the criminal or fires a warning shot to prevent the crime from occurring. This means that a million times a year North American citizens have properly used their guns to prevent a rape, murder, or robbery. And any honest policeman will admit that the police usually cannot stop a crime in progress; they can only try to capture the criminal after the crime is committed.

In reaction to the growing legal attacks on gun ownership, the city council of Kennesaw, Georgia, passed a law in 1982 requiring every adult in their city to own a gun. The only exceptions were the disabled, convicts, or conscientious objectors. The city elders passed this exceptional law to prove that the possession of firearms by normal citizens would prevent crime. This is in contrast to the liberal media's viewpoint that the legal ownership of guns somehow contributes to the criminal's use of firearms.

Naturally, the national media suggested that this "insane" law would lead to gun fights and slaughter on the streets of Kennesaw. The liberal *Washington Post* newspaper indignantly called the town "the brave little city of Kennesaw, Ga., soon to be the pistol-packing capital of the world."[1] In contrast to these predictions of disaster, however, the citizens of Kennesaw have not experienced a massive increase in crime or violence during the last 12 years. Only two murders occurred in Kennesaw in the last decade. Only one of the murders was committed with a gun, and it was done by out-of-state criminals. The other murder was committed with a knife. Apparently prospective criminals have wisely avoided Kennesaw rather than take the chance of being confronted during a crime by a well-armed citizen. While this strategy is not appropriate nationally, the history of Kennesaw suggests that the growing crime problem in North America is not caused by the possession of guns by law-abiding citizens.

The Reversal of Our Civil Rights

The U.S. Bill of Rights provides protection against government harassment through its constitutional guarantee of "freedom from unreasonable search and seizure." The Fourth Amendment to the U.S. Constitution declares: "The right of the people to be secure in their persons, houses, papers, and effects, against unreasonable searches and seizures, shall not be violated." However, the U.S. Supreme Court ruled in 1990 that police checkpoints to apprehend drunks are legal. Police can now place roadblocks to intercept cars and interrogate all drivers. Despite the fact that studies show that 99 percent of drivers are not drinking, police can now demand that all drivers submit to sobriety tests. In addition, they can search your car if they choose to do so.

These police actions are more in line with the practices of communist states than the police activities that Americans have taken for granted over the last 200 years. These police actions, which assume the citizen is a criminal and not innocent, have a parallel in the governments' practice of secretly monitoring all of our bank deposits and withdrawals to discover the one-tenth of one percent of citizens who are money launderers or drug dealers. In both cases, the assumption of government agents is that honest, law-abiding citizens are assumed to be guilty until they can prove themselves innocent. These intrusive procedures and legal assumptions are a total reversal of the "assumption of innocence" philosophy that defined our North American democracies for two centuries.

Surveillance Technology

Surveillance cameras that constantly monitor our highways, streets, parking lots, and buildings are altering our way of life. These intrusive cameras are eliminating the privacy that most of us have previously taken for granted. Our privacy is being progressively eroded as the use of security cameras to provide traffic safety and crime control has been expanded to include surveillance of employees at their desks, in washrooms, and throughout a factory or store.

The strong corporate arguments in favor of such continuous employee and customer monitoring include crime prevention, protection of staff, and employee drug-prevention programs. However, the final result is that many employees are now living a life that is little different from that described by George Orwell in his frightening novel *1984*. The truth is that modern technology has produced surveillance possibilities that are far more pervasive than those faced by the characters in George Orwell's prophetic novel.

How do you feel about government officials, the police, or other inquisitive individuals knowing every private detail of your life? The complete record of your travel destinations; your choice of books, newspapers, movies, or pay TV; your traffic tickets; your medical tests; and every purchase you make is now electronically recorded and "on file" for anyone who can access the computer data file. In fact, the technical capacity of the government to monitor every aspect of your life far outweighs your ability to protect your privacy. Despite the growing public concern with the issue of privacy in our computer records, the governments of the United States and Canada have continued to permit a massive intrusion into the private lives of their citizens.

The widespread introduction of corporate security systems that require the use of employee badges containing an implanted computer microchip has given companies the potential to monitor the location and activity of every worker at all times. The computer can record the exact time that an employee enters his office and can quietly monitor his or her every move throughout the day. Sensors placed at strategic locations throughout the building can record the location and duration of every movement by the badge wearer. New, sophisticated office phone systems allow your boss to secretly monitor any private phone calls you might make. Many computerized office phone systems contain a record of all possible legitimate business phone numbers. If an employee dials an unauthorized number to make a personal call to a friend, the office phone system will record the call and produce a report that can be used by the supervisor at the next employee evaluation.

The International Labor Organization in Geneva recently warned, "Workers in industrialized countries are losing privacy in the workplace as technological advances allow employers to monitor nearly every facet of time on the job." The study claimed that the United States was the worst offender. Similarly, the American Civil Liberties Union stated, "Criminals have more privacy rights than employees. Police have to get a court order, whereas in the workplace, surveillance can be conducted without safeguards."

Additionally, computer network supervisors in many fully computerized companies can secretly monitor the actual keystrokes and productivity of every individual employee who uses a desktop computer in his or her daily work. Employees who are aware of such surveillance tactics often complain about the stress they experience knowing that they are being secretly monitored every minute of the day. In many companies, the use of random drug testing and secret cameras, together with intrusive psychological questionnaires, creates a very unhealthy environment of fear and mistrust.

Several of my friends who work in private investigation companies and industrial counterespionage have shown me some of the incredible technological advances in surveillance devices. A new pinhole camera can be placed behind a wall to monitor the next-door room audibly and visually. It is almost impossible to detect the lens unless you examine every wall, floor, and ceiling surface with a magnifying glass because the camera lens is the size of a pinhead. These new cameras can photograph silently in almost total darkness. Another new surveillance camera can be secretly concealed in a small mobile telephone with the camera lens aimed through the tiny hole normally used for the microphone. Thus a businessperson who is carrying on negotiations with a group of visitors can leave the room and secretly monitor the conversation of his or her visitors while he or she is gone.

There are surveillance devices that can now enable you to monitor everything that occurs in your home or office while you are away—at the cost of only a few hundred dollars. One remote monitoring device, the XPS-1000, allows you to call your phone number from anywhere in the world by dialing your phone with a special activation code. The device will not ring your phone. However, from that moment on, you can monitor every sound in the building. Another tiny device, a microtransmitter surveillance bug powered for three months by a miniature battery, can be secretly left in any room. The device will broadcast up to 1,000 yards to a radio receiver on any FM frequency you have chosen.

These developments mean that if someone truly is determined to monitor your activities, they can do it. The concept of privacy these days, then, is a mere illusion.

Police Confiscation of Property

Police forces across the United States are now seizing automobiles, homes, and currency before any trial or court hearing has taken place. As a result of recent changes in the laws of forfeiture, the police now have the legal right to confiscate everything you possess without the necessity of a trial, a conviction, or even a charge! Across the nation, police are seizing over 5,000 bank accounts, houses, automobiles, farms, and corporations every single week. *USA Today*, every Wednesday in section D, carries a list of the latest week's property confiscations by the Drug Enforcement Administration (DEA). Thus you can read, every week, about the latest seizures of cash, bank accounts, homes, and cars by only one of the government police agencies permitted to confiscate property. Every year, additional government agencies are joining in on this easy and profitable attack on the property of Americans. One of the primary motivations of the police departments is the simple fact that they get to keep the confiscated loot whether or not you are actually guilty of the offense they believe you might have committed.

The U.S. government agencies that are involved in the confiscation of property include the FBI, the Food and Drug Administration, the Coast Guard, the Post Office, the Securities and Exchange Commission, the Bureau of Land Management, the Department of Housing, and many more. Thousands of state and local police departments have joined in this "legal" theft of property and currency as a means to gain substantial additional funds for their budgets. There is great potential, then, for corruption when an officer fails to turn in the loot he or she has confiscated.

The excellent monthly intelligence journal, the *McAlvany Intelligence Advisor*, is edited by my friend Don McAlvany. The journal recently reported that motorists who were stopped by police for a minor traffic violation on Highway I-95 in Volusia County, Florida, were asked, "How much cash are you carrying?" If the driver innocently answered that he or she was carrying more than a few hundred dollars, the police officers would seize it. The Volusia police claim that carrying significant amounts of cash is "suspicious behavior."[2]

Under the current laws of Florida and the United States, "suspicion" is all the police need to confiscate your money. If you are carrying costly jewelry, or happen to be driving an expensive car, they can confiscate your car as well, despite the fact that no crime has been committed and that no one was charged with a crime. Incredibly, during the last four years, Volusia County, Florida, has legally seized $8 million from unsuspecting tourists. The reason for the focus on tourists is that they are less likely to put up a battle in court when they have to travel back to the state where their property was seized.

Police forces in other cities and states throughout America are also involved in the confiscation of cars. Over 4,000 cars are confiscated every year in Houston, Texas, while 10,000 cars are seized annually by police in New York. Police forces are making similar seizures across the nation. You can contest the seizure of your property in court if you have the money, tenacity, and time to prove that you are innocent. You also must prove that your possession of that property was not "suspicious." This requirement that you prove your innocence before you can retrieve your seized property is a complete reversal of the legal presumption of innocence that underlies our justice system.

The U.S. Drug Enforcement Administration (DEA) and local police forces now operate surveillance units at virtually all U.S. airports. Almost every employee working at an airport, from the airline clerks to the baggage handlers, can receive a ten-percent informer's fee for reporting a customer who buys a ticket with cash or looks suspicious. DEA surveillance operations, which use secret cameras, are now being set up at all airports and most major hotels. These operations watch for people who display unusual or "suspicious" amounts of cash.

The legal concept behind civil-asset forfeiture is the fiction that property, and not individuals, can be guilty of legal offenses. This contempt allows the government to disregard all of your constitutional rights. When the police seize your assets, in effect, they confiscate your "guilty property," but they often do not charge you personally. Their goal is simply to seize your property. By not charging you with a crime, they hope that you will go away and let them keep the property.

Even if you are never charged with a crime, you will probably never see your property again. Business owners have had their assets seized because one dishonest employee used their office phones, without their knowledge, to make an illegal bet or engage in a drug deal. It doesn't matter to the police agencies that the owner did not know about the illegal actions of the employee. The police do not care that a businessperson is an honest citizen who hates illegal acts. In the upside down world of civil-asset forfeiture, all that matters to asset-hungry police agencies is that the property has become legally "tainted." Under the existing laws of the United States, this means that the property is now subject to forfeiture because it was involved in an illegal act.

In a recent debate in Congress, a senator from Illinois declared that his research to date indicated that over 80 percent of the people who had "suspicious" property seized from them were never even charged with a crime! To gain some idea of the size of this threat to your property, the *Washington Post* reported that the U.S. Marshal's service alone presently holds 30,000 confiscated cars, homes, boats, and corporations. These outrageous seizures of property are occurring throughout America despite the U.S. Constitution's clear safeguard against "unreasonable search and seizure."

The National Identification Center

Congress and the White House have secretly agreed to build a National Identification Center in Virginia, and the original completion date was sometime in 1996. This center will enable federal law enforcement and intelligence agencies to monitor every aspect of our lives with an advanced computer system. Sophisticated computers will record and consolidate the hundreds of existing computer records the government possesses on every citizen. Ostensibly, this new identification center will be used primarily to monitor the compliance of citizens with new gun control regulations. However, the benefits of a national computer center containing data files on every American are obvious for elitist government officials who wish to establish a police control over America.

Congressman Neal Smith, from Iowa's fourth district, revealed the government's secret plans in a newsletter to his constituents in October 1993. While discussing the handgun control laws that he supports, Smith claimed responsibility for helping to

create a new National Identification Center that will
be used to monitor citizens for gun control and
"other" purposes. He wrote:

> The Subcommittee on Appropriations which I chair has been
> actively pursuing an effective solution to this problem.
> . . . But the program we are implementing will take more
> time. The solution to screening people . . . is to have a Na-
> tional Center computerized so that local law enforcement of-
> fices can instantly access information from all states. In other
> words, all states that supply that information to the National
> Center will have a positive identification system which will
> identify any applicant. . . . We have invested $392 million so
> far in such a Center, about a four-hour drive from Washing-
> ton, D.C., and we hope to have it completed and equipped in
> about two years. . . . We hope all states will be in the system
> by 1998 and will supply the information on a continuing
> basis. . . . Meanwhile, we will continue to establish the Na-
> tional Identification Center for this and other law enforce-
> ment purposes.[3]

The National Identification Center will allow all
governmental intelligence agencies, including the
ATF and FBI, to identify and monitor all registered
gun owners. But what are the "other" law enforcement purposes they intend to pursue? This center is
only one component of an all-encompassing system
of police control that is being established nationwide. The supersecret government agencies, the National Reconnaissance Office and the National
Security Agency (NSA), now have the capability to

monitor every single phone call and fax transmission worldwide.

During the year-long hunt for the Colombian drug lord Pabula Esctavar, U.S. intelligence agencies scanned and monitored the Colombian telephone system and South American radio bands for any call containing Esctavar's voice. After almost a year of silence Esctavar made the fatal mistake of speaking on the phone for about thirty seconds. Within ten seconds of beginning his call, NSA intelligence specialists were able to select his voice out of hundreds of thousands of simultaneous phone calls throughout South America through voice print analysis. (Every human voice has a unique "voice signature" that is as individual as your fingerprints. If the intelligence agencies have a recording of you speaking for less than one minute, they can isolate your unique voice print from millions of other voices.) Government agents instantly targeted Pabulo Esctavar's voice and triangulated the precise location of his phone. Within minutes, Colombian police commandos stormed his hideout and killed him.

In addition to spying on our phone calls, the government wants to introduce the so-called "clipper chip," which will allow intelligence agencies and the FBI to unlock the secret encryption codes of every communication system and computer program in America. Over the last decade, mathematicians have developed sophisticated encryption programs that allow the average business owner or computer user to safely encrypt his or her confidential information so that no one can read the private files. This "clipper chip" program will provide police and intelligence agencies with a "back door" to break your encryption code and read your confidential files.

The clipper chip is now being installed in telephones, televisions, and other consumer electronic products throughout America. The government has already invested $500 million in technologies—digital communications and fiber optics the size of a human hair and capable of carrying a million phone calls simultaneously—that ensure its ability to monitor your private telephone calls with impunity. In Canada, the supersecret Communications Security Establishment (CSE) has received permission to continue surveilling the federal communication system and decoding advanced computer encryption codes used by businesses and individuals.

Government Surveillance

As reported in my book *Prince of Darkness*, the National Security Agency has denied that it can listen to all phone calls and radio messages throughout the world.[4] However, Mike Frost, a former interception intelligence specialist working with the top-secret Canadian Communications Security Establishment (CSE), is one of several intelligence sources that has confirmed that the NSA has this capability.

Frost was trained during the 1980s at the special National Security Agency school outside Washington,

D.C., where he was taught how to install sophisticated listening devices on the roofs of U.S. embassies and other sites worldwide. Frost admitted to the *Toronto Sun* newspaper that he installed these devices in many national capitals to monitor communications and phone calls worldwide.[5] In North America, the NSA phone surveillance program code name is "Oratory." In Britain, the BBC reported that the MI-6 interception technology is call the "Dictionary Program." The Cray supercomputers recording and monitoring millions of our phone calls simultaneously are listening for the use of any of 400 key words that have been programmed into the computer system. If a phone caller uses one or more of these key words in his or her conversation (such as explosive, bomb, gas, gun, drugs, White House), then the computer will record that particular phone call for later analysis. During the following day that phone call will be analyzed by a human intelligence specialist operator to determine if the call has any bearing on national security matters.

The vast majority of the monitored phone calls do not contain the key words and are immediately dumped without being listened to by a human operator. However, if the call is of interest to the intelligence agencies, they will thereafter monitor all future calls to and from that particular phone number. When this monitoring capability is integrated with a voice-print analysis, the National Security Agency can instantly identify and monitor the phone calls of any targeted individual within five seconds of the moment he or she begins a phone call from any phone on earth.

While those of us who enjoy our privacy and freedom may resent this kind of intrusion, we must also realize that our governments have no choice today but to monitor all communications in a world where terrorists can instantly attack and destroy not only whole buildings but also whole cities.

Foolproof Identification Devices

Following several tragic incidents of babies being stolen from maternity wards, hospitals worldwide have been exploring technologies that will make it more difficult for an unauthorized person to steal a newborn baby. The *Edinburgh Evening News* reported on June 20, 1994, that babies at Edinburgh's Capital Hospital now have a miniature electronic monitor attached to the snug strap placed on a baby's wrist. If someone attempts to take the baby away from the controlled maternity areas, an alarm will summon the hospital security staff. The paper reported that "police have welcomed the use of the lightweight, washable device currently undergoing trials at Simpson Memorial Maternity pavilion. . . . It is the latest in new age child protection, developed to stall kidnap bids."[6]

Of course, a determined kidnapper could find a way to remove the electronic monitor from the child's wrist. The final solution to this problem will probably involve a miniaturized computer chip that can be inserted beneath the skin of the newborn baby—a chip that will be permanent and nonremovable. In addition to protecting babies from kidnapping, such an identification device would provide a lifelong ID for police, health, and possible financial purposes. In fact, patients in several South Korean hospitals now have a tiny computer ID chip implanted in their fingertip as a foolproof identification system. Nurses with an electronic scanner can verify the patient's identity to prevent an operation on the wrong person.

Magnetic Fingerprints

Scientists have discovered that just as each person has fingerprints that are different from those of all the other people on earth, so also do magnetic media, credit cards, computer hard drives, and electronic security pass cards possess totally unique magnetic properties at the microscopic level. These minute differences can be detected, recorded, and used to identify whether or not a particular credit or security card is an original or an almost-perfect counterfeit. With banks losing over $1 billion every year to credit card counterfeiters, there is a great need to develop foolproof, anti-counterfeit magnetic fingerprints to provide absolutely secure identification. With such technology, the government will be able to track every single citizen from the cradle to the grave with no possibility of anyone escaping the electronic surveillance net.

Smart Cards

Technology is developing at such a rapid rate that we may soon carry a single ID smart card containing a computer chip that will allow us to make phone calls, unlock our houses and cars, and buy anything from newspapers to televisions. MasterCard International is introducing a massive campaign to promote the use of smart credit cards by its 22,000 affiliated banks and over 12 million retail merchants that participate in their system worldwide. One of their motives is to reduce the spiraling losses due to credit card fraud—losses that now amount to over $500 million a year.

An article in *Popular Science* magazine in November 1994 reports that college students are already using MCI's new campus smart card system.[7] MCI authorizes colleges to issue students a single smart card that will simultaneously serve as their photo ID, door key, credit-debit card, and bank automatic teller card. With this smart card, a student can register for classes, take out library books, pay for cafeteria meals, and even pay for tuition. It is called the Campus Connections Card. It looks like a standard credit card with the addition of a digitized photo of the owner. However, it contains two special magnetic stripes: one that allows point-of-sale transactions, the other for debit transactions. Florida State University was the first campus to make extensive use of the system, but MCI is planning to introduce the card nationwide through a large number of colleges.

These multiple-use smart cards are just the beginning of a process that will culminate in every citizen using one single smart card to replace the wide variety of credit-debit and identification cards most of us now carry. The final step will be the replacement of the smart card with a tiny computer chip placed beneath the skin. This proof is a means of identifying people and authorizing financial transactions. This, of course, will make cash obsolete. One of my confidential sources works at the VISA headquarters and has revealed that they are studying the future use of a new credit system that will actually use a miniature computer chip embedded beneath the skin instead of the standard credit-debit card.

One of the new technologies in the smart-card field is called a "stored-value card," a kind of electronic wallet. These stored-value smart cards contain a tiny computer chip that electronically stores a preset amount of money that you can use to purchase anything you want. Rather than use cash, people will purchase such credit-card size smart cards for $500, for example, and purchase items by offering the cashier their stored-value card. The merchant will run the card through the reader and deduct the amount of that purchase, leaving the remaining balance to use to purchase other items.

An article in the *New York Times* on September 6, 1994, reported that stores and banks support this new system because it will eliminate cash transactions that are expensive to handle and subject to theft.[8] Increasingly, telephone companies are selling prepaid stored-value telephone calling cards that allow the purchaser to pay for long-distance charges on public phones.

Over 80 percent of the 360 billion purchases made each year by American consumers are made with cash. A recent study showed that 90 percent of these transactions involved purchases of less than $20. In light of the overwhelming amount of small purchases, the advantages of using these money-purchase smart cards is obvious. Electronic Payment Services, the bank-owned company that runs the MAC cash machines, is building a nation-wide electronic smart-card system. A few years ago this technology cost $10 per card. This made the cards economically unviable. However, the cost has dropped to the point where they can now produce these smart cards for less than $1.

The planned system would allow a customer to call their bank by phone and verify their identification by inserting the smart card in the slot in their special home phone. The card would be electronically credited with another $500 or whatever amount the customer requests to be transferred from their bank account to the smart card.

Many banks in Europe and Asia support the introduction of a smart-card system that will replace cash forever. Several large banks in Britain are introducing a sophisticated "Mondex" smart card that will store your money in up to five different European or North American currencies and will allow you to travel across Europe without worrying about carrying local currencies.

One of the latest inventions is a form of electronic currency that can be used by members of the internet, linking tens of thousands of interconnected computers and millions of consumers on the information highway. A European firm has created "DigiCash" that can be purchased from a participating bank and then used electronically to purchase goods or services from other internet patrons or companies. Their plan is to make the electronic currency anonymous. It would, theoretically, be untraceable but a merchant could verify that it was a legitimate credit issued by a recognized bank. However, the bank would be unable to identify the purchaser.

These technologies are being introduced by governments as preliminary steps on the road to the cashless society of the New World Order. The prophecies of the Bible tell us a world government will arise in the last days—a government led by the Antichrist, the world's last dictator, who will rule the earth in the years leading to the return of Jesus Christ. The prophets also foretold that money would cease to exist in the last days. It would be replaced by a cashless system that will use numbers instead of currency that allows you to buy and sell. Revelation 13:17 tells us that in this new system, "no one may buy or sell, except one who has the mark or the name of the beast, or the number of his name."

We are now rapidly approaching the moment when these ancient Bible prophecies can be fulfilled through the introduction of the 666/Mark of the Beast financial system of the Antichrist. In the following chapters, we will explore the prophecies and the economic trends that are rushing us toward the final crisis of human history.

PART 4

The Coming Economic Crisis

CHAPTER 13

The Secret Agenda
of the New World Order

The General Agreement on Trade and Tariffs (GATT), the North American Free Trade Agreement (NAFTA), and the World Trade Organization (WTO) are significant agreements that are leading the world step by step toward a one-world government. These recent trade agreements have now placed the economic future of the United States and Canada under the control of foreign officials and organizations that do not share our values nor our love of free enterprise. Multinational companies have worked behind the scenes for years spending vast sums of money and employing thousands of lobbyists to make sure that Congress and the White House would assure the passage of these critical trade agreements that serve their globalist economic and political agendas.

The Move Toward a One-World Economy

The North American
Free Trade Agreement (NAFTA)

It comes as no surprise to those who have studied
the implications of NAFTA that a large number of
North American-based multinational corporations
are beginning to move factories and jobs to Mexico
and South America. The reasons are obvious; these
companies can either base their plants where labor
is cheap and there are no unions, no pensions, and
no health benefits; or they can build in North
America where they are faced with high wages,
strong unions, expensive health benefits, and large
pension obligations. In terms of pay alone, Mexico's
minimum wage is a mere 58 cents an hour. So you
can guess where the company board will choose to
build its next plant, especially when the company
can avoid many corporate taxes by locating in a
foreign jurisdiction.

With the help of NAFTA, then, these companies
are able to transfer existing American jobs overseas
to gain the tremendous advantage of low-cost wages
and benefits. Then they ship the foreign-made products back to the United States for sale to the American consumer at prices that no Made-in-America
manufacturing corporation can possibly match. Welcome to the world of free trade!

Former U.S. Secretary of State Henry Kissinger (a
member of the Trilateral Commission) was one of the
architects of the New World Order. As an expert in

diplomacy, Kissinger is a world-renowned authority on the true intent of international treaties. Here is his evaluation of the real meaning of NAFTA:

> What the Congress will soon have before it is not a conventional trade agreement, but the hopeful architecture of a new international system. A regional Western Hemisphere Organization dedicated to democracy and free trade would be a first step towards the New World Order that is so frequently cited but so rarely implemented.

The General Agreement on Trade and Tariffs (GATT)

President Clinton recently transferred significant control of the American economy away from the U.S. Congress and into the hands of the new 117-nation World Trade Organization (WTO). The WTO was created at the conclusion of the Uruguay round of negotiations to replace GATT. First, Clinton surrendered control of the American troops stationed in Somalia and Bosnia. These U.S. soldiers are now working under foreign commanders in service to the United Nations. Amazingly, when 15 American soldiers were killed in a helicopter accident in Iraq, Vice President Gore told the startled parents that their sons had not died for America, but they had given their lives "in the service of the United Nations."

Clinton has since signed "enabling" legislation that will force the U.S. economy to be "coordinated" with the foreign bureaucrats who work for the WTO.

Step by step, then, the U.S. economy is being placed under the control of international global interests as part of Clinton's planned reduction of American sovereignty.

In a recent interview, Peter Sutherland, the former director general of GATT, admitted that "the old GATT procedure effectively had no ability to impose sanctions on the guilty." In other words, under the old GATT system, the United States could impose trade sanctions and restrictions as part of a diplomatic campaign against countries such as Nicaragua or China for their violations of human rights. While this was technically against the rules of international trade, GATT had no legal capability to stop America. However, under the new agreement, America must follow the rules imposed by the World Trade Organization. So if the United States should ever try to violate these rules in the future by using trade sanctions, then the WTO will automatically impose trade sanctions on American exports. These restrictions on U.S. economic policy will severely limit the ability of a future American president to influence another country's actions through trade sanctions.

As Peter Sutherland points out, "The new system will have an appeals body to rule. . . . The judgment on appeal will have to be accepted . . . sanctions can be imposed upon the recalcitrant country."[1] To understand what a change this new WTO regime will bring, consider this situation: In 1989 when Chinese authorities massacred the students who demonstrated for democracy in Beijing, America expressed its displeasure by imposing trade sanctions on China. However, in the future, America cannot use trade and economic sanctions as foreign policy. This is one more significant surrender of national sovereignty in preparation for the coming one-world government.

The World Trade Organization (WTO)

The WTO legislation allows foreign bureaucrats to exercise control over the economy and business of the United States. History shows us that whoever controls the currency and economy of a nation actually controls that nation. The power-hungry bureaucrats at the United Nations and their friends at the European Union and the new World Trade Organization are delighted with the prospect of gaining this kind of control over the United States.

If you believe the GATT and NAFTA represent a threat to American jobs and the sovereignty of the United States, then you will be even more upset when you understand the danger of the up-and-coming World Trade Organization. The ostensible purpose is to liberalize trade relations among nations by lowering tariffs and opening markets to all competing nations. In January 1995 the World Trade Organization in Geneva, Switzerland, replaced GATT with a mandate to enforce international trade rules. Their real purpose is to "put some real teeth" in the rules of the international trade organization. In the past, nations that didn't like a GATT ruling could ignore it and impose tariffs or sanctions as they saw fit in their own national interest.

The September 15, 1994, issue of *The New Amer-*
ican pointed out the dangers of the WTO.

> The truth is that the WTO bureaucracy would have sufficient
> power to pressure nations to change their domestic laws. WTO
> was designed to eliminate a nation's option to ignore GATT
> dispute panel rulings, as the United States had done in an Au-
> gust 1991 case.... The United States promptly ignored the
> GATT panel ruling, continuing its ban of tuna from Mexico.[2]

In the future every nation, including the United
States and Canada, will be forced to obey the rulings
of the WTO panels even if it requires massive
changes in their federal, state, or provincial laws.
The article in *The New American* also noted,

> Senator Jesse Helms observed that under the WTO, dozens or
> perhaps hundreds of state laws could be attacked by foreign
> countries. As a matter of fact, the European Union issued a
> book entitled *Report on United States Barriers to Trade and*
> *Investment*. This report contains 111 pages of federal and
> state laws that the EU claims are barriers and that the Euro-
> peans may challenge in the WTO.[3]

This dangerous attack on the U.S. government's
control over America's economy and business is embedded in a treaty that is so complicated that the
document covers 22,000 pages of text! Incredibly,
only one out of 100 U.S. senators even took the time
to read through this document, which is the greatest

single attack on the sovereignty of America in 200 years. The lone senator who actually read the treaty voted against it.

If the true intent of the WTO was simply to reduce tariffs, this could be expressed in only one page of text. Obviously, hidden in the tens of thousands of pages of legal language are thousands of special exceptions and lucrative deals for the multinational companies whose lobbyists have worked for years to bring this trade agreement to fruition. In the future, any nation that is found guilty of violating the decisions of the WTO dispute panel will find itself hauled before the world body and forced to either change its laws, pay massive fines, or face mandatory worldwide trade sanctions that forbid all other nations to trade with the offending country.

In all the history of mankind there has never been an attack against the sovereignty and independence of the nation-state that compares to the impact of the World Trade Organization treaty. Despite the treaty's vast implications, the U.S. Congress that was voted out of office in the November 1994 election met in special session after the election to vote for this treaty *without any debate.* They voted for this unpopular treaty despite the fact that 99 senators had failed to even read the text.

Ask yourself: Who were these senators representing when they chose to approve this treaty without debate? Many of these senators were Democrats who had lost the mid-term 1994 elections. If you think the Republican win in that congressional

election changes everything for the better, think
again. Consider the question: Why did both Republican House Leader Newt Gingrich and Senate Republican Majority Leader Bob Dole agree with President
Clinton to pass the GATT and WTO legislation
without any debate?

The Clinton Administration is totally committed
to American membership in the World Trade Organization, where the majority of the membership
is comprised of Third World nations. Other international organizations, like the United Nations Security Council, permit America and the other super-
powers to protect their national interest through
limited membership and a veto over actions that
they perceive as being against the national interest of
their nation. However, in the WTO, every state in
the world, including small nations such as Mongolia
or Monaco, will have the same voting power as
America. In any future trade dispute, America will
have only one vote among 117 nations. Furthermore,
the United States will have no veto over the actions
of this trade body.

To get an idea of how the vast majority of the WTO
nations view the United States, consider the fact that 76
percent of them voted against the United States during
the sessions held at the United Nations in 1993. There
is no reason to believe that their attitude will be any
different in the World Trade Organization. And this
time, in the WTO, America will not have a veto to protect itself against the actions of other nations. Phyllis

Schlafly, in *The Phyllis Schlafly Report* (June 1994), commented on the real reason the globalists want America and Canada to join the WTO:

> The WTO is designed to function as the global trade pillar of a triumvirate that will plan and control the world's economy. The other two pillars are the World Bank, which loans capital to developing nations, and the International Monetary Fund (IMF), which supervises the flow of money around the world. The three-legged plan to plan and control the world's economy was devised at the Bretton Woods Conference at the end of World War II. The World Bank and the IMF got off the ground rapidly (largely financed, of course, by the United States), but the planned global trade arm, then called the International Trade Organization (ITO), was blocked by U.S. senators who concluded that it would diminish U.S. sovereignty and interfere with U.S. domestic laws.[4]

The basic philosophy behind GATT and the WTO is to reduce the tariffs imposed by nations that are endeavoring to protect their industries from cheap foreign imports. However, in the case of textiles, the reduction of tariffs will basically destroy the American textile industry. The WTO will allow foreign manufacturers (who pay their workers only five percent of the wages of American workers) to sell their cheap textiles in American stores, thereby eliminating the jobs of up to one million textile workers in the United States.

The Move Toward a Cashless Society

Global Money Transfers

The largest international banking system in the world, the Society for Worldwide Interbank Financial Transmission (SWIFT), has unveiled a new system that will allow companies and individuals to transfer large amounts of money worldwide in only seconds. SWIFT handles 90 percent of the world's international monetary transfers between 950 major banking institutions. Over $6 trillion is transferred across international borders in one-and-a-half million financial transactions every 24 hours. The European Union strongly supports these efforts to streamline international transfer payments as a vital step on the path to a worldwide superstate.

The U.S. Government's War Against Cash

The U.S. Treasury Department is engaged in a continuous worldwide war against people who seek to counterfeit American currency. The amount of counterfeit money produced each year is rising astronomically. In 1992 the U.S. Treasury Department confiscated $30 billion in counterfeit money overseas. In 1993, the amount recovered rose to a staggering $120 billion.

According to the National Research Council, millions of dollars in counterfeit U.S. currency is produced annually by new high-tech computer printers and copiers. Iran and Iraq are engaged in the massive counterfeiting of tens of billions of dollars in U.S.

currency every year. Recent reports claim that Iran can now produce "super bills" from stolen U.S. Treasury plates that are indistinguishable from genuine currency. A fascinating article in the November 1994 issue of *Popular Science* described the technologies that have made the Treasury Department's task very difficult. The new Canon color copiers are astonishing in their technical ability to reproduce currency accurately.

In an attempt to eliminate the use of these sophisticated copiers by counterfeiters, the Canon company has introduced several innovative technologies. One involves a sensor that recognizes currency and prevents the copier from duplicating it. In addition, new Canon copiers encode an invisible micro-miniature code number in all copy images—a code that is invisible to the naked eye. This technology will allow Secret Service investigators to examine a copier-produced counterfeit bill and determine the serial number of the copy machine and the identity of the person who purchased it.

In its never-ending war to protect American currency, the Treasury is planning to introduce a number of new technologies that will counterfeit-proof the new currency sometime in 1996. One of the most significant technologies is the plan to print currency with some kind of machine-readable bar code that may be hidden within an intricate design on the bill. Another plan is to purposely introduce moire-inducing patterns in the currency's design—patterns that will produce distortions when copy or scanning equipment tries to duplicate the bill. The Treasury is using micro print only six thousandths of an inch wide, which is virtually impossible to duplicate.

Other new anti-counterfeiting technologies involve the use of iridescent planchettes and special magnetic security threads that cannot be reproduced by a computer or a copier. Both the United States and Britain have introduced the magnetic threads in their larger-denomination bills, which means that they can now be detected in large quantities by airport security scanners. In addition, they are using watermarks and special colored fibers that respond to ultraviolet or infrared light, which allows bank scanning machines to detect and verify them. Special color-shifting inks that change color when you view the bill from different angles are already being introduced in higher-denomination bills that will replace the current bills in circulation.

The Treasury Department is also using magnetic inks that allow sensors in money-counting devices and vending machines to verify the authenticity of a bill. The red and blue micro-fibers found in the 1990 Series bills can be detected in luggage by special airport scanners. And the Canadian government mint introduced tiny square holograms created from thin layers of ceramic molecules. These holograms shift from gold to green depending on the viewing angle, and will not reproduce on the new color copiers.

Plans to Replace U.S. Currency

During the last few years a number of preliminary tests were done to measure the public's response to the idea of replacing U.S. $50 and $100 bills with new counterfeit-proof currency that is barcoded. When introduced, the proposed plan will allow only ten days for citizens to make the switch. People with more than $1,000 cash in their possession will be required to file a special form with the Treasury Department to justify replacing their obsolete currency with the new bills. If a citizen cannot prove that his or her holding of U.S. currency is legitimate, the Treasury will not replace the old currency.

In 1990, the Federal Reserve sent specialists to the Soviet Union to advise the government on monetary policy. As a result of their suggestions, Gorbachev ordered all Soviet citizens to turn in their 50- and 100-ruble notes within a week and exchange them for new currency. If a Soviet citizen could not prove that he had acquired his or her money legally, the banks would not issue the citizen new replacement currency. In that one week, the Soviet government eliminated one-third of the nation's outstanding currency. As a result of the government decree, the life savings of many Soviet citizens were wiped out.

Under the U.S. plan, the treasury forms for people who have large amounts of cash will be forwarded to the IRS to help target them for a future IRS audit. Some government officials have gone so far as to suggest that $5, $10, and $20 bills will also be replaced. The government's plan is to flush out hundreds of billions of dollars from the underground economy used by tax evaders and drug dealers.

On October 3, 1989, an amendment to bar code U.S. currency was passed by the Senate. This bill empowers the Treasury to use the latest optical-scanning technology to trace all cash with denominations greater than $10. Eventually, the serial numbers of all $100, $50, and $20 bills will be read by optical scanning devices similar to those used today at grocery store counters. A computer readable strip on the currency will identify the individual who received the currency from the bank teller. Senator John Kerry (D–MA) introduced the amendment and defended his actions as follows: "This is necessary because money laundering is not isolated to drug use." In discussing the bar code measure, he ominously declared: "It provides a mechanism by which our government, our law enforcement agencies, our financial institutions, and foreign institutions as well, can efficiently track U.S. currency—bill by bill—without any undue administrative burden.

In a few years, then, most stores and businesses will have a bar-code currency reader that will identify the bar codes on all the currency you offer in payment for goods and services. The store's computer will be linked with the IRS, allowing their computer to compare your purchases with your declared income on your tax forms. Because of this technology approved by the U.S. Congress, your financial privacy will be eliminated forever.

CHAPTER 14

The Coming
Economic Collapse

I am not a prophet, so I cannot predict when the governments of both the United States and Canada will "hit the wall" financially. That moment will occur when the national debt and its compounding interest charges have risen so high that the total tax revenue of the country will not be enough to pay the interest on the national debt. Sometime prior to that event, our governments will find that they are unable to borrow international funds because foreign lenders will realize that they will never be repaid. Many Third World countries have already found themselves in this scenario and have declared a moratorium on their debts because they simply cannot pay the staggering interest charges, let alone the principle. In addition, the Second World nations—Russia and many Eastern European countries—are at the point where they are unable to meet their interest obligations. Eventually, after decades of growing deficits, the governments of the First World—Western Europe and North America—will be forced to admit that they too are broke.

A nation cannot continue to borrow forever, going deeper and deeper in debt each year. There comes a point when economic collapse or hyperinflation is the only remaining option. Because a national government has the ability to print money, our politicians will most likely succumb to the temptation to "print money" to delay the inevitable economic collapse. The temptation will be overwhelming to inflate the currency to allow the government to continue paying its bills. Using hyperinflation, the government can gradually repudiate its national debt by repaying bondholders with devalued, inflated currency.

The Current "Recovery" Is an Illusion

The present economic "recovery" is based to a large degree on the continuing speculative binge in the financial markets. The majority of capital investments during the past few years have been focused in the areas of computers and communications equipment. Computers have represented an astonishing 50 percent of the increase in fixed investments by American business. The problem, however, is that computers increase productivity by eliminating jobs, not creating new ones. Construction and equipment activity remain relatively weak these days compared to past economic recoveries.

Recently, the White House boasted about the great increase in American jobs under President Clinton's economic stewardship. For example, they announced that an additional 760,000 jobs were created between March 1993 and March 1994. The U.S. Labor Department also claimed that 194,000 new jobs were created in October 1994. However, these so-called "official" government figures are pure fiction! When these figures were closely questioned by *Business Week* magazine (November 1994 issue), the Labor Department admitted that an astonishing 85 percent of those 194,000 new jobs were created out of thin air without a shred of documentation. The government admitted that their normal monthly surveys of American companies detected only 29,000 new jobs in October. The Clinton administration "fudged" these figures by adding hundreds of thousands of imaginary jobs on the assumption that they may have missed some newly created jobs in their survey.

While it may be justifiable to adjust an official figure by ten percent, it is ludicrous to inflate monthly new job figures by 600 percent (from an actual 29,000 to an "official" 194,000 jobs). This is only one example among many that should awaken readers to the unreliability of government economic figures.

Despite the optimistic economic claims of the White House, business profits these days are not strong. During the past few years, profits of companies have been substantially less than they were during every other economic recovery since World War II. Inflated earnings from the banking sector and the stock market have distorted the true picture of corporate earnings. A lot of what we are hearing about in the media is a "smoke and mirrors" recovery.

The truth is that both Japan and North America are now experiencing a long-term structural depression that began about 1990. We should keep in mind that there was a similar short-term rebound in the early 1930s following the 1929 crash. The present recovery is not based on strong savings and increased capital growth as it should be, but rather on the greatest financial speculative market in this century. This market was fueled by extremely low interest rates and the monetary policy of the Federal Reserve. This hyperstimulation of the financial markets prepared the ground for the great speculative bubble that is only now beginning to break.

To put this in focus, the present financial speculation in America is much greater than the speculative growth that took place in the Japanese financial markets from 1987 to 1989. The Japanese market then dropped 62 percent, costing Japanese investors a staggering $3 trillion in investment losses. The stock market collapse triggered a drop of 50 percent in Japanese real estate values, producing a loss of $7 trillion. That is a preview of the economic collapse that can take place in North America during the last half of the 1990s.

Growing Risks in the Financial Markets

When the American financial markets crumble, global financial markets and the world economy will be wiped out. The staggering size of the U.S. corporate and government bond markets, together with the speculatively high price levels in the stock market, are extremely dangerous.

However, these bond and stock markets are paragons of conservative strength in comparison to the monstrous American financial derivatives market. Over the last decade, Wall Street and the larger banks have created an astonishing number of new, highly leveraged, speculative financial vehicles called derivatives. These derivative contracts are designed to create massive profits for their Wall Street investors at the total risk of the poor investor. Beginning with real estate investment trusts, the brokers created junk bonds, leveraged buyouts, options, and securitizing of debt. These creative and highly leveraged investments are so speculative and dangerous that they may trigger the greatest economic collapse in history. To give you an idea of the amount of money involved, the American derivatives market is now worth $21 trillion. And the amount of money at risk in the worldwide financial derivatives market has now exceeded $42 trillion.

Aside from the inherent risk involved in having such an enormous amount of funds invested in one area, there is also great danger in that these novel and little-understood financial vehicles are not regulated by the Stock Exchange or government regulators! Banks, brokerage houses, and insurance companies are creating hundreds of sophisticated financial derivative contracts that have never existed before. These contracts are being made without any rules to limit their risk. Many experienced investors and some financial brokers who understand well the stock and bond markets do not fully understand how these complicated contracts are supposed to work.

The extremely low U.S. interest rates from 1989 to 1993 encouraged over 61 million investors to take their money out of low-interest bank accounts and money market funds and plunge into the stock market in the hopes of earning higher yields. People moved out of low-risk, low interest CDs, T-bills, and money market vehicles and put their money into the high-risk stock market through mutual funds earning an average of 15 percent annually. In the future, when the financial markets fall, many of these investors may lose their life savings.

Unfortunately, many banks have followed the actions of individual investors by abandoning conservative strategies and plunging into the long-term bond market in hopes of making large profits for their shareholders. However, the transfer of a trillion dollars out of conservative low-interest bank deposits and into speculative stocks, bonds, and financial derivatives has set the stage for a spectacular economic collapse that will exceed the 1929 crash. One of the present consequences of this speculative binge has been a disastrous drop in the amount of cash and liquid assets held by the average American household— a drop to the lowest level in three decades. This suggests that the average citizen is unprepared for the economic roller coaster ride that lies ahead. Rising interest rates in the last 18 months have already wiped out $1.5 trillion in the bond market. Further interest rate increases will cause a bond market collapse that could destroy many banks, insurance companies, and pension funds.

Monetizing Debt to Produce Inflation

The inflationary process used by the government to "monetize the debt" has, as its underlying purpose, the creation of money for government programs without the political backlash that usually results from raising taxes. In effect, this process allows the government to repudiate its past debts by producing inflation, so that holders of government bonds are repaid in cheaper, inflated dollars.

Every year the federal government spends hundreds of billions more than it raises in taxes. They make up the difference (the deficit) by borrowing money from the private sector, selling interest-bearing notes called treasury bills (T-bills) and bonds to investors. The banks buy these treasury bills from the U.S. Treasury to generate safe interest income. The U.S. Federal Reserve system will then buy back some of these bonds from the local banks.

But where does the privately owned Federal Reserve find the money to do that? Believe it or not, they actually produce these dollars "out of thin air" in the Federal Reserve system computers. President Truman had a sign on his White House desk that said, "The Buck Stops Here." However, according to Bob Woodward's latest book, Federal Reserve Chairman Alan Greenspan has a plaque on his desk with the slogan "The Buck Starts Here."

The Federal Reserve publishes its figures every Thursday, including a list of "U.S. Government securities bought outright." The *Wall Street Journal* reports that the Federal Reserve system buys between $1 and $2 billion worth of government debt every week. Between 1990 and 1993, the Federal Reserve monetized the government's debt by purchasing over $90 billion of T-bills from the government. The Federal Reserve then allows the banks to use this money as new reserves. Using the three-to-one leverage provided by the fractional banking reserve system, the banks can use these new reserves as a basis to lend their customers huge new loans multiplied many times over the amount of the actual reserves. When these loans are made to customers, the official bank assets will increase thereby, and the money supply will be increased by this amount. This financial "sleight of hand" transforms government debt into an increase in monetary supply. This "monetization" of government debt is the root cause of inflation—not the rise in wages and retail prices that inevitably follow such inflationary actions by the federal government.

Inflation robs us of our savings and makes economic planning and calculations almost impossible. Inflation punishes savers, such as the holders of long-term bonds, and favors those who borrow money because they will ultimately repay their loans with inflated, cheaper dollars. Obviously, the greatest benefit is felt by the biggest debtor of all, the government. History reveals that inflation is the government's favorite method of repudiating its debts. The economist Maynard Keynes made this observation in his book *The Economic Consequences of the Peace:* "By a continuing process of inflation governments can confiscate, secretly and unobserved, an important part of the wealth of their citizens."[1]

Throughout history, inflation has always been produced by the actions of the government. It can never be produced by citizens or businessmen. Despite the government's attempts to deflect the blame onto greedy labor unions and price-gouging retailers, the truth is that inflation can always be directly attributed to the government, which is the sole authority with the lawful power to issue legal tender. In a recent issue of their *LBMC Report*, Lewis Lehrman and John Mueller wrote,

If we ask why prices have risen almost fourfold since 1971, the nontechnical answer is that the banking system has 'monetized' over $2 trillion in Treasury debt since then. . . . And if we ask why federal deficits have mushroomed in the meantime, the answer is that our legislators have gotten used to a monetary system which permits public debt to be monetized on such a vast scale.[2]

Predicting Future Inflation Rates

In the last several years, vast profits have been earned by happy investors who were in mutual funds that were investing in both stocks and bonds. This is because low inflation rates and low interest rates created an almost ideal investment atmosphere. But a rise in inflation would threaten this investment climate. This means, of course, that every investor wants to know where inflation rates are headed. Wayne Angell, the chief economist at Bear Stearns, a major Wall Street firm, has developed a brilliant economic model that can predict future inflation trends. In a fascinating article in the October 1994 issue of the *National Review*, the writer tells us about this incredible formula that predicts the future rate of inflation based on the fluctuations in the price of gold.[3]

Without taking into account any other economic conditions except the price of gold, this formula can actually predict about 80 percent of the change in the inflation rate one year into the future. For example, to determine the Consumer Price Index 12 months from now, we simply calculate as follows: Take the price of gold today—say $390 an ounce—and multiply 390 by 0.024 and subtract 5.32 = 4 percent. This formula indicates that with the price of gold at $390 today, we can expect an inflation rate at this time next year of approximately four percent. As a rule of thumb, for every $10 increase in the price of an ounce of gold, we can expect inflation to increase another one-fifth of one percent. For every $50 increase in the price of gold, we can expect a one percent rise in inflation rates. In other words, if gold rises to $440, we can expect an inflation rate of five percent.

Because the future rate of inflation is such an important factor in our investment decisions, I included a simple chart that will help you project the rate of inflation one year in advance (based on the Wayne Angell/Bear Stearns' inflation formula).

If the price of one ounce of gold is:	The predicted inflation rate 12 months from today is:
$340	3%
$390	4%
$440	5%
$490	6%
$540	7.6%
$590	8%
$640	10%
$690	11%

The True Cost of Inflation

In the period from 1992 to early 1994, the Federal Reserve system allowed the monetary base—the bank reserves and currency—to grow at an annual inflationary rate of ten percent. Their new target for this year is 8.7 percent. In addition to the obvious danger that rising inflation poses to the whole economy, the stock market will take a beating when mutual fund and stock investors realize that inflation is eroding the real value of their shares. Moreover, the fear of rising inflation and interest rates is already wreaking havoc in the bond market mutual funds.

Because of low inflation during the last several years, many people have forgotten the devastating effect relentless inflation can have on their life savings. When the inflationary spiral begins to run upward again, the average citizen on a fixed-pension income will suffer devastating losses to their true retirement income. The following chart shows the effects of inflation on the purchasing power of $10,000 of pension income:

Annual Rate of Inflation	Your Reduced Purchasing Power After 10 Years	After 15 Years	After 20 years
5%	$6,139	$4,810	$3,769
7.5%	$4,852	$3,380	$2,354
10%	$3,855	$2,394	$1,486

Even with a relatively restricted inflation rate of only ten percent, the purchasing power of a $10,000 pension payment would be reduced to only $1,486 of today's purchasing power in just 20 years.

The U.S. National Debt Crisis

The "official" U.S. national debt stands at $4.3 trillion. Government economists naturally prefer to leave off the balance sheet several enormous financial obligations, such as the trillion dollars it borrowed from the Social Security trust fund, in addition to unfunded government pension funds for military and civilian employees. However, when you add in these "off-budget" financial obligations, the real U.S. national debt is a staggering $7.5 trillion. The interest alone on this debt costs American taxpayers $615 billion every year. This comes to $1.7 billion every day, or $70 million every single hour.

How was this debt created? Incredibly, only ten percent of it was created by Congress spending more money on defense and social programs than they raised in taxes. The other 90 percent was created directly by compounding interest on the original debt.

So that you can better grasp the nature of the problem caused by our compounding national debt, consider these figures: In 1980 when the Gross National Product (GNP)—the total value of all goods and services produced in America that year—reached $2.7 trillion, the national debt of $910 billion amounted to 33 percent of the GNP. Only ten years later, in 1990, when the GNP reached $5.4 trillion, the true national debt had multiplied *six* times to reach $6 trillion, which is 110 percent of the GNP. By 1995, when the GNP reached $6.5 trillion, the true national debt has grown to $8 trillion, or an astonishing 125 percent of the GNP. It is obvious that this rapidly compounding national debt will eventually destroy the economy.

Today, a huge portion of your federal taxes goes toward paying the interest on the national debt. When the privately owned U.S. Federal Reserve system raises interest rates, then Americans will have to pay enormously higher taxes to cover the additional interest costs on the exploding national debt. Who is hurt the most when interest rates rise? The middle class, because it pays out a much greater portion of its income in interest payments than those who are rich. In addition, the middle class benefits the least from rising rates because they seldom have much money invested in interest-bearing bonds and savings accounts. On the other hand, people who are very rich benefit from high interest rates as they reap huge rewards from the rising interest returns on their bonds. And they suffer the least damage because they seldom need to borrow funds.

Rising interest rates, then, increase the growing disparity between the very rich and the rest of us. The top 20 percent of North American wage earners have seen their incomes rise markedly during the last ten years, while the incomes of the remaining 80 percent have fallen significantly.

When you add up the total indebtedness of America today, including the federal, state and local governments, plus the debt of all corporations and individuals, the nation now struggles under a staggering debt load amounting to $15.6 trillion. Since 1980, the indebtedness of individuals, corporations, and the local and state governments have increased more than 400 percent. However, during the same period, the federal government's debt increased by an incredible 500 percent. While some people argue that this rising debt is normal considering the growing economy, the truth is that the debt is spiraling out of control as it rises far more quickly than the economy or people's savings. Each year, Congress has less and less room to maneuver. Over 61 percent of the annual budget goes to pay interest on the national debt and entitlement programs for welfare, Social Security, and medicare payments. Meanwhile, the average family now spends over 20 percent of its monthly income on debt repayments.

The speculative bubble in stocks, bonds, and financial derivative investment vehicles is directly related to the explosive growth in debt during the last 15 years. This huge debt load will limit our options and massively increase the economic pain when the crash finally does come. Most individuals and corporations are in bad shape to face the coming economic disaster because they haven't put aside any cash reserves in savings. The average homeowner in America has the lowest amount of cash on hand that we have seen since 1900. When the crash comes, massive bankruptcies will hit businesses and homeowners as they find themselves unable to pay the interest on the huge loans they've accumulated in the past few years.

The Massive Tax Grab

Huge increases in government welfare expenditures have placed an unbearable burden on taxpayers. In addition, the cost of compounding interest on the trillions of dollars of national debt is taking a greater and greater share of the total tax revenues. A recent study by the Fraser Institute in Canada revealed that the average Canadian family's tax demand rose by an astonishing 1,200 percent in the last 33 years. Back in 1961 the average Canadian family paid only $1,675 in taxes each year, while today a family pays $21,228 in taxes. Income taxes and hidden taxes are now the largest single expenditure for families. In fact, we spend more on taxes today than we spend on housing, food, and clothing combined.

The Federal Reserve's Miscalculations

History shows that most major financial crises were triggered by the actions of central banks that tried and failed to manage the economy that was in conflict with market forces. The Federal Reserve almost always acts too late, or too soon, and does too little, or too much. The financial bubble of the early 1990s was caused by the Federal Reserve holding down interest rates to abnormal levels from 1990 to 1993. The economic writer Kurt Richebacher points out that "the greatest financial and economic disasters in history have generally been courted by prolonged periods of abnormally low interest rates."

After three years of very low interest rates, beginning in the fall of 1993, the Federal Reserve raised long-term interest rates from 5.8 percent to 9.05 percent. This triggered enormous losses among those who were invested in mutual funds, stocks, and bonds. Then in 1994 the Federal Reserve raised the federal funds bank interest rate six times. Wall Street experts had projected low interest rates and low inflation for that time, but they were wrong! Since World War II, interest rates have more than doubled from their lowest level in the cycle. As 1995 got underway, the Federal Reserve continued to increase interest rates in its so-called "war against inflation."

Government-authorized inflation figures are usually understated and false. The Sindlinger inflation study, based on 5,000 in-depth household and business surveys every month, claims that the true inflation rate is almost three times larger than the government statistics claim. In addition, the study shows that the true unemployment rate is almost ten percent, which is almost 50 percent higher than the official numbers.

We should be wary, then, of trusting government statistics. The government's statisticians have dozens of clever ways to distort unemployment and other economic figures so that they favor the administration in power. For example, they will count part-time workers as full-time employees. They will not count as unemployed those who become discouraged and cease looking for work. Using "smoke and mirrors" accounting techniques, the government economists create hundreds of thousand of phantom jobs that do not exist. For example, during the 1992 election campaign, the U.S. Department of Labor released figures showing that over one million Americans had lost work that year. These false figures helped defeat President Bush by convincing the voters that these jobs were lost under his leadership. In addition, despite clear statistics proving the recession was over by mid-1991, then-presidential candidate Bill Clinton denied that the recession had already ended. Instead, Clinton kept proclaiming his winning political slogan, "It's the economy, stupid!" However, as soon as the election was over, it was no accident that the Labor Department "discovered" that the million lost jobs were simply a computer error and that job loss was negligible in 1992. Welcome to the world of politics!

If our leaders had been watching Japan, they would have noticed the warning signs that preceded the financial crisis in which Japan now finds itself. However, they have ignored Japan's experience with low interest rates in the mid-eighties which led to its dangerously speculative financial market in the late 1980s. The disastrous U.S. stock market crash in the late 1920s was created in the same way. And both the 1929 U.S. market and the 1980s Japanese market collapsed, leading to deep depressions.

The Federal Reserve now realizes that they have created a potentially disastrous speculative situation in the financial markets. They are trying to moderate the market by raising interest rates. The Japanese Central Bank came to the same conclusion several years ago and put the brakes on Japan's economy by massively raising interest rates. The unintended result was an economic disaster with staggering losses of trillions of dollars in the financial and real estate markets of Japan. It appears that North America will follow the same agenda.

In a strange replay of history, the Federal Reserve is now afraid that the U.S. economy is heating up and may fuel a major inflationary rise in the future. They are raising interest rates now to keep inflation from harming the banks. In the fragile and dangerously over-extended financial environment we face today, the shock effect caused by massive interest rate increases may be the needle that will pierce the financial market's balloon and trigger the economic collapse they fear. Already the Federal Reserve is signaling that it interprets rising commodity prices and the news that American factories are nearing 85 percent of productive capacity as danger signs of possible renewed inflation in the coming months.

Tragically, history reveals that governments and central banks have an almost perfect record of misunderstanding economic signals and taking hasty actions that inevitably trigger the very financial crises they fear. One of the great danger signals is the evidence that liquidity has disappeared as investors abandon bank deposits and money market funds for investments in securities and mutual funds. Recently, the Federal Reserve governor, Lawrence Lindsay, was quoted saying, "Low savings and a shift in household finances to less liquid assets are a threat to continued economic recovery.... Households are less liquid than at any time in memory." Any informed historian will tell you that almost every financial collapse in the last 100 years was triggered by the lack of financial liquidity.

As the Federal Reserve raises interest rates, the economy will suffer a major contraction and financial markets will fall. In an ideal world the government and the Federal Reserve would simply adopt a laissez-faire approach and let market forces affect interest rates. However, this will never happen because the financial elite that run the government and the Federal Reserve are liberal socialists who believe they need to control every aspect of the economy. Their desperate desire for this control will bring about the very disaster they fear.

The Coming Stock Market Crash

We are now facing the greatest risk of a massive stock market crash since 1929. At the same time, millions of naive, inexperienced investors are pouring their life savings into a staggering array of mutual funds. Over 31 million new investors placed their savings into the stock market during the last four years, buying stocks or mutual fund shares at the end of the speculative stock price cycle. And the situation is far more dangerous today than it was in 1929. A much larger percentage of family wealth is now invested in the stock market than before the crash of 1929. In addition, the 1929 meltdown of the stock market did not immediately lead to a worldwide collapse of other stock markets because national markets were not integrated then. Few multinational companies were traded on multiple national stock markets at the time. However, today, the global stock and bond markets are so completely integrated that markets in Hong Kong or Europe will react instantly to a crisis that takes place in the New York market. A major crash on Wall Street or the London Exchange can now trigger an instant worldwide financial collapse.

The U.S. stock market is already in the danger phase that historically has led to a major bear market. The history of the Dow Jones over the last 100 years suggests that vertically rising bull markets such as we have enjoyed for the last four years almost always end with a speculative explosion that is followed by deeply declining bear markets. Following the 1929 crash, share prices on the U.S. stock exchange fell 89 percent over the next two-and-a-half years. It is interesting to note that although investors suffered major financial losses when the initial crash occurred, they continued to realize even greater losses as the market kept falling for the next several years. People who got out of the market after taking their initial losses were saved from enduring the constantly dropping share prices that followed for years afterward. Many investors, however, refused to bail out and sell their stocks because they hoped that somehow the market would rebound and they would recover their losses. Consequently, these investors rode the market all the way to the bottom and were wiped out. That brings us to a fundamental rule of investment losses: Your first loss is your best loss. Analyze your loss, learn the lesson, and get out!

There is yet another sign that we are experiencing the most overpriced stock market in U.S. history: The Dow Jones Industrials, at the time of this writing, are trading at approximately 39 times the amount of their dividends and 21 times their earnings (or P/E ratio). We must go back to the months before the crash of 1929 and the collapse of October 1987 to find equally speculative high stock prices.

The Price/Earnings ratio is a measure of the price of the share compared to its earnings. If a share of ABC Ltd. is trading for $100 per share and its earnings are $10 per share, then the stock has a P/E ratio of 10. If you bought a share in that company, you would earn back your investment in only ten years. Historically, that is a fairly normal P/E ratio (which normally ranges from 10 to 15). Recently, however,

the Price-Earnings ratio (P/E) of the Standard and
Poor's 500 stock index exceeded 27, which was the
highest P/E ratio in the last century.

Let me put this in simple terms: If you bought
shares with a P/E ratio of 27, you would have to invest and collect dividends on those shares for the
next 27 years to earn back the amount you paid. In
the investment world, a P/E ratio of 27 normally indicates an overpriced share. Around the globe, other
stock markets are equally overvalued with an average P/E ratio of 28. Stock prices worldwide are so
high that it will take almost three decades for a share
to earn back its purchase price.

These high share prices are supported by sheer
speculation instead of underlying fundamental values and earning power. The amount of money that
has poured into the stock market during the last few
years has inflated share prices to levels that are simply not sustainable. This means that these share
prices will eventually fall to a much lower level in
the near future; it is just a matter of time as to when
the crash will occur.

During the 12 months ending April 1994, investors and speculators unleashed a tidal wave by
pouring over $110 billion of new money into global
stock markets and forcing share and bond prices to
rise to dangerous levels. The speculative mania that
has affected the U.S. stock market is now moving
into the global markets. Unfortunately, a majority of
these investors have never before invested in the
stock market, so they are unaware that a brutal
down market could cause them to lose a substantial

portion of their hard-won life savings. Many of these new investors have purchased their mutual fund shares from a bank that recently entered the field of mutual fund investments to make up for the massive cash withdrawals from bank deposits. One poll found that over 70 percent of people who purchased their mutual fund from a bank mistakenly believed that their investment was insured by federal deposit insurance. They are wrong! There is no insurance on these funds from deposit insurance.

In 1988 there were 34 million American stock investors. In only seven years this has risen to 65 million Americans in the stock market today. Significantly, more than half of these investors are very new to the stock market. Most of them have invested in the stock market through one or more of 4,430 mutual funds.

In 1987, mutual fund investments were comprised of $180 billion in equities. Eight years later these mutual funds have grown to a staggering $2 trillion worth of stocks and bonds. Since 1992, investors have withdrawn over $750 billion from federally insured low-interest bank accounts and invested these funds in the volatile stock market. Over the last five years an average of $11 billion was withdrawn from the banks every single month and placed in the stock market. This unprecedented tidal wave of new money has helped to drive the price of shares to spectacular and speculative heights.

One of the danger signs that the stock market is reaching its peak is that over 80 percent of the money now in mutual funds was invested in the last 36 months. Therefore, most of these new investors are buying at the top of the market. The risk of widespread financial disaster in America is greater today because so many people are in the stock and bond markets. Back in 1929 only ten percent of Americans owned stocks, yet the 1929 crash and the resulting Great Depression wiped out the life savings of tens of millions. The percentage of money which Americans have invested in stocks and bonds has grown in the last 20 years from only 21 percent of the average household's assets to 41 percent today. Over thirty million new investors have taken a significant percentage of their life savings and placed these funds into the most speculative, overpriced stock market in history.

An additional risk comes from the enormous amount of money that millions of North Americans are now investing in foreign countries. These people invest primarily through international mutual funds ($130 billion in 1993 alone) that buy foreign shares earning an average of less than one percent in annual dividends. Obviously, their sole motivation is large capital gains; not dividend income.

As you can see, then, we are now in a dangerous position where there is great potential for enormous losses. When you consider the financial devastation from the 1929 crash, when only a few people owned stocks, then you can appreciate the possible magnitude of the economic collapse that lies ahead. When the stock markets begin to crash, it will be almost impossible to sell your stocks or to redeem your mutual fund shares because everyone else will be trying to sell at the same time. After the collapse, when share prices have dropped to a fraction of their current values, the smart money will begin buying up the market at bargain-basement prices. In contrast, the average investor will find that his life savings have been wiped out.

Many large banks and insurance companies are exposed to the potential of devastating losses from their unwise and speculative investments in the stock and bond markets. These supposedly conservative banks and insurance companies now hold over $1 trillion worth of equities and bonds purchased at high prices in the last few years. The insurance industry holds almost $500 billion in municipal bonds that are now dropping in value because of rising interest rates. Sixty-one million Americans have invested over $2 trillion in the stock markets. When people begin to see that the stock market is crashing, a huge panic will sweep the country. With so many of these investors new to the stock market there is little likelihood that they will "bite the bullet" and ride out their losses. It is much more likely that they will sell as stock prices plummet, making a bad situation even worse. The only people who will win are those who were wise enough to move their funds out of the stock market and mutual funds before the economic collapse.

Many people think the Great Depression was caused by a number of bank failures in the period from 1929 to 1933. We are now told that we no longer have to worry about that happening again. Milton Friedman and many other economists have suggested that a depression is now impossible because the Federal Reserve system would prevent it. However, it wasn't the bank failures that triggered the great Depression. The impact of these bank failures was relatively small. The real trigger for the Great Depression was the 1929 stock market crash and the brutal bear market that followed, wiping out approximately $85 billion in investments. This was a staggering amount of money because the dollar in 1929 was worth almost $10 in today's currency.

The people who had the foresight to remain liquid (that is, keep their assets in cash) survived the Great Depression and recovered. In fact, during the Depression era over 10,000 Americans became millionaires ($1 million at that time was the equivalent of $10 million in today's dollars). They saw the warning signs before the 1929 crash, preserved their cash, and got out of debt, stocks, and investment real estate before the collapse of prices. They were then in a position to acquire quality real estate, equities in solid companies, and other investments at a fraction of their previous price.

The Banking Credit Crisis

Thomas Jefferson once said that "banking establishments are more dangerous than standing armies." During the 1930s a great number of banks failed because of their exposure to bad investments in real estate, nonpaying loans, and massive withdrawals by their customers. From 1928 until 1932 a total of 4,700 banks failed. President Roosevelt proclaimed a bank moratorium on March 6, 1933, leaving millions of people without access to their cash. While some people later received a portion of their funds, many others lost everything they had deposited in their bank.

Congress responded to these bank failures by establishing an insurance system to guarantee the funds deposited by bank customers. The Federal Deposit Insurance Corporation (FDIC) was created in 1933 and now insures bank deposits up to $100,000 per customer for member banks. However, not all banks are insured. It is a voluntary system, and over 500 U.S. banks are not insured by the FDIC. Member banks have a sign on the door proclaiming their membership. However, during the recent savings and loan (S&L) crisis, the FDIC was absolutely overwhelmed with claims. This failure forced the federal government to directly bail out the S&L system at a cost of 700 billion dollars.

Despite the warning signs from the savings and loan collapse, the Federal Deposit Insurance Corporation remains greatly underfunded. Today, the FDIC has assets of approximately $1 billion to insure $4 trillion in over 14,000 bank and S&L accounts. This amounts to less than two-and-a-half cents of FDIC assets to insure every $100 of insured deposits!

The present insolvency of the FDIC makes it a certainty that millions of people will lose their life savings in a future banking collapse. No one should deposit more than $50,000 in any one bank in light of today's risk. Place your large deposits in several different banks after you have verified that the bank is financially sound. You can obtain this verification through one of the bank rating services listed in the Resources section at the end of the book.

Many banks have recently been forced by the federal banking examiners to merge with larger banks in an effort to prevent the total failure of the banking system. However, knowledgeable sources tell us that thousands of banks are extremely vulnerable because of unwise real estate investments and Third World loans. Many of these international loans are already far behind in their payments. Billions of dollars of these loans are nonpaying and have been rescheduled to allow developing nations additional time to make their loan payments.

The Financial Derivatives Market

Many banks, in their desire to increase their profits, have participated in incredibly dangerous investments in the financial derivatives market. Unfortunately, these volatile derivative investments can easily result in losses of billions of dollars.

In contrast to direct stock investments and bonds, financial derivatives are totally artificial financial vehicles. Financial derivatives derive their value from their underlying traditional investments, such as stocks and bonds. These derivatives include such diverse financial vehicles as interest rate swaps and options, currency futures and options, stock index futures and options, collateralized mortgage obligations, commodity futures, interest-only mortgages, principal-only mortgages, synthetic securities, Eurodollar futures, and yield curve notes. These new derivatives investments are so complicated that many of them can be calculated only by computers. More importantly, these derivatives are so highly leveraged that a one-percent rise in the value of the underlying security will produce a 100 percent gain in the equity invested. However, a one-percent decline will totally wipe out your entire investment. When U.S. government bonds recently declined more than ten percent, if you had bought one of these derivative bond investments with a 100-to-1 leverage, you would have lost ten times the amount you originally invested! Several years ago, *Time* magazine ran a article entitled "The Secret Money Machine—Seven Years After the Crash" that pointed out the extreme dangers of exotic financial derivatives. This article described derivatives as "computer generated hyper-sophisticated financial instruments that use the public's massive bet on securities to create a parallel universe of side bets and speculative mutations" so vast that the underlying $1 trillion involved is more than three times the total value of all stocks traded on the New York Stock Exchange in a month and twice the size of the nation's gross domestic product.

However, in the last few years the size and complexity of the financial derivatives market has exploded. Today, over $21 trillion is at risk in America and an astonishing $42 trillion is at risk worldwide. To place these figures in perspective, the total value of all stocks traded on the New York Exchange amounts to only $6 trillion. We should remember that the stock market crash in 1987 that resulted in the loss of $1 trillion of investors' funds was precipitated by a massive drop in the financial derivatives market. During the last year the largest Japanese steel company lost $1.3 billion in a derivatives trade while the largest steel company in Germany lost $1.4 billion. Then, Orange County, California, lost $2 billion while the 270-year-old Barings Bank of England was forced into bankruptcy when they lost $1.3 billion in one week on a derivatives trade by one 28-year-old employee. This incredibly dangerous derivatives market could very well be the trigger for the coming financial collapse that the Bible indicates will occur in the last days.

PART 5

Escaping the Economic Chaos to Come

CHAPTER 15

Financial Principles for Christians

Christians often have an ambivalent attitude toward the subject of money and financial planning. On the one hand, we all spend a considerable portion of our time and a great deal of energy earning our livelihood; yet, most Christians feel the need to downplay the importance of money in their lives. The great American humorist Mark Twain used to say, "Where I was brought up we never talked about money because there was never enough to furnish a topic of conversation."

Christians often assure each other that "money isn't everything" and that "money can't buy happiness." And while many of us are willing to share an astonishing amount of information regarding our personal lives, most of us would never consider telling our closest friend about our income or bank balance. On the other hand, some people have

focused so exclusively on the area of finances that
they have almost made money their sole measure
of whether or not God is blessing their lives.

We as Christians need to acquire a balanced and
biblically based attitude about finances. Obviously,
money is important. But we need to recognize that
financial resources are simply a tool that the Lord
has placed in our hands as a trust to be administered.
Someday, we will give the Lord an accounting of our
stewardship of the finances He entrusted to us.

A Christian's Attitude Toward Money

Many Christians have never evaluated their attitude
towards money and financial planning in the light
of God's Word. As a consequence, they often possess
erroneous and harmful attitudes that hinder their
financial success and peace of mind. Several of these
erroneous attitudes include the following:

1. Many Christians think that the Lord is uncon-
   cerned with their money and financial matters.
   Nothing could be further from the truth.
   Money is such an important aspect of our daily
   lives that God has provided ample instructions
   concerning our finances. The Bible contains
   many detailed guidelines on how a believer
   should handle his finances.

2. Some Christians have created an artificial division between the sacred and the profane in their
   finances. Some believers say, "This ten percent

of my money belongs to God but the other 90 percent belongs to me to spend in any way I please without regard to God." They believe that it is fanatical or extreme to involve God in every area of their finances. However, the Lord demands control over every single area of a Christian's life. Everything we have belongs to Him. All that we now possess or ever shall own is simply given in trust to us by the Lord.

3. Many Christians believe that prosperity is somehow suspect and that becoming financially successful is "unspiritual." Some teach that the poor are more spiritual than those who succeed financially. Some Christians assume that people who succeed financially must spend every single moment thinking about their finances and that they must have "made money their god." The truth, however, is almost exactly the opposite. Those who are in deep financial trouble often spend far more time each day worrying about money than those who have achieved some measure of financial success. Christians who have achieved financial stability are free to focus on far more important things than how they will pay their bills at month's end. Financial success can actually be spiritually liberating in a Christian's life, enabling him or her to focus on the truly important spiritual goals in life.

4. Another fallacy is the idea that we should passively await the day that "our ship comes in."

Some people spiritualize this to justify their lack of financial discipline and savings by claiming that, if God wants them to succeed, they will one day wake up and find that they have supernaturally acquired financial independence. But the Bible does not support the idea of passively awaiting a financial miracle that solves all our financial problems. The Lord commands us to work to provide for the needs of our families.

The area of finances is one where the attitudes of man and God differ markedly. While man's attitudes are usually self-centered, the Lord calls on us to live our lives based on the eternal values relative to heaven. Matthew 16:26 tells us, "What is a man profited if he gains the whole world, and loses his own soul? Or what will a man give in exchange for his soul?"

While the Lord tells us that "it is more blessed to give than to receive" (Acts 20:35), most men live their life as if it is more blessed to receive than to give. God tells us that those who sacrifice for Him in this life shall "receive a hundredfold now in this time . . . and in the age to come, eternal life" (Mark 10:30). But people often believe that if they surrender something, it is lost forever.

The Lord taught us in the parable of the rich man and the beggar that those whose only desire is to accumulate financial property will ultimately lose everything they value. In contrast, our materialistic age encourages people to measure a person's value solely based on their ability to make money or acquire possessions. During a trip to California I noted a bumper sticker that summed up this prevailing materialistic philosophy: "Whoever dies with the most toys—wins!" However, the Word of God reminds us that "one's life does not consist in the abundance of the things he possesses" (Luke 12:15).

Ultimately we need to let God's Word shape our attitudes towards our finances and possessions. Do we act as if we are the owners of the property and money that pass through our hands? Or, do we look at our property and income as stewards who have been entrusted with the care of valuable possessions that belong to God, who will someday demand a full accounting? As Christians, the answer is clear. All we own and all that we shall ever possess should be held lightly because they are not our own. We are just passing through this life. Our eternal destiny is in heaven. The Lord commands us, "Do not lay up for yourselves treasures on earth, where moth and rust destroy and where thieves break in and steal; but lay up for yourselves treasures in heaven, where neither moth nor rust destroys and where thieves do not break in and steal" (Matthew 6:19-20).

When we examine the Scriptures, we discover a number of helpful and biblical principles related to our financial strategies and plans. As in every area of our Christian life, we need to find a correct and balanced position based on "the whole counsel of God."

God Will Supply Our Needs

We see affirmation of that in Philippians 4:19, where the apostle Paul said, "My God shall supply all your need according to His riches in glory by Christ Jesus."

One of the most fundamental of biblical truths is that God is vitally concerned with our practical, daily economic needs.

Within the pages of Scripture is a complete set of principles that should undergird our basic financial strategies during these last days when the world undergoes a major economic collapse. While we await and expect the rapture at any moment, we must also be ready for the Lord to tarry for a number of years and be prepared to live through the economic roller coaster that lies ahead. In such times, we need to understand that our ultimate source is not our salary or our investment savings but, rather, our Father in heaven. He will guide us, through His Word and His Holy Spirit, to know what we need to do to protect ourselves, our families, and our churches in the difficult days that lie ahead. King David reminds us, in Psalm 37:25, about God's unchanging faithfulness to His children. "I have been young, and now am old; yet I have not seen the righteous forsaken, nor his descendants begging bread."

Diligence and Hard Work

Throughout the Scriptures, God commands us to be diligent in our handling of our business and finances.

It is interesting to note that you cannot find a single biblical hero who is weak, indecisive, or lazy. While it is God who prospers our efforts, He expects us to do our part. In the book of Proverbs we find a number of passages that describe this principle:

- "Be diligent to know the state of your flocks, and attend to your herds" (Proverbs 27:23). The Scriptures promise God's blessing if we faithfully work to accomplish our task.

- "He who tills his land will have plenty of bread" (Proverbs 28:19). The Word of God commends our diligent efforts to prepare for our future needs.

- "Go to the ant, you sluggard! Consider her ways and be wise, which, having no captain, overseer or ruler, provides her supplies in the summer, and gathers her food in the harvest" (Proverbs 6:6).

Although God has promised to care for us, we are also told via the parable of the servants and the talents that we are to invest the resources He has placed in our hands to achieve the maximum return (that is within reason). The two faithful servants who invested their talents to achieve a positive return were commended and honored for their faithfulness. The servant who hid his one talent in the ground was severely reprimanded for his laziness and lack of stewardship. The master said:

You wicked and lazy servant . . . you ought to have deposited my money with the bankers, and at my coming I would have received back my own with interest. Therefore take the talent from him, and give it to him who has ten talents. For to everyone who has, more will be given, and he will have abundance; but from him who does not have, even what he has will be taken away (Matthew 25:26-29).

This teaching of our Lord clearly commands us to be good stewards of our resources. This parable also clarifies Christ's teaching on interest and saving money at financial institutions. While God condemns usury (criminally high interest rates), He portrays favorably the servant who invested his master's money with the bankers to gain a good return.

As You Sow, So Shall You Reap

In Christ's parable of the sower, He taught that the economic results we achieve are directly related to the seeds we sow. Some Christians believe that we should simply pray with faith and expect the Lord to supply our every need whether or not we have acted as good stewards through faithful work, planning, or investments. However, the Lord expects each of us as Christians to work and invest the fruits of our labor. The Bible instructs us as follows: "This I say: He who sows sparingly will also reap sparingly, and he who sows bountifully will also reap bountifully" (2 Corinthians 9:6). Once we have faithfully and diligently done our part, we can prayerfully ask the Lord to bless our efforts and give us wisdom regarding our investments.

The Law of Giving and Receiving

If we hold on to our possessions too tightly we will likely lose them. Every possession we have is simply a trust to be administered for the Lord. Those who understand and accept this principle will be open to helping their neighbors through gifts and practical assistance. After many years of professional financial planning with clients, I have seen overwhelming evidence that people who are generous in their gifts to the Lord and in their help to neighbors will receive abundant blessings from God. But remember: When we give, our motive should be to give without any regard to receiving anything back.

Our Lord promised that people who joyfully give to others will receive in return many times the amount they gave. "Give, and it will be given to you: good measure, pressed down, shaken together, and running over will be put into your bosom. For with the same measure that you use, it will be measured back to you" (Luke 6:38).

The Love of Money

A biblically balanced attitude toward our money and possessions is vital to our Christian walk. Money and possessions are important tools to provide for the practical needs of our life and our families. Unfortunately, we live in the most materialistic society in human history. Our modern Western culture measures a person's worth to a great extent by his riches and lifestyle. Television and advertising seduce the values of many people to the point where they believe their happiness and true worth depend on their having acquired the latest car or clothes. We must consciously resist the sinful materialism of our age lest money and possessions become our "god."

The Word of God says that "the love of money is a root of all kinds of evil, for which some have strayed from the faith in their greediness, and pierced themselves through with many sorrows" (1 Timothy 6:10). People who are obsessed with money are not walking in the will of God. However, we should not misunderstand that Scripture passage. It isn't saying that money itself is the root of evil. It is the *love* of money that is sinful. Many passages in the Scriptures command us to act with prudence and diligence. We are exhorted to work hard and make wise investments. God commended the faithfulness and financial stewardship of Abraham, Isaac, Jacob and many others. The Lord restored Job's huge fortunes and blessed him twice as much as before: "The Lord blessed the latter days of Job more than his beginning" (Job 42:12).

The real question for each of us regarding our finances is this: Whom will we serve? Ultimately, we will either choose to serve Christ or choose to serve ourselves. Scripture tells us that no one can serve two masters; for either he will hate the one and love the other, or else he will be loyal to the one and despise the other. You cannot serve God and mammon" (Matthew 6:24).

Will we serve Jesus Christ through our diligence and faithful stewardship of the economic resources He allows us to control? Or will we allow materialism and lust for money to overtake us and rob us of the joy of the Lord? As Christians we need to handle our possessions and finances faithfully and prayerfully, for someday we will give an accounting to our Lord Jesus Christ for how we handle our financial life, decisions, and priorities.

Tithing and Giving Your Firstfruits

The Old Testament commanded the Jewish people to pay ten percent (a tithe) to the Temple of the Lord. As Christians, we are living in the age of grace and are not subject to the old law. However, the principle of bringing our firstfruits to the Lord is still applicable to believers in the church age: "Honor the Lord with your possessions, and with the firstfruits of all your increase; so your barns will be filled with plenty" (Proverbs 3:9,10). When we give ten percent of our firstfruits to God we are simply recognizing that the Lord really owns 100 percent of all we possess.

The Bible instructs us to pay our tithes to the local church, "the storehouse," where we are being spiritually fed and blessed. God, through the prophet Malachi, gave this command in the closing book of the Old Testament:

"Bring all the tithes into the storehouse, that there may be food in My house, and prove Me now in this," says the Lord of hosts, "If I will not open for you the windows of heaven and pour out for you such blessing that there will not be room enough to receive it" (Malachi 3:10).

God has promised that He will bless us abundantly if we will be faithful to Him with our tithes. After many years in financial planning I can tell you that every financially successful Christian I know has learned by experience that we simply cannot give more to the Lord than He will return to us. Tithing is one of the fundamental principles we need to implement in our financial planning and priorities. It is the most important key to your financial prosperity as a Christian.

Giving Alms

Another key principle for your financial prosperity is to be willing to give to others when they experience a financial crisis. The Apostle John wrote, "Whoever has this world's goods, and sees his brother in need, and shuts up his heart from him, how does the love of God abide in him? My little children, let us not love in word or in tongue, but in deed and in truth" (1 John 3:17,18). Your attitude towards your money is a reflection of your attitude toward the Lord.

The Christian who constantly blesses the people around him will find himself blessed by God. Too often we think of giving only in terms of placing money in the offering plate or donating to a registered charitable fund. However, we need to be practical in our personal giving. The next time you see a Christian brother or sister in financial difficulties, prayerfully consider helping in a practical way by giving $100 as well as praying with him or her. Don't worry about the fact that you won't receive a tax receipt that allows your gift to become an income tax deduction. The Lord keeps far better accounts of our giving than the income tax authorities. "The generous soul will be made rich, and he who waters will also be watered himself" (Proverbs 11:25).

Providing for Your Family

Some Christians avoid insurance planning and the preparation of a will under the mistaken notion that these are unnecessary because "God will provide." The Bible clearly teaches that we are responsible to protect our families as much as we possibly can. If we were unable to protect them, then we could safely trust the Lord to take care of them. However, the Lord will hold us responsible if we do not follow the biblical command to take whatever steps we can to provide protection for our family.

Wills and insurance policies are simply financial tools to protect our family in the event of a premature death. Since none of us have a lease on life, we need to make provision for the possibility that we may not live long enough to accumulate enough assets to make our families financially secure. The apostle Paul commanded believers to provide financially for their spouses and children: "If anyone does not provide for his own, and especially for those of his household, he has denied the faith and is worse than an unbeliever" (1 Timothy 5:8).

In a later chapter in this book we will explore how we can best protect our loved ones and, at the same time, save money on our insurance and taxes. But I want to assert once again that preparing a will for both husband and wife is an absolute necessity today. If we fail to provide direction for the distribution of our estate, then the government will step in to distribute our assets according to their own formula. To keep that from happening, all responsible Christians should have a will for themselves and their spouses. In Proverbs we read these approving words about those who faithfully plan for their family's future: "A good man leaves an inheritance to his children's children" (Proverbs 13:22).

God Can Put a Hedge Around You

In the midst of the economic dangers surrounding us today it would be easy for many Christians to lose their sense of peace and simply surrender to despair regarding the coming financial collapse. However, as believers, we can confidently look to the Lord to protect us from unusual dangers. The Bible tells us that God made a hedge around Job as one of His faithful servants (Job 1:10). Since God's nature does not change, we can know that the Lord still places hedges around each of His followers today. While this does not guarantee that we will never suffer a devastating accident, illness, or economic loss, we do know that nothing can happen to us as Christians without God allowing it in His permissive will.

Satan acknowledged God's supernatural protection of His servant Job in the following words: "Have You not made a hedge around him, around his household, and around all that he has on every side? You have blessed the work of his hands, and his possessions have increased in the land" (Job 1:10). While God expects us to be diligent and prudent, ultimately, our finances and our economic destiny lie in His hands.

Avoid Get-Rich-Quick Schemes

Today, there are many people offering dubious financial schemes in the marketplace as well as within the church. Remember the maxim: If it sounds too good to be true, it is. If someone promises you a fabulous return on your investment, the likelihood is that you will lose your shirt. Scripture warns us against get-rich-quick schemes. In Proverbs we read, "A faithful man will abound with blessings, but he who hastens to be rich will not go unpunished" (Proverbs 28:20).

If someone in your church approaches you about some financial scheme, then go immediately to your pastor or a senior board member for advice. If they advise caution, then pay attention to their warning.

Never Cosign for a Loan

Another financial trap is the appeal by someone for you to guarantee their loan by cosigning at the bank. Never cosign! Virtually everyone I know who has cosigned for a loan has lived to regret his action. If the individual fails to make a single payment, the bank will immediately force the cosigner to pay the whole loan balance. Then it's up to you to obtain the payment of the loan from the person. The Bible specifically warns against cosigning a loan: "My son, if you become surety for your friend, if you have shaken hands in pledge for a stranger, you are snared by the words of your own mouth; you are taken by the words of your mouth" (Proverbs 6:1-2).

Trust the Lord Completely

Financial prosperity can be a great gift from God that enables you to provide funds for missions, your church, and vital evangelism projects. It can also free you to devote significant time to do volunteer work for the Lord instead of working your whole life for a salary. The Lord promised the Israelites great economic blessings if they would just follow in obedience to His commands:

> The Lord will grant you plenty of goods, in the fruit of your body, in the increase of your livestock, and in the produce of your ground, in the land of which the Lord swore to your fathers to give you. The Lord will open to you His good treasure, the heavens, to give the rain to your land in its season,

and to bless all the work of your hand. You shall lend to many nations, but you shall not borrow (Deuteronomy 28:11,12).

The most important principle we can follow in our financial life is to place our trust in our heavenly Father, prudently follow His biblical principles, and look to Him to direct our path. "Trust in the LORD with all your heart, and lean not on your own understanding; in all your ways acknowledge Him, and He shall direct your paths" (Proverbs 3:5,6).

CHAPTER 16

Financial Strategies for the Last Days

From the moment you begin your working life until retirement at age 65, you will earn a considerable fortune. Although many of us have never considered this, most of us will earn in excess of a million dollars throughout our working life. Consider the incredible resources that God has entrusted to your hands:

Between now and age 65 you will earn the following amount:

Your Age Today	YOUR MONTHLY INCOME			
	$2,000	$3,000	$4,000	$5,000
25	$960,000	$1,440,000	$1,920,000	$2,400,000
30	840,000	1,260,000	1,680,000	2,100,000
35	720,000	1,080,000	1,440,000	1,800,000
40	600,000	900,000	1,200,000	1,500,000
45	480,000	720,000	960,000	1,200,000
50	360,000	540,000	720,000	900,000
55	240,000	360,000	480,000	600,000

These figures reveal the enormous economic resources you have the opportunity to administer during your life. But the question is: How much of this fortune will you retain to use for your retirement? Ultimately, it is not what you earn, but what you save and invest that will produce financial success or failure in your later years. If you can discipline yourself to save even ten percent of your monthly earnings, you can invest these funds to help achieve true financial independence for you and your family.

The Goal: Financial Independence

Why do so many people fail to save and invest? Saving money is still a good idea. Who knows—perhaps one day money will be valuable again!

Financial independence can be defined as accumulating an amount of capital that will produce a stream of guaranteed income that is sufficient to meet your financial needs without the help of a salary. Financial independence is a practical goal that can be achieved if you let some fundamental principles of finance go to work for you.

The reason the majority of people reach retirement without achieving financial independence is that they neglect to properly invest the resources God gave them during their working years. They do not plan to fail; they simply fail to plan for financial success! Many people have had the experience of trying and failing to develop a workable budget and savings plan. They cash their paycheck, pay their bills and living expenses, and hope to save some money out of the surplus that is left at the end of the month. The problem is, you will never have any cash left to save at the end of the month.

For most of us, the only practical solution is to change our entire saving strategy. The principle is simple but fundamental; when you cash your paycheck, pay yourself first by depositing ten percent of your check into your savings account. Then pay your outstanding bills and living expenses out of the remaining funds. For people who are living hopelessly from paycheck to paycheck, this simple but profound change can mark the first step on the road toward financial success.

You may feel that you cannot afford to save ten percent of your income because you are too deep in debt. But in reality, you cannot afford to delay beginning your savings plan. The best way to end your financial bondage to debt is to take control of your finances by beginning your savings plan today. If you cannot commit to saving ten percent of your income, then begin at five percent and gradually increase the percentage over time. However, the key is to begin today. Will there ever be a better time to begin taking control of your financial destiny? Promise yourself that you will begin today to follow a plan that will lead you and your family to financial freedom.

Budgeting

Perhaps you've heard the saying, "When your outgo exceeds your income, then your upkeep will be your downfall."

The second step to gaining control over your finances is to establish a basic budget that will allow you to set targets, establish goals, and maintain financial discipline. Many people have no idea where their money goes; it just seems to disappear every month. Someone once said, "Living on a budget is exactly the same as living beyond your means except now you will have a record of it."

A budget is a way to take control of your money and begin using your God-given resources to achieve your financial goals. I am not suggesting that you should record every single penny you spend. Rather, plan a budget that helps you to make basic decisions about allocating your income and keep track of your expenses in that budget. Many banks and bookstores have excellent budget books available that will help you plan your monthly and yearly expenditures.

The key to successful budgeting is to be flexible and realistic about the actual amounts you are spending on various categories. Estimate your income conservatively, but overestimate your expenditures. A budget should not be a financial straitjacket, but a simple way to keep track of where your money is going so that you will be able to take control and redirect it in a manner that enables you to achieve your goals.

Here's another maxim about budgeting: "A budget is a financial plan adopted to prevent part of the month being left at the end of your money."

You should ask yourself these basic questions at the end of each year:

1. Have I succeeded in saving a significant portion of my money during the last year?

2. Have I succeeded in paying off a significant portion of my debts?

If your answer to these two questions is yes, then you are beginning to move in the right direction in your financial life. However, if you answered no to both questions, then you need to make some changes in your budget and strategy.

Living on Credit

Credit is a useful financial tool that can help you to purchase a car or home that you could never own otherwise. However, the misuse of credit has brought many people to the brink of financial disaster. Marriage counselors tell us that arguments over money, debts, and credit card bills are a major reason that many marriages end in divorce.

Because our finances are such an integral part of our lives, learning to control our use of credit and creating financial stability can enormously improve our marriages as well as our spiritual lives. The Bible warns about the dangers of debt because of the financial bondage it can create. In the book of Proverbs we are commanded to pay our bills when they are due. We should not delay our repayment if we have the means to repay. "Do not withhold good from those to whom it is due, when it is in the power of your hand to do so. Do not say to your neighbor, 'Go, and come back, and tomorrow I will give it,' when you have it with you" (Proverbs 3:27,28).

If you are unable to pay a debt on time, call your lender—then confirm in writing that you have a legitimate problem. Indicate when you will make the required payment. Lenders will often cooperate with you if you are suffering a temporary problem. However, lenders become annoyed when a creditor falls behind and does not explain the situation. Your reputation for paying your bills on time is vital in building your financial independence. Reliability in paying your bills is also critical to your Christian testimony.

Gaining Control of Your Credit

Taking the following steps will go a long way toward keeping your credit under control:

1. Ask yourself: Do I really need to buy this item with credit? Can I purchase it with cash? If you are going to buy something with credit, first calculate very conservatively how much of your income you can safely devote to credit payments. Remember to include a safety margin of over ten percent of your monthly income to be kept in reserve above normal expenses, tithing, and existing credit obligations.

2. Shop very carefully for credit because interest rates, user fees, and credit terms vary widely among banks and other financial institutions. Check the total cost of your credit cards against the cost of cards offered by other lenders. Shop as carefully for your credit as you would for a desired item in a store. The true

annual interest cost for many credit cards is outrageous. Some credit cards charge the user as much as 18 to 24 percent interest or higher. Avoid using the overdraft privileges offered by many banks. The interest rate for this benefit is often extremely high.

3. Avoid the credit card trap that encourages many consumers to habitually carry unpaid credit card balances from month to month. They are paying extremely high interest rates for these unpaid balances. Wise users of credit cards pay off their full outstanding balance every single month and thereby use the bank's funds interest-free.

   Ideally, you should use no more than two or three credit cards, including one of the major universally accepted ones such as VISA, MasterCard, or American Express. If your credit card balances are so high that you cannot pay them off in a few months, consider arranging a personal bank loan or personal line of credit at a much lower interest rate to pay off the outstanding balances on your credit cards. Then repay the new low-interest bank loan as quickly as possible. Don't ever allow your newly paid-off credit card balances to creep up beyond the level where you can repay them at the end of each month.

4. Avoid using credit for consumer items that depreciate quickly, such as a television or

appliances. If you cannot afford to pay cash, perhaps you should simply wait a little while until you can save up enough money to make the purchase. Paying with cash tends to reinforce in your mind the actual cost of your purchase.

5. Use credit primarily for the purchase of major items, such as a home or a car—items that you could not purchase otherwise.

6. Whenever you borrow, make sure that you arrange to pay off the loans as quickly as you can to minimize the cost of borrowing. The homeowner who arranges to make advance prepayments on his mortgage can save an enormous amount of future interest charges and pay off his mortgage years earlier. This strategy is covered in greater detail later in this chapter.

Credit is a lot like fire. When you are in control of it, you'll find it to be a valuable servant. However, if your credit gets out of control, it can ruin your life financially. While other people or the economy usually have a minimal influence on your finances, credit can have a major impact.

You can improve your own financial future in a major way through changing your (1) attitudes, (2) goals, and (3) actions. First, your attitude should include a strong desire to succeed, a willingness to overcome obstacles, and an ability to continually analyze your plans and their results. Next, you should begin to take control of your money by setting definite financial goals. These goals should be high enough to motivate you but they must also be realistic enough so that you can truly believe that they are attainable. Finally, you need to follow through with a set of balanced financial strategies based on the Word of God and a sound analysis of the special risks and opportunities in today's economy. Ask yourself, "If I achieve the same financial results in the next five years, as I have this past five years, will I be satisfied?" If your answer to this question is no, you need to commit to changing your financial strategy.

Setting Goals Is Vital to Financial Success

Setting financial goals is necessary if you truly want to succeed financially. You cannot succeed by being a spectator; you need to study your financial options, make decisions, and then invest.

Financial success can be described as the progressive realization of your predetermined financial goals. However, many studies reveal that most people have inadequate and vague financial goals. A major study revealed that 27 percent of Americans have no financial goals at all and usually arrive at retirement with less than $25,000 in assets plus a meager government pension. Sixty percent of people have only the vaguest of financial goals; they will barely survive with modest personal assets of $50,000 plus their government pension. Ten percent of those surveyed have some verbal financial goals but never put them in writing. However, it is fascinating to note that this group still accumulates an average of

$250,000—more than ten times the retirement assets of those who have no goals at all. Finally, only three percent of Americans have clearly defined, written financial goals. As a result, this select group accumulated considerably more than one million dollars in personal assets at retirement! The bottom line is this: If you are not setting goals to succeed financially, then you are actually planning for failure. The choice is yours.

It is worthwhile to sit down and establish some meaningful financial and life goals at least once every year. Then a year later, you should review your accomplishments compared to your written goals from a year earlier.

One of the highlights my wife, Kaye, and I celebrate annually around New Year's Day is another year of ministry. We go to a favorite restaurant, bring along our Goals and Objectives book, and record the accomplishments that we made during the past year. Then we prayerfully discuss and outline our new goals and objectives for the year to come.

These goals cover three time intervals and encompass several distinct categories. The time intervals are 1) short-term (less than one year), 2) intermediate (two to three years), and 3) long-term (five to ten years). The categories include: 1) financial: savings and asset buildup, debt reduction, and income objectives; 2) Ministry: a new book, new videos, conferences, foreign mission trips, and so on; 3) Personal: vacations, education, physical, and so on; 4) Material: home improvement, car, computer equipment, and so on.

Setting goals together and recording our accomplishments as God blesses our endeavors makes for one of the most satisfying moments of the year. It is an opportunity to prayerfully ask the Lord for His direction in our lives in relation to future goals and objectives. In addition, this exercise reminds us of the tremendous blessings God has granted us. We who live in North America should recognize that we enjoy enormous economic blessings and advantages than are greater than those that 98 percent of the world's population have ever experienced in all time. We should thank God every day for His rich blessings to us and recognize our responsibilities as stewards of the abundant resources the Lord has placed in our hands.

How well are you doing with your finances? You should calculate your net worth at least once every year to see how much progress you are making toward achieving your goal of financial independence. Add up your total assets and deduct the amount of your total debts to arrive at your net worth. For example, if you have $220,000 in total assets—including your home, car, furniture, investments, and so on; and you owe $120,000 on your mortgage, car, credit cards, and so on; then you have a net worth of $100,000.

It is very motivational to note your progress year after year as you begin to improve your net worth by increasing your assets, reducing your debts, and implementing your financial goals and plans. The annual review process can motivate you to continue maintaining the financial discipline that is necessary to achieve financial independence.

A Word About Investing

Investing and the Power of Compound Interest

The astonishing power of compound interest is fundamental to your investment strategies for achieving financial independence. Significantly, Baron Rothschild, one of the richest men in history, called compound interest the "eighth wonder of the world." If you allow yourself to become mired in growing debt, however, compound interest works against you. But it can be a wonderful tool for multiplying the investment funds you set aside each month.

For example, if you could save $1,000 every year (only $83.33 per month) from age 35 to age 65 at an average of ten percent interest, you would accumulate $164,494—a significant addition to your Social Security or government pension plan. Now, your bank savings account should be only a temporary place to store your funds while they accumulate. Once the account has grown to $2,500 to $5,000, you should explore other investment options that will pay much higher interest or investment returns than your regular bank savings account.

Government Savings Bonds

One of the safest and easiest investment choices for the conservative investor is government savings

bonds offered by both the U.S. and Canadian governments. Since these savings bonds are backed by the
taxation power of the federal government and the
government must pay the interest due if they wish
to borrow additional funds in the future, these savings bonds are virtually without risk for the next five
years or so (until the government begins to hyperinflate the currency).

Government savings bonds can usually be purchased in various denominations from any financial
institution. Some government savings bonds pay
regular interest every year, while others compound
the interest over the duration of the bond. Usually,
compound savings bonds provide a higher rate of return. Also, instead of buying a $5,000 government
savings bond, consider buying five $1,000 bonds.
This strategy gives you the option of surrendering
one or two of the smaller bonds rather than surrendering the $5,000 bond when you need some
emergency cash.

Tax-Free Municipal Bonds

In America, one bond investment that offers major
tax advantages is tax-free municipal bonds that are
issued by cities to raise funds. If the city issuing the
bond is in sound financial shape, this can be an excellent way to invest your funds conservatively
while earning tax-free interest. You can check on the
financial risk for a particular city's tax-free municipal bonds through Standard and Poor's or Moody's
Bond Rating Service. Ask your broker for a research
report and a bond rating. The safest bond rating

available is AAA. Avoid investing in bonds that are rated below A-grade.

This type of investment has advantages for a taxpayer in the 28 percent tax bracket or higher for the next five years or so until hyperinflation begins.

Treasury Bills

Treasury bills (T-bills) are government-backed investments that are fully secured by the taxation authority of the federal government. They, too, are safe investments for the next five years until we reach the period of hyperinflation.

T-bills are investment vehicles in which an investor lends the government a significant amount of funds for a period of 91, 182, or 364 days at a competitive interest rate. T-bills have the same level of security as government savings bonds but are usually available only in large denominations of $50,000 or more.

Rather than paying an interest rate, T-bills are sold to you at a discount and the government returns the full amount to you at maturity. The difference represents your interest return. For example, if you purchase a 180-day T-bill for $97,000, six months later the government might pay you $100,000, depending on interest rates. This $3,000 gain (interest) is exempt from state and local taxes for Americans; however, you are subject to federal income tax on these earnings.

In the past, only wealthy investors were able to purchase Treasury bills. However, various stockbrokers have recently started a secondary market in

T-bills that allows small investors to place several thousand dollars in T-bills. You can purchase T-bills from any investment broker, bank, or directly by mail from the Federal Reserve. T-bills are especially advantageous for investors who live in a state that levies high state income taxes.

Corporate Bonds

Bonds issued by corporations function in the same manner as those issued by governments except they are not backed by the same level of security. Corporate bonds are usually secured by the assets of the issuing corporations. However, it is very difficult for the average investor to accurately determine the true financial strength of a corporation from simply reading its published financial and annual reports. In light of the many corporate bond defaults in the last few years, I would recommend that you avoid corporate bonds at this time unless you are a professional investor.

Common Stocks and Mutual Funds

Over 63 million Americans are now invested in the stock markets. While millions of people own shares directly, most investors have placed their money in one of the more than 4,000 mutual funds that have started since 1980. Rather than own the shares directly, a mutual fund investor owns units of the mutual fund. The mutual fund itself actually owns the shares or other investments. Other investors prefer to purchase individual equities and stocks directly in the hopes of earning either dividends or capital gains.

Based on the excellent average returns of 17 percent per year or more that have been earned by many mutual funds during the last few years, many naive investors have come to believe that they will automatically achieve great returns and run little risk by continuing to invest in mutual funds. They are very mistaken. Most mutual fund companies point to their past track record and imply that this is an indication of expected future results. However, after five or so years of great returns, the markets are at an all-time speculative high and are ripe for a crash.

We are presently experiencing the greatest speculative stock market in this century. I believe it is only a matter of time before we see a major drop in the price of shares. The stock market is now so high that average shares are trading at a Price/Earnings ratio of 27. This means that average share prices are so high it would take 27 years to receive enough dividends to earn back the price you paid for the stock. A more normal Price/Earnings ratio is between 10 and 15. Since today's dividend earnings are so low compared to the share price, investors are buying these inflated stocks at high prices in the vain hope that share prices will go still higher. That is a prescription for disaster. In addition, the stock and bond markets are both threatened by the volatile financial derivatives market, which has $42 trillion at risk at this time.

The managers running these mutual funds have abandoned to a great degree the fundamental safeguards that were designed, after the 1929 crash, to protect these funds from future disaster. For the last 45 years mutual funds have operated under restrictions that prohibited them from engaging in risky and speculative practices. However, since 1990, competitive pressures have driven many of these funds to drastically alter these restrictive rules to allow them to purchase into very risky investment strategies. For example, many mutual funds are now speculating unwisely by purchasing securities on margin and selling shares short. These funds are also buying shares for the first time in very high-risk companies that are less than three years old. Some mutual funds are speculatively buying shares in other mutual funds rather than making direct investments in the shares of companies. Several funds have even gone so far as to allow the mutual fund to purchase shares of companies in which the officers and trustees of the mutual fund have acquired significant share positions. This leaves the mutual fund open to massive conflicts of interest between the best interests of the individual fund investors and the managers of the fund. All of these factors together suggest that, at the moment, mutual funds are not a safe place to put your funds.

As I pointed out in chapter 14, I believe that we are standing on the brink of a major stock and bond market collapse. Unless you are a professional investor, I would strongly recommend that you consider transferring your existing investments in stocks or mutual funds into more conservative and secure investments until after the stock market experiences a significant correction. After the stock market drops, there will be excellent opportunities for prudent investors to purchase shares of stock in solid corporations at a fraction of the cost before the market crash.

Money Market Funds

These investment funds are a form of mutual fund offered by stockbrokers and financial institutions. Money market funds invest your money in short-term financial securities such as T-bills, bonds, or commercial short-term loans offered by corporations. Instead of owning a bond or T-bill directly, an investor will own a unit in the money market fund that actually owns the underlying T-bill or bond. The usual minimum investment will be around $1,000 with the earned interest either paid out to the investor every month or reinvested to purchase additional units of the fund.

Money market funds calculate the interest generated by the fund's investments every day. A major advantage of these funds is that they are highly liquid, but they are subject to severe losses when interest rates are as volatile as they are today. A disadvantage, however, is that they are not protected by federal deposit insurance. While money market funds are extremely easy for investors to use, one of the dangers is that you as an investor own only units or shares in the fund. You do not directly own the underlying financial security, such as the government T-bill or savings bond. Also, if the managers of the money market fund guess incorrectly about the direction of future interest rates, you could lose a substantial portion of your investment. And, in a day when many of these funds are taking big risks by investing in the unregulated financial derivatives market, it may be wise to avoid such funds at this time. Instead, consider investing directly in whatever investments you judge are appropriate as far as the level of risk and possible rate of return.

Term Deposits

Term deposits are offered by various financial institutions, including banks, as a vehicle for investing larger amounts of money ($5,000 plus) for 90, 180, or 364 days. Term deposits tend to pay less interest than Guaranteed Investment Certificates (which we'll read about in a moment), but they have the virtue of not being locked in. Term deposits can be surrendered for cash at any time before their maturity date, although you will lose a significant amount of the interest you would otherwise have earned at maturity.

Term deposits issued by strong financial institutions offer excellent security. They are a good, safe place to "park" your investment funds for 90 days to six months while waiting to see which way the financial market is going before you select longer-term investment vehicles.

Canadian investors might consider investing funds in a U.S. Dollar Term Deposit sold by Canadian banks if they believe that, due to the continuing constitutional crisis in Quebec, the Canadian dollar is likely to drop lower in value over the next few years.

Guaranteed Investment Certificates; Certificates of Deposits

Guaranteed Investment Certificates (GICs) or Certificates of Deposit (CDs) are sold by banks and other financial institutions as a medium-term investment. The advantage for most investors is the guaranteed rate of compound interest and the higher rate of interest offered for the longer-term GICs. The disadvantage is that your funds remain locked in for one to five years. However, there is a way you can obtain your money if an emergency arises. As long as the GIC is transferable, a number of stockbrokers will offer to purchase your GIC at a discount.

GIC certificates are medium-term vehicles that should be purchased by investors who are prepared to invest these funds for several years or more. The business section of the newspapers publish the various interest rates offered by various financial institutions on Guaranteed Investment Certificates. These investment vehicles are ideal when interest rates are high but should probably be avoided if interest rates are volatile. It is essential that you check out the financial strength of the bank offering the GIC (see the list of references at the end of the book).

Protection for the Future

The Inflation-Interest Rate Strategy

When the banks' prime lending rate (the rate charged to their best customers) has risen more than three percent in a few months, it is a good indication that we are entering a period of high interest and high inflation. In such a situation, you'll want to consider placing your money in shorter-term investment vehicles, such as T-bills or short Term Deposits at a strong bank at the highest interest rate available. When these investments mature, you should keep renewing them as long as interest rates continue rising. Then, when you believe that interest rates have peaked, transfer your funds into the highest interest-rate long-term investment available, such as a Guaranteed Investment Certificate issued by a strong bank. This strategy will lock in those high interest-earning rates for a number of years.

The Risk of Hyperinflation

There is a growing danger of hyperinflation in North America in the late 1990s as our governments finally "hit the wall" financially after decades of irresponsible borrowing. In the United States the national debt now exceeds $7 trillion and the compounding interest on that debt is growing rapidly. In Canada, the national debt exceeds $680 billion and the interest charges are growing so quickly that our total federal tax revenue will soon be insufficient to cover it. Some economists have calculated that the total federal tax revenues in both the United States and Canada will be insufficient to pay the interest on our national debt by 1998 or 1999. At that point the government will be forced to hyperinflate the currency in order to produce the needed additional funds to pay for social services, interest charges on the national debt, and the daily cost of operating the government.

The warning signs preceding hyperinflation will be apparent for some time before the crisis takes place. We will witness growing wage demands, rapidly rising prices, large swings in stock prices, a declining value in our currency against the stronger Japanese and German currencies, and ever-growing government deficits.

Though hyperinflation will wipe out most investors, there are still a few survival strategies available for the prudent person. Once you determine that we are heading into a period of hyperinflation, consider selling as many of your fixed long-term investments as possible so that your assets are more liquid. You may have to pay substantial surrender charges to withdraw your fixed term funds. However, in a time of raging hyperinflation, if you hold onto investments in bonds, pensions, annuities, and fixed-income funds, you will lose significantly more than the surrender charges would cost.

Hyperinflation will destroy the economies of the United States and Canada as it has many other economies in this century. Following World War I, the Weimar Republic of Germany experienced the nightmare of raging inflation from 1918 to 1923. That crisis destroyed the life savings of most of the German people. Prices rose astronomically and millions lost their jobs. This set the stage for the rise of Adolf Hitler. To give you an idea of how severe the inflation was, a pound of butter cost one German mark. By 1923 the same pound of butter cost hundreds of millions of marks. People had to use wheelbarrows to carry the enormous stacks of paper marks needed to buy their groceries. Factories paid their workers every two hours and let them off work so they could quickly buy food before the newly printed marks became worthless! In the photo section I show a 100 million mark German bank note from 1923 that would not cover the cost of a lunch!

Since that time, other sophisticated countries—including Brazil, Argentina, Chile, and Russia—have also experienced hyperinflation. Argentina was one of the world's strongest economies in the first decade of this century. However, since World War I, the currencies of Brazil, Chile, and Argentina have devalued to the point where they are worth less than one-tenth of one percent of their value in 1915.

During the coming period of hyperinflation, the stock market will become quite volatile as inflation surges higher. Mutual funds should be avoided during hyperinflation by all but those who have the strongest of nerves. In a time leading toward hyper-inflation, you should first liquidate your fixed long-term assets. Then consider transferring your cash into precious metals, stable foreign currencies, and other conservative investments in countries that are not experiencing hyperinflation. Increasing your investment in precious metals from ten percent to as much as 35 percent of your investment assets may be appropriate. As for foreign currencies, the Swiss franc, the currency of Switzerland, is fully backed by gold and is therefore a strong and stable currency. An investment in a Swiss franc bank account, annuity, or bond, though it pays a lower interest rate, will provide you with unparalleled security.

Always keep in mind the wise phrase, "This too will pass." Even after a disastrous period of hyperinflation, the crisis will someday end and stability will return. Those who have avoided losses and retained their assets and cash by wisely shielding themselves from the ravages of inflation will be in a position to purchase quality investments at phenomenal discounts.

Gold and Silver

Gold possesses a number of characteristics that makes it the best financial investment available for storing monetary value over a long period of years. Fortunately, governments cannot print gold the same way they print paper currency. Consequently, over the centuries, gold has retained an almost constant value, and people have relied on it as the ultimate safeguard for their assets.

Gold has the following characteristics: It is indestructible, compact, scarce, and portable. The chairman of the U.S. Federal Reserve system, Alan Greenspan, told Congress in February 1994, "Gold is a different type of commodity because virtually all of the gold that has ever been produced still exists." He continued,

> Therefore changes in the level of production have very little effect on the ongoing price, which means that it's virtually wholly a monetary demand phenomenon. It's a store of value measure which has shown a fairly consistent lead on inflation

expectations, and has been over the years a reasonably good
indicator. It does this better than commodity prices or a lot of
other things.

This is a rather amazing admission about the value
of gold from an international banker!

The tremendously inflationary monetary expan-
sion created by the Federal Reserve during the last
few years virtually guarantees that we will face massive increases in inflation in the last years of the
1990s. This strongly suggests that the prices of gold
and silver are likely to rise substantially in the years
ahead. Gold and silver, then, should form part of a
balanced, long-term investment strategy.

Gold is not a speculative investment vehicle for
quick profits. Back in 1979 and 1980, the prices of
gold and silver rose to the highest levels in history:
$875 for an ounce of gold and $53 for an ounce of
silver. Naturally, after millions of investors had
watched the exhilarating rise in gold and silver
prices for several months, they belatedly decided to
buy near the top of the market in the naive hope of
"buying high and selling higher." But in the months
that followed, the prices of both precious metals collapsed to $287 an ounce for gold and $3.51 for silver.

Consider investing in precious metals over the
long-term as part of your balanced portfolio. Gold
and silver should form between ten and 25 percent of
your normal investment portfolio. The basic ratio-
nale for placing some of your investment funds in
gold and silver is prudence and insurance. For thousands of years, both metals have remained the stable

and universal medium of exchange. Back in the early 1920s a man could buy a good-quality suit with an ounce of gold. Despite the massive financial changes during the last 70 years, an ounce of gold will still buy a good-quality suit today.

Unlike paper currency, which is always subject to devaluation by government-produced inflation, gold and silver remain in limited quantity so they will not lose their true values. In the event of hyperinflation, an investment in gold and silver will provide significant protection for an investor. In the case of a complete financial collapse, the person who wisely purchased precious metals in the form of gold and silver coins will have purchasing power when other people will be left with increasingly worthless currency.

Aside from a minimum of ten and 15 percent of your funds in precious metals, you should also consider increasing your purchases of gold and silver when you see signs of rising inflation and severe economic problems. The warning indicators that hyperinflation is approaching are significant rises in real wages, rising basic commodities prices, and massive government deficits.

As we approach the late 1990s, both the United States and Canada will find their national debts at a level that forces the governments to spend almost all our tax money on the interest on their debts. At the point when international borrowing becomes extremely difficult for the governments, their Treasuries will begin to secretly hyperinflate currency. In such a scenario, the rate of inflation will skyrocket beyond anything ever experienced before in North American history. Those investors who wisely placed significant funds in gold and silver will be well rewarded.

In 1935, President Roosevelt made it illegal for Americans to own gold bullion. But they could still own semi-numismatic gold coins because they were legal tender as coins and they had collector value because of their rarity. Though President Ford made bullion ownership legal again in 1974, many financial planners believe that investors should hold their gold in the form of semi-numismatic coins because of the historic precedent set by Roosevelt's confiscation of bullion in 1935.

People who choose to invest in gold bullion can purchase it in small units, bars, or wafers of various sizes. Since there is a charge for each bar on top of the price of the gold itself, it is to your advantage to buy the largest bar you can afford. Be sure the gold bar is stamped by a reputable refiner such as Johnson Matthey or Handy & Harman. These refiners guarantee the purity of their gold (usually .9999 fine).

Avoid newspaper or mail offers to buy gold or silver. Many investors lost their money when they sent a check in response to an advertisement and never received the gold. Purchase your gold from a large dealer or bank after shopping around for the lowest commission and bar charges. A safety-deposit box is recommended for storing your precious metal investments. And remember, the cost of the safe deposit box is tax-deductible.

Many investors prefer gold or silver coins because of their portability, universal liquidity, and negotiability. For example, one-ounce gold coins are readily available from dealers and banks. Recommended one-ounce coins include the Canadian Maple Leaf, the South African Krugerrand, and the American Eagle. In addition to the price of the gold itself, the coin's price will include a premium of ten percent or more for a one-tenth-of-an-ounce coin, while a one-ounce coin will bear a three-and-a-half percent premium. When you resell the coins you will recover some portion of the premium. Obviously, it is to your advantage to purchase larger coins to avoid excessive premium charges. Also, depending on the province or state you live in, you may have to pay sales tax on your gold purchase.

Purchase your gold or silver coins from a reputable dealer or large financial institution after checking for the lowest premium available. You'll also want to get protective holders so your coins don't get scratches; that would reduce their value to another purchaser. And finally, it is unwise to leave your gold or silver in the possession of the seller in return for a certificate. Demand physical delivery of your bullion or coins. A number of investors have lost their complete investment when the dealer "holding their coins" subsequently went bankrupt.

The secret to financial success in the precious metals market is simple: Buy low and sell high! Everyone knows that rule but very few investors actually follow it. Most people buy high and sell low. The public was not interested in buying gold when it was available for only $35 an ounce. However, when gold reached its market high of $700 to $800 an ounce, suddenly everyone wanted to buy. Unfortunately, by that time, it was too late to buy. Their intent was to buy high, but sell even higher. This practice usually ends in disaster, for once the price begins to drop the poor, hapless investor rides the market roller coaster all the way down while hoping against hope that the price will rebound any day.

Don't get carried away with media and market hype. Watch the herd of investors and avoid following their mistakes. Remember, everything changes. While the majority of investors act as though either recession or the boom will continue forever, they are always wrong. Recessions always end and market booms will eventually crash. You should purchase gold and silver as a long-term investment that acts as a financial insurance policy.

Real Estate: Making Your Home Your Best Investment

Home ownership is one of the great pleasures of life. In addition, it is one of the best financial investments available to the average investor. One of the keys to success in real estate is to lock in your profits when you first purchase the property. If you buy the right property at the right time at the right price, you will virtually guarantee yourself a profitable transaction. Research is the key. Find the best real estate agent in your community and cultivate a good relationship with him or her. Buy quality real estate from a motivated seller—someone who has a legitimate motive to sell his or her property at a good price. You can discover the seller's motivation through friendly, probing questions. Listen carefully. Once you understand the seller's motive, you can then try to help them obtain what they want while you obtain what you want. Try to arrange a win-win situation where both the seller and the buyer act with integrity and receive what they want out of the deal.

How Much Can I Afford to Spend for My House?

To determine how much of a home you can afford, you should consider this rule of thumb: Your down payment should be approximately 25 percent of the price of the house. Mortgage lenders usually calculate your ability to afford a given mortgage payment by applying a formula they call the Gross Debt Service Ratio. The basic rule is that you can afford to spend only a maximum of 30 percent of your gross monthly income on your mortgage payment along with your real estate taxes.

Another measure of your ability to comfortably handle your mortgage payments is known as the Total Debt Service Ratio formula. This formula says that your total payments for indebtedness—including other loans, credit cards, and mortgage payment plus real estate taxes—should not exceed 40 percent of your gross monthly income.

These ratios that are used by mortgage lenders are also excellent guidelines you can use to determine how much you can afford to spend on a home.

How to Make Your Mortgage Work for You

Home ownership is one of the most powerful tools you can use to achieve financial independence. Most of us could never purchase a house unless we borrowed the funds through a mortgage loan with a financial institution. Unfortunately, most mortgage amortization schedules require payments over a period of 25 to 30 years, which means the average homeowner ends up paying a total of two to three times the original price of the house!

In the first few years after buying a home, virtually all of your mortgage payments will go toward paying the interest costs with almost no reduction of the outstanding mortgage balance (or the principal). For example, with a typical 25-year $100,000 mortgage bearing an interest rate of 8.5 percent, the homeowner will make payments of $805 every month for 25 years. This homeowner will have paid a total of $241,568.13, before they own the home free and clear.

When you buy a home, ask your mortgage lender to provide you with a full amortization schedule showing the actual amount that goes toward principal from each mortgage payment. This schedule should help motivate you to prepay your mortgage as quickly as possible so you can achieve some remarkable savings in the long run.

Prepaying Your Mortgage

Making voluntary prepayments on your mortgage is one of the most significant investment decisions you can make toward improving your financial life. Your savings on future interest charges will be astronomical. In effect, you are actually depositing your prepayments into "your own private bank" by increasing your equity in your home. If you should ever need to access emergency funds you can easily borrow against your increased home equity.

Consider the following situation for Bob, a typical homeowner who has a 25-year $100,000 mortgage at nine percent interest. By making a prepayment of only $1,200 every year, Bob can save $50,365 in interest *and* pay off his mortgage seven years ahead of schedule. Since most other available investments are taxable, assuming a tax rate of 40 percent, Bob would have to earn 15 percent before taxes on his $1,200 annual taxable investment to achieve the same economic benefit as prepaying $1,200 annually on his nine-percent mortgage. There are very few other investments that will provide you with the same security and flexibility and guarantee such a high rate of return.

Here are three successful strategies you can use to enhance your investment in your home.

1. Increase your monthly mortgage payment at renewal. One of the most effective strategies you can follow is to renegotiate your mortgage on renewal to arrange the shortest possible amortization schedule (payment period) and the largest possible monthly payment that you can comfortably afford. Using the example of the homeowner on the previous

page, who paid $805 a month, by simply increasing the monthly payments by $200 to $1,005 this same homeowner will save $67,840 in future interest charges. In addition, he or she will pay off the mortgage ten years early (in only 14.5 years).

2. Request that your bank allow you to make your mortgage payments once every two weeks rather than once a month. Although you are paying virtually the same amount over the year, the fact that each biweekly mortgage payment is applied to the outstanding mortgage two weeks earlier results in substantial savings. In addition, you will pay down your mortgage even faster because you will have added the equivalent of one additional month's payment every year on this system.

3. Make an annual prepayment of up to ten percent of your outstanding principal every anniversary date of your mortgage. The full amount of these prepayments will be applied to paying down your outstanding principal, which will save enormously on your future interest charges and allow you to fully own your home years ahead of schedule.

Prepayment of your mortgage is simply one of the best financial strategies you can use. The earlier you begin prepayments, the greater the financial benefit. Even a small prepayment in the early years of your loan will save a huge amount in future interest payments.

The day you finally pay off your mortgage will be one of the great milestones in your financial life. When you make your last payment, make sure your lawyer gets a written statement from your mortgage lender that your mortgage was paid in full. In addition, your lawyer should check with the local title registry office and remove the mortgage registered against your property.

Renewing your mortgage is another way to save some money. Shop around for the best rates available several months in advance of your renewal date because it can take a number of weeks to transfer a mortgage to another lender. If you believe that interest rates are declining, choose a short-term mortgage (six months or one year would be appropriate). Later, when you believe interest rates have reached a low point, you should lock in these low rates by renewing your mortgage with the longest term available.

How Canadians Can Make Their Mortgages Tax Deductible

For many years, American homeowners have been allowed to use the interest portion of their mortgage payments as an income tax deduction. Unfortunately, in Canada, the government will not allow homeowners to deduct the interest they pay on their mortgage. However, for astute investors, there is a little-known technique that can, in effect, make your mortgage payments tax deductible. The Canadian Income Tax Act allows a deduction from your income taxes for any interest payments you make on investment loans that are arranged for the purpose of earning income that will be taxable.

Let's assume that a Canadian has a $100,000 home mortgage and that he has also accumulated $100,000 or more in bonds, stocks, and other investments. He should liquidate his $100,000 in various investment vehicles and use this cash to pay off his mortgage. The house would now be mortgage-free. Then he would go to his bank and borrow $100,000 in a new investment loan for the purpose of making new investments. The investor would now use the increased equity in his home as collateral security for the new bank loan. Since this $100,000 loan was obtained for the purpose of purchasing T-bills, GICs, stocks, and so on, this person can legally deduct the interest portion of the loan payments. In a roundabout way, the investor has in effect made his mortgage payments deductible against his income tax. The Canadian courts have confirmed that this is acceptable.

Another option for Canadians who have a self-directed Registered Retirement Savings Plan is to invest the funds from the RRSP into the mortgage. If the interest rate on your mortgage is higher than the return you could obtain by investing in alternative outside investments, this could be a worthwhile investment and tax strategy. However, the income tax rules for this procedure are quite strict, so you should definitely consult your accountant to make sure it is worthwhile in your case. Your accountant can make sure that the detailed paperwork and special mortgage insurance is completed correctly.

CHAPTER 17

Preserving Your Assets in Dangerous Times

Estate planning can be defined as the orderly arrangement of your financial and legal affairs to assure that your estate is properly distributed to your beneficiaries with a minimum of legal problems and unnecessary estate taxes. Your purpose should be to create a plan today so that your debts can be paid off and your properties can be transferred to your heirs by gift, trust, or will. In addition, your plan should provide an adequate income to guarantee that your beneficiaries will be able to maintain a normal lifestyle after you are gone. The purchase of adequate life insurance will help assure your loved ones that they will be able to stay in their home and continue the lifestyle they enjoy today.

Some people fear that estate planning is expensive and appropriate only for those who are wealthy. However, with taxes, laws, and the economy being what they are today, we need to plan our estates as responsible stewards of the assets God has entrusted to us. Estate planning is not solely concerned with the issues of death and the provision of adequate income for our beneficiaries. We should also plan for the efficient ownership of all family properties during our lifetime. As Christians we are required by the laws of God to pay our fair and legal share of taxes. However, as citizens, we also have the legal and moral right to arrange our financial affairs in a manner that reduces our taxes. The U.S. Supreme Court ruled in the case of *Gregory vs. Helvering* (293 U.S. 465) that "the legal right of a taxpayer to decrease the amount of what otherwise would be his taxes, or altogether avoid them, by means which the law permits, cannot be doubted." Estate planning for most investors, then, should include individual tax counseling by an accountant and professionally prepared tax returns.

Estate Planning

If your estate is worth creating throughout your lifetime, then it is certainly worth spending a few hours every year with a professional insurance and financial planner to protect these assets for you and your family. In preparing your estate plan, it is important to consider your goals. For 18 years I was a Chartered Life Underwriter in the financial planning profession before being called into full-time ministry. During those years I would ask my clients the following questions to help them clarify their financial strategies, goals, and concerns:

How do you feel about:

1. Your obligations to your family?

2. Your spouse's ability to handle your estate assets after you are gone?

3. Your spouse making major family decisions in your absence?

4. Your family receiving a guaranteed annual income from your investments after you pass away?

5. The ability of your current retirement plans to meet your goal of a comfortable retirement?

6. The ability of your existing group insurance coverage, together with your personal life and disability insurance, to fully protect your loved ones if you should become disabled or suffer premature death?

Will Planning

Oftentimes we take the subject of wills lightly and laugh at jokes like the one about the man whose last will and testament began, "Being of sound mind, I spent it all." However, an up-to-date will is a vital part of your Christian stewardship. Many Christians do not have updated wills that reflect their current life situation and responsibilities. Unfortunately, if you do not prepare a will of your own and you die "intestate" (without a properly prepared and signed will), then the courts will distribute your assets among your next of kin according to a rigid formula that does not take into consideration the special needs of individual family members. In addition, the cost of distributing your assets will be much higher than if you had a proper will. If you do not have an immediate family and you die without a will, the government will seize your property in a procedure called "escheat." A properly drawn will, then, protects your heirs, minimizes taxes, and provides for the proper distribution of your assets to your beneficiaries.

If you are your family's primary breadwinner, you will need to make sure that your estate plan will provide an adequate ongoing income for your family to replace the salary you previously earned. Very few people will accumulate sufficient investment funds in their estate before their death to both pay any estate taxes and provide a guaranteed income for their family for a number of years. Premature death can intervene before you have time to accumulate a significant estate, leaving your family without the needed assets or guaranteed income. The solution to this problem is to have a well-written will and adequate amount of life insurance.

Who needs a will? Virtually everyone who is married, single, divorced, or widowed. In today's legal society, both spouses need to have a carefully drawn will that will provide for the proper distribution of the estate following the death of either spouse. Both husband and wife should be familiar with all their insurance policies, the location of all bank accounts, and the contents of safe-deposit boxes. Nothing is sadder than a widow living in poverty while the cash, stocks, and bonds of her deceased husband lie undiscovered in an unknown bank or safe-deposit box.

I strongly suggest that you utilize an attorney rather than use a mass-produced will form from a stationery store. The following questionnaire will help guide you through the preliminary steps you can take prior to visiting your attorney. By preparing yourself in this way, your attorney will find it much easier to advise you because you have already carefully considered most of the key issues regarding your estate. The questionnaire does not cover every eventuality, but it does draw attention to most of the points you should consider. A properly drawn will is so vital to the future of your family that it is most unwise to take the chance of making an error that your family will have to pay for.

Information for your will:

1. Full Name
   Spouse's Name
   Full names of children

2. Is it probable that other children may be born before you next amend your will?

3. Whom do you wish to appoint as your executor and trustee?

4. How do you wish to dispose of your house? To your spouse absolutely; to your spouse for life

with or without the power to sell or exchange; to your child or children equally; or should the house be sold and the proceeds added to the residue of the estate.

5. How do you wish to dispose of your household goods, personal effects, automobile, and so on? To specified beneficiaries? Or should these assets be sold and the proceeds added to the residue of your estate?

6. Do you wish to leave any specific bequests to particular individuals, charities, churches, or missions?

7. Do you wish to make special provisions in the event your spouse does not survive you for a period of 30 days?

8. Do you have any particular instructions regarding your burial? (Discuss this with your spouse so he or she will know your wishes.)

9. Do you own any real estate located outside of the country?

10. How do you wish to dispose of the residue of your estate after all debts, taxes, and special bequests are made?

    METHOD A. By outright gift or bequest to one or more persons? (For example, to your wife and/or children.)

    METHOD B. By providing a life income from your estate to one or more beneficiaries and then later distribute the capital or residue in a particular manner? (For example, to your wife for her lifetime and then later to your grown children.)

11. Whom do you wish to name as a guardian if you and your spouse die while the children are minors? This is vital. Find another like-minded couple who share your values and mutually agree that you will act as guardians for the other couple's children if they should both die prematurely.

12. In your will, do you want to provide for the expenses your guardian will incur in caring for and educating your children?

13. List the details of any other wishes, trusts, or provisions.

If you and your spouse carefully fill out this questionnaire (one for each of you) and discuss it with a qualified lawyer, he can prepare a will that properly protects your family and provides for the wise distribution of your estate according to your wishes. In addition, your attorney can advise you on how you can minimize taxes that might otherwise decrease your estate.

You should update your will after any major life change that alters the way your estate should be distributed when your die. For example, if a beneficiary or an executor dies or leaves the country, you should update your will. In addition, if you acquire or sell a business, your will may need to be updated.

It's true that if there are no major changes to your life situation and your will becomes decades old, it will still be valid. However, in this day of continuing changes in taxation and laws, it is prudent to review your will with a competent attorney every five to ten years.

Joint Ownership

Joint ownership of property is probably the most common method people use to transfer property at their death—partly because there is no initial cost to this method. Many individuals plan to transfer their property to their beneficiaries by adding their names to the title of the property as joint owners. However, while this is a popular option, there are many dangers to this method of estate planning. I strongly advise against joint ownership of property except for joint home ownership for husbands and wives. That's because joint ownership is the greatest source of problems when an attempt is made to transfer the property to someone other than the spouse.

While it is easy to add someone's name to a title on a property, if you change your mind, you cannot remove that person's name without his or her written permission or a court order. If you add your son or daughter's name to the title on your home in anticipation of transferring the home to your child at your death, you may face financial disaster if that child falls into deep debt or divorces his or her spouse. Your child's creditors could force the sale of your home or the spouse your child divorced might demand his or her share of your home as "joint marital property." Or, your co-owner might transfer his or her half of the title to someone else without your approval or knowledge. Also, if you choose to add a minor child as joint owner, you will be unable to sell or refinance the property without a court's approval because a minor cannot legally sign on his or her own behalf.

In light of the many horror stories where parents have lost their property through unwise use of joint ownership of property, I strongly advise you to consider waiting until your death to transfer your properties to your beneficiaries. Hold onto your property until you die. Many parents have transferred properties to children while still alive to avoid taxes and have lived to regret it. Situations change, and you may find that you need that property. Be prudent.

Living Trusts

Living trusts are actually "inter vivos revocable trusts" that allow a person to distribute his estate at his death without the legal and financial costs of probating a will. The courts can take as long as two years to probate your will through your executor, whereas a living trust can go into effect immediately. In addition, probating a will can produce executor and probate costs equal to as much as ten percent of your total estate. And probate exposes your affairs to the knowledge of other people because these are "public documents."

In relation to living trusts, "inter vivos" means that the trust comes into effect while you are still alive. That's unlike a testamentary trust, such as a will, that takes effect only at your death. Living trusts are also revocable, which means that as long as you are alive, you retain total control to change or cancel the trust. Your living trust becomes the owner of the assets you transfer to the trust, and it continues to live on legally after your death. Living trusts are not new nor are they a tax gimmick. They have been used successfully for hundreds of years to protect estate assets.

In the United States, many people are asking their lawyers to set up a living trust that will allow them to control their estate while they are alive, maintain total privacy, and avoid probate costs and delays in distributing the estate following their death. The advantage of a revocable living trust is that you can avoid probate at death while still controlling what happens if you become incapacitated before death. When you transfer assets into a revocable living trust you keep your estate out of probate court because, in effect, you no longer own those assets.

Your lawyer will inventory your assets and advise you of the best way to protect your estate from taxes and achieve your goals of protecting your interests while you are alive, even if you become incapacitated. In addition, he will include the proper clauses to allow for the transfer of your estate to your beneficiaries following your death.

When you and your lawyer set up your living trust, you will become the grantor or settlor and remain the only one who can make changes to your trust. You can choose to be the trustee of your trust, or you can make your spouse your co-trustee. If you die or become incapacitated, your trustee continues to control your estate without ever needing the probate court to get involved. Some individuals choose to appoint a professional corporate trustee, such as a trust company.

Regardless of who is appointed trustee, as long as you are medically competent, you can change the trustee at any time. In your trust document, you will name some trusted individual to act as the successor trustee in the event you become incapacitated. When you die, this successor trustee will act in the same manner as an executor for a will, except he or she will escape the costs, publicity, and the legal delays of reporting to a probate court.

In your living trust, you can name individuals or organizations as beneficiaries of the proceeds of your estate when you die. If you should become incapacitated by disease or accident your successor trustee will step in to administer your estate for your benefit as long as is required. However, because you have a living trust, there will be no court-appointed administrator. The person you select as your successor trustee has a legal fiduciary responsibility to act responsibly in your best interest financially.

FINAL WARNING

An Enduring Power of Attorney

Many people are in danger of losing control of their property or business in the event of an incapacitating injury or disease. In many states and provinces the government trustee will immediately step in and seize control of your assets and business should a doctor or hospital determine that you are temporarily incapacitated due to an accident, surgery, or illness. In the event of an accident or illness, the hospital or doctor is required by law to notify the government trustee that you are incapacitated. Also, your business can be destroyed in only a few months if your spouse is unable to pay the bills as they fall due. You don't want to shrug off the possibility that this would ever happen; statistics indicate that the risk of incapacity at some point in your life is significant.

The only way to prevent a government-appointed trustee from intervening in your affairs is to sign an Enduring Power of Attorney. In this document you can appoint your spouse or some other trusted individual to act on your legal behalf, continue operating your business or estate, and pay your bills. See your attorney to arrange for the mutual signing of an Enduring Power of Attorney with your spouse.

A "Living Will" or Power of Attorney for Personal Care

One of the growing concerns in this age of medical miracles is that a hospital will use their sophisticated medical technologies to keep you alive in a coma long after any hope of a meaningful life has disappeared. I strongly recommend that you discuss with your spouse and family whether or not you wish for a hospital to do that. In addition, you can appoint your spouse or a trusted friend to make decisions and "give or refuse to consent to treatment" that endeavors to maintain your life. This can be done by creating, with the help of your lawyer, a "living will" or a Power of Attorney for Personal Care. This will assure that your wishes will be carried out at a time that you are incapacitated and unable to communicate.

Life Insurance

Most of us recognize the importance of insuring our homes or cars against fire, accidents, and other perils. However, many people fail to properly insure their income, which supports everything else in their lives. You should find a qualified professional insurance broker or agent who can analyze your insurance needs and provide you with proper life insurance and disability insurance.

Our ability to earn an income is the greatest single financial asset we possess. The reality we all face is that our income will one day end due to retirement, disability, or premature death. While a wise investment program can accumulate enough capital to provide a guaranteed income when we retire, there is still the possibility that premature death will keep us from providing financial independence for our families.

Men who leave their wives and children without a proper guaranteed income seldom intended that result. They just never got around to providing the protection that was needed.

What kind of income will your family need to maintain their standard of living?

Annual gross income	Percentage of the gross income required to maintain the standard of living
Up to $24,000	65%
$24,001 to $32,000	60%
Over $32,000	50%

In addition to providing a guaranteed income, your life insurance policy should be large enough to pay off all your outstanding debts and mortgages. A debt should last no longer than the person who created it. The ability to pay off your house mortgage and any outstanding debts or business loans at death is one of the most obvious benefits of life insurance. A mortgage-free home is one of the greatest gifts a husband can give to his family when he is no longer there to bring home his paycheck.

Some husbands feel there is little need for life insurance because their wives are young and could easily remarry. However, statistics reveal that remarriage is actually very unlikely. Between the ages of 21 and 30 less than 25 percent of widows ever remarry. Less than 10 percent of widows between the ages of 30 and 40 will remarry (L.I.A.M.A. Study, 1971). If a widow has children, the odds against re-marriage are even greater. Therefore, families need a proper insurance plan to guarantee that the widow and children will continue to enjoy a home and the necessities of life.

How can you determine the proper amount of life insurance you need? While there are a number of sophisticated formulas that you can use, there is a fairly straightforward calculation that helps to deter-mine the amount of insurance needed to protect your family. (See page 442 for formula.)

Insuring Your Spouse

Another area of life insurance that many husbands fail to consider is insurance on their wives. When a wife dies before her husband it creates a financial hardship that may destroy the plans they shared for educating their children or a comfortable retirement. If a wife is working outside the home, her income should be fully insured in the same manner as the husband's. That's because a couple's lifestyle, includ-ing their mortgage and retirement plans, depend on the wife's income equally as much as the husband's. The loss of her income could wreak financial havoc. A solution to guaranteeing her income is a joint life insurance policy that will pay off whoever dies first. A joint term insurance policy can often provide sub-stantial savings on your insurance premiums be-cause it's cheaper than buying two separate policies.

Life Insurance Formula

- How much money will my family need
  to pay my debts?

- What is my annual income today?   **A**

- What percentage of my income do I   **B**
  want my family to receive?

- How much income is needed to fulfill   **%**
  ____% of my income?

- Assuming my family can earn 5 percent   **C**
  after taxes from the proceeds of my insurance policies, how much insurance is
  needed to provide the annual required
  income? _____

- Calculation: (Assume your widow will   **D**
  invest the insurance at 5 percent net)

- At 5 percent interest return: multiply
  the needed income _____ C × 20=

- Add the amount required to pay debts   **E**
  _____ A to the amount needed to pro-
  vide a guaranteed income _____D to
  calculate the total amount needed for
  insurance =

- How much group and personal life in-   **F**
  surance do I now have?

- Subtract the amount of your existing   **$**
  insurance _____F from the total insur-
  ance needed _____E to determine the
  amount of additional insurance needed
  to meet you family needs.

                        New insurance needed: **$_____**

Protection from Estate Taxes

Life insurance is also a useful financial tool for wealthy individuals who find that our government's demands for estate taxes will leave their heirs "cash poor." In effect, Uncle Sam has a "mortgage" on everything you own. Very often large estates must be sold in a hurry to provide cash to pay the taxes due at death. However, if an individual purchases adequate life insurance to pay these taxes, his estate can be preserved for his heirs. If you do not provide for estate taxes through adequate insurance, the taxes may wipe out what you've worked so hard to build up for your family.

Insurance Discounts and Rates

While most Christians would obviously ask for the lower insurance rates available for nonsmokers and nondrinkers, very few realize they can ask their insurance companies to give them a nonsmoker's discount on insurance policies they bought years ago. These special discounts are often applicable to fire and auto insurance policies as well. In addition, always shop around for the best insurance rates available. You may find very significant differences in the various insurance premiums you are quoted by different companies.

Term Insurance or Permanent?

There are two main types of life insurance: term and permanent. Permanent insurance, including whole life and universal life policies, combine pure term insurance protection with a savings element. Due to the low interest rate earned on permanent insurance policies, most financial planners suggest that you buy pure term insurance and place your investment dollars elsewhere.

Term insurance rates are very inexpensive and quite competitive, so you should have your insurance broker or agent shop around for the best possible rates. Many companies will issue an insurance policy for $100,000 protection for a 35-year-old male nonsmoker for an annual premium of less than $180, or $15 per month. These low rates make it possible for anyone to provide adequate insurance protection for their family.

Renewable term insurance policies are available for periods of one, five, ten, or twenty years. In addition, you can purchase term insurance to age 65 or sometimes even higher ages. Someone who is age 60 or older may be required to purchase a permanent insurance policy to acquire protection that will continue beyond age 70. Wealthy individuals may still need insurance past age 70 to make sure they have enough to cover estate taxes so they can keep their estate intact for their families.

Maximize Your Group Insurance

If your employer offers group insurance, ask if you can obtain coverage that is higher than the standard insurance amount of one or two times your annual salary. When you begin a job, or at an annual renewal, you may be able to exercise an option to increase your group insurance coverage. It is worthwhile to obtain the maximum group insurance offered because of the low rates available. Make sure the beneficiary named on your group insurance and company pension card is correct.

Disability Insurance

Many individuals fail to include disability insurance in their financial planning. Someone who is 35 years old is six times more likely to suffer a long-term disability than to die prematurely before the age of 65. A person between the ages of 35 and 65 has one chance in three that he will suffer a disability longer than 90 days (*Journal of AMN Society of C.L.U.*, Vol. 8, No. 1). And the average length of disability is at least five years.

For many individuals, such a long-term disability would quickly exhaust their savings accounts and their ability to borrow funds. Several studies reveal that the average family would be broke if they missed only five monthly paychecks. Even if you saved ten percent of your income for ten years, disability lasting one year could wipe out all your savings.

Make sure you get a long-term disability insurance policy, either through your group insurance at work or by purchasing an individual disability policy from your insurance broker. These policies can provide tremendous security against a financial disaster.

Retirement Planning

While we are focused on the daily task of making a living, we often forget that the years are passing and we will someday reach the end of our working life. And there is a good chance that you will live for a number of years past your retirement. Mortality studies indicate that 70 percent of all people between the ages of 25 and 45 will live to age 65 and higher. In addition, the studies reveal that 38 percent of those who reach age 65 will live to age 80 or more.

When your ability to earn a salary ends, how will you provide an adequate monthly income that allows you to live a lifestyle similar to the one you enjoy today? Obviously, the government's pension plans are less than adequate to provide the level of income you need to continue with the same standard of living you enjoy today. In addition, there is a significant chance that the government's pension plan will fail within the next 20 years because of the huge unfunded liabilities that exist in the government pension fund. These government pension plans are basically broke; all of the money we have contributed to these government plans has been spent by the politicians.

The only way you can ensure that you and your spouse will enjoy the financial rewards of a well-earned retirement is to begin planning today for the time when your regular paycheck will end. You need to set aside just a little of the money you make each month and invest it in a carefully selected retirement plan so that it will be there for you when you retire.

How much is needed for
a comfortable retirement income?

To begin your retirement planning, answer the following questions:

- Do you have a retirement program?

- When do you want to retire?

- How much monthly income do you want to receive during retirement?

- How much monthly income will the government's social security pension plan provide?

- What is the shortfall between your monthly income goal and what the government's plan will provide?

Monthly income required	ASSUMED NET INTEREST RATE AFTER TAX ON YOUR RETIREMENT FUND			
	5% Return	6% Return	7% Return	8% Return
$1,000	$ 240,000	$ 200,000	$171,428	$150,000
$2,000	$ 480,000	$ 400,000	$342,856	$300,000
$3,000	$ 720,000	$ 600,000	$514,284	$450,000
$4,000	$ 960,000	$ 800,000	$685,712	$600,000
$5,000	$1,200,000	$1,000,000	$857,140	$750,000

One of the biggest and best tax breaks available to you as a taxpayer is the tax deductibility of the contributions you make to government-approved retirement pension plans (in the United States, Individual Retirement Account [IRA], and in Canada, the Registered Retirement Savings Plan [RRSP]. These tax-sheltered funds will accumulate at a tremendous rate using compound interest and can help you produce a guaranteed income that supplements your government pension plan.

A significant advantage is earned by those investors who make their annual investment at the beginning of each year rather than waiting till the last day of the year. In only 30 years the investor who diligently makes his annual deposit in January rather than December will accumulate almost ten percent more money by retirement. It is never too soon, and it is certainly never too late for you to start investing in a retirement plan to achieve your goal of future financial independence.

Tax-sheltered Retirement Savings Plans

Most successful investors pay almost 50 percent of their highest dollar in taxes. For example, compare the case of two brothers: Bill invested a full $5,500 each year for 35 years in a tax-sheltered investment at 10 percent interest while his brother Mike, with the same financial resources, failed to use a tax shelter. After paying 50 percent in income taxes on the $5,500 he had available to invest, Mike invested the remaining $3,750 at 10 percent interest for the next 35 years but without the benefit of a tax shelter. At the end of 35 years, Bill accumulated a total of $1,690,000 in his tax-sheltered retirement fund compared to only $258,000 for his brother Mike. What an incredible difference in investment results!

Although both brothers had the same amount to invest every year for 35 years at ten percent interest, the brother who took advantage of the tax shelter accumulated an additional $1,432,000 in retirement funds simply because he protected his investment from taxation! If he can earn a ten-percent return on his investment funds after age 65, this $1,432,000 in extra investment earning will generate $11,933 in additional income each and every month for life. This amounts to a total of $143,196 in extra pension income every single year throughout Bill's retirement.

While Bill's retirement pension fund of $1,690,000 will generate $16,900 of monthly income and will be fully taxable at a probable 50 percent tax rate, he will still have $8,450 of after-tax monthly income to live on until he dies. On the other hand, brother Mike, who chose to invest his $5,500 each year without a tax shelter, will have accumulated a fund of $258,000 that will produce a retirement pension of only $2,150 every month. The brother who utilized the tax shelter to accumulate his retirement funds will have almost four times the monthly income throughout his retirement!

That example confirms that sheltering your pension investment from taxation is one of the major keys to success in retirement planning. You may want to consider placing each year's pension deposit in a separate investment vehicle to maximize your flexibility in the future. For example, if at some point you need emergency funds, you could simply collapse only one year's pension deposit of $10,000 or so rather than collapse your complete fund. Also, with the first option, you'll pay income tax on only one year's worth of pension money instead of many year's worth.

Another advantage of depositing your pension in separate investment vehicles is that if you choose to take a year's sabbatical, you could withdraw some of your tax-sheltered pension funds to provide an income while you study or volunteer for an extended mission trip. Although these withdrawn funds will be taxable, if you are not earning other income that year, the tax burden will be light.

When you retire you can then withdraw your pension funds and pay tax on the total amount. Of course, a retiree does not know how long he or she will live. If you fear that your pension will not last the entire length of your retirement years, you must live conservatively and use only the interest generated by your investments. The problem with that arrangement is you may not have enough income to enjoy retirement. Yet, if you use the interest and also dip into the principal, you may exhaust your funds before you die.

With people living longer and longer, this is a real dilemma for most retirees. The best solution is to purchase a guaranteed life annuity from a life insurance company. This annuity will guarantee you a monthly income until you die. The monthly check that the insurance company will pay you is a blend of principal and interest and guarantees you a maximum monthly income throughout your life. This is the best method for maximizing your monthly income while guaranteeing that the monthly checks will continue as long as you live. If both spouses are living, a joint life annuity will provide a guaranteed income as long as either spouse remains alive.

Tax-Savings Strategies

Income tax rates have risen to very high levels. We could almost rightly say that "It's almost reached the point where if you take a day off work you are in danger of falling behind in your income tax payments."

In Canada, the government—at all levels—now takes an average of more than 50 percent of all income earned by the average Canadian. The original Canadian Income Tax Act was introduced in 1917 as a "temporary" measure to pay the war debt from World War I. The rate of taxation was originally only 1.6 percent with the first $3,000 in income exempt from all taxation. Since the average Canadian earned $760 in 1917, most citizens paid no tax whatsoever. A citizen with $5,000 in income would pay only $80 in annual taxes!

In the United States, government taxes at all levels usually take over 45 percent of the money earned by its citizens. In both countries, then, the average taxpayer works till May each year before earning a single dollar for himself and his family.

Many studies reveal that the average taxpayer unintentionally overpays on his or her income taxes. If you carefully plan your financial situation and obtain the best taxation advice available, you can save thousands of dollars in unnecessary taxes. Today the tax codes are so complicated that very few citizens can utilize all of the various exemptions and deductions that are legally available to them without professional advice. Any competent tax planner or accountant will earn his fee several times over by gaining significant tax savings for his client.

You may have heard the line about the rumors that the tax department has developed a new simplified tax form to replace the cumbersome existing ones. The proposed new tax form would have only three lines:

A. What did you make last year?
B. What did you spend?
C. Send the government B.

We may laugh at these kinds of jokes, but the reality is that taxes eat up a large portion of our income. To save money, here are some basic strategies you may want to discuss with your tax counselor, accountant, or financial planner.

1. Keep all receipts and vouchers related to your home-repair expenses. You may sell your home later as an investment property and your vouchers and receipts will validate expenses that would adjust your adjusted cost basis to your advantage to minimize your capital gains tax.

2. Leasing versus owning a car. If you intend to keep a car more than two years, leasing is often to your advantage from a taxation standpoint. If you change your car every year and a half or so, owning is often the better tax break.

3. Consider establishing an office in your home if you run a business. You may deduct part of the rent, or part of the mortgage interest, in addition to the utilities and equipment. You must save your receipts and document all of your business expenses.

4. Pay off nondeductible items or loans first and borrow for deductible items or loans. For example, use the money you have saved in your investment fund to prepay your mortgage or other nondeductible loans early. Then borrow the necessary funds from your bank to invest in new investment vehicles. The interest on this new loan will be tax deductible because the loan is for investment purposes.

5. Never prepay above the amount required on your income tax payroll deductions. You receive no interest from the government on your prepayments and no tax benefit. Always hold onto your money as long as you can. If you usually receive a significant income tax refund each year, you are giving the government an interest-free loan of your money.

6. Make the maximum deposit to your government retirement savings plan for yourself and your wife as an essential part of a balanced financial plan.

7. Claim all the deductions that are permitted for investment purposes, including brokerage fees, safe-deposit box charges, and so on.

8. Split the major breadwinner's income with your spouse and children. This "income splitting" will cause the resulting income to be taxed at a lower tax rate in the hands of family members with smaller incomes.

Financial Strategies for the Last Days

What strategies should Christians consider for living in the last days? Proverbs 27:12 tells us "A prudent man foresees evil and hides himself; the simple pass on and are punished."

1. Reduce your debt and build your liquid cash reserves as quickly as possible.

2. Avoid all weak financial institutions, including savings and loans, banks, insurance companies, and trust companies. Check out your bank's strength by ordering a Weiss or Veribanc Report (usually $15 to $25 per report. These resources are listed at the end of the book).

3. Avoid mutual funds and stocks at this time because of the danger of a stock market collapse during the next few years.

4. Avoid investing in corporate and rental real estate at this time because of the depressed market during the 1990s.

5. Your own home is an excellent long-term investment. Prepaying the mortgage on your

home is one of the best financial strategies you can follow.

6. Avoid corporate bonds, commodities, and other complex, high-risk derivative investments that are difficult for the average investor to properly evaluate.

7. Government bonds, treasury bills, guaranteed investment certificates, and fixed-term deposits issued by strong banks are excellent investment options for the next five years or so.

8. Follow a basic budget plan, save ten percent of your monthly income.

9. Begin to tithe ten percent of your monthly income in obedience to God's plan.

10. Consider investing 20 percent of your investment funds in gold and silver coins as a financial insurance policy.

11. Complete wills for you and your spouse. Acquire adequate life and disability insurance.

Those who are prepared for the dangers of an economic collapse will be able to avoid the worst dangers in the years ahead. In addition, they will be able to protect their homes, their businesses, and their families' financial assets by following a prudent and conservative course of action. After an economic collapse, an investor with ample cash will be able to acquire excellent real estate and shares in solid companies at a fraction of the prices before the crash.

Do Not Worry About Your Finances

Finally, after you have done all you can to protect your financial assets, you need to place all your financial matters in God's hands and trust Him. "Do not worry, saying, 'What shall we eat?' or 'What shall we drink?' or 'What shall we wear?' For after all these things the Gentiles seek. For your heavenly Father knows that you need all these things. But seek first the kingdom of God and His righteousness, and all these things shall be added to you" (Matthew 7:31-33).

An important note: Keep a proper perspective on your financial matters by realizing that all of these concerns are only temporary. Although these economic issues are important today and God commands us to act with diligence, there is coming a day when they will all pass away. Our ultimate destiny as Christians is the heavenly city of God, the New Jerusalem. The only key to heaven is our faith and trust in the salvation that Christ won for us on the cross almost 2,000 years ago. While our salvation is based solely on the blood of Christ that was shed for us, all Christians will be judged at the judgment seat of Christ regarding their faithfulness to His commands. Those who have been faithful will receive crowns and mansions that will last forever.

What Is Your Treasure?

When the final accounting of our life is made before the throne of God, our finances and material possessions will count for nothing. On that judgment day, all that will matter are the souls we have won to the Lord, the obedient service we have rendered to Christ, and the things we have done for our brothers and sisters in the Lord. These deeds of righteousness done out of love for Jesus Christ will be the treasures that will count for eternity. Christ commanded us: "Lay up for yourselves treasures in heaven, where neither moth nor rust destroys, and where thieves do not break in and steal. For where your treasure is, there your heart will be also" (Matthew 6:20,21).

PART 6

New Insights from the Ancient World

CHAPTER 18

Three Fascinating Discoveries

Over the last 30 years I have been fascinated with Bible prophecy because it authenticates the Scriptures as God's inspired Word and it points to the imminent return of Jesus Christ to usher in the Messianic kingdom.

I am always delighted when God leads me to new information that confirms His Word. In my ongoing research into recent archaeological discoveries and the writings of early church leaders I have made several exciting new discoveries that I want to share in this chapter. We will explore a number of interesting discoveries about the following subjects: the finding of a teaching about the pre-tribulation rapture from the first centuries of the early church; the archaeological discoveries of the tombs of Mary, Martha, and Lazarus, which proves the historical accuracy of the

Gospels; and the proof that miraculous healings, the raising of the dead, and the charismatic gifts were common among believers during the first three centuries following the resurrection of Christ.

The Pre-Tribulation Rapture and the Early Church

Ultimately, the truth about the timing of the rapture will be found *only* in Scripture. That shouldn't surprise us; we all know well that one of the most pivotal events in the church age, the Protestant Reformation, was based on a return to the authority of the Bible. The Latin phrase *Sola Scriptura*, meaning "Scripture Alone," became the rallying cry of the reformers who ignored centuries of tradition and church councils in their insistence that truth could be discovered only in the Word of God. While the resolution of our discussion about the rapture must be based on our interpretation of Scripture, it is also important to answer the errors of those who disparage "the blessed hope" of the rapture with misinformation about the modern rediscovery of the truth about the pre-tribulation rapture.

Many post-tribulationist writers have attacked the pre-tribulation rapture doctrine by claiming that it cannot be true because no church writer or reformer ever taught this doctrine until approximately 170 years ago. While the real question for sincere students of Scripture must be whether or not the Bible truly teaches this doctrine, the argument that no one ever saw this "truth" throughout 1,800 years of church history has been very effective, causing many Christians to abandon their belief in the pre-tribulation rapture. The only problem with this post-tribulationist argument is that it is wrong.

Many contemporary writers claim that the pre-tribulation rapture theory first originated around A.D. 1830. They ascribe the theory's initial creation to either Emmanuel Lacunza (Ben Ezra, 1812), Edward Irving (1816), Margaret Macdonald (1830), or John Darby (1830). For example, Dave MacPherson in *The Incredible Cover-Up* (1975) stated:

> Margaret Macdonald was the first person to teach a coming of Christ that would precede the days of Antichrist. . . . Before 1830, Christians had always believed in a single future coming, that the catching up of I Thessalonians 4 will take place after the Great Tribulation of Matthew 24 at the glorious coming of the Son of Man when He shall send His angels to gather together all of His Elect.[1]

Reverend John Bray, in *The Origin of the Pre-Tribulation Rapture Teaching* (1980), declared:

> People who are teaching the pre-tribulation rapture teaching today are teaching something that never was taught until 1812. . . . Not one of those early church fathers taught a pre-tribulation rapture. . . . I make the offer of five hundred dollars to anybody who will find a statement, a sermon, article in a commentary, or anything, prior to 1812 that taught a two-phase coming of Christ separated by a stated period of time, such as the pre-tribulation rapturists teach.[2]

These writers, among others who despise the teaching of the pre-tribulation rapture, dogmatically assert that it was taught for the first time in 1830 by John Darby and the Plymouth Brethren or one of the other individuals already mentioned.

A number of these authors will have to drastically revise the next editions of their books because of two remarkable textual discoveries that conclusively prove that a number of Christian teachers taught a pre-tribulational rapture centuries before John Darby's time. During the summer of 1994, after more than a decade of searching, I discovered several fascinating manuscripts that contain clear evidence that the pre-tribulation rapture was taught in the early church.

Ephraem and the Pre-Tribulation Rapture

For all the saints and Elect of God are gathered, prior to the tribulation that is to come, and are taken to the Lord lest they see the confusion that is to overwhelm the world because of our sins (*On the Last Times, the Antichrist, and the End of the World*, by Ephraem the Syrian, A.D. 373).

The early Christian writer and poet, Ephraem the Syrian, (A.D. 306 to 373) was a major theologian of the early Byzantine Eastern Church. He was born near Nisbis, in the Roman province of Syria, near present-day Edessa, Turkey.

Ephraem displayed a profound love of the Scriptures in his writings as illustrated by several of his written comments quoted in the *Works of Nathaniel Lardner* (Vol. 4, 1788). For example, Ephraem wrote, "I esteem no man more happy than him, who diligently reads the Scriptures delivered to us by the Spirit of God, and thinks how he may order his conversation by the precepts of them."

To this day, Ephraem's hymns and homilies are used in the liturgy of the Greek Orthodox and Middle Eastern Nestorian churches. While the 16-volume Post-Nicene Library includes a number of homilies and psalms by Ephraem, the editors noted that he also wrote a large number of commentaries that have never been translated into English.

Ephraem's fascinating teaching on the Antichrist has never been published in English until now. This critically important prophecy manuscript from the fourth century of the church era reveals a literal method of interpretation and a teaching of the pre-millennial return of Christ. More importantly, Ephraem's text revealed a very clear statement about the pre-tribulational return of Christ to take His elect saints home to heaven to escape the coming Tribulation. In addition, Ephraem declared his belief in a personal, Jewish Antichrist who will rule the Roman Empire during the last days, a rebuilt Temple, the two witnesses, and a literal Great Tribulation lasting 1,260 days. It is also fascinating to note that he taught that the War of God and Magog would precede the tribulation period. I discovered another text by Ephraem, called *The Book of the Cave of Treasure*, that revealed his teaching that Daniel's seventieth week will be

fulfilled in the final seven years at the end of this age
that will conclude with Christ's return at the Battle of
Armageddon to establish His kingdom.

**Writings on the Last Time, the Antichrist, and the
End**   The following section includes key passages
from Ephraem's important text, which was written
about A.D. 373. These words were translated by
professor Cameron Rhoades, of Tyndale Theological
Seminary, at my request.

1. Most dearly beloved brothers, believe the Holy Spirit who
speaks in us. Now we have spoken before, because the end of
the world is very near, and the consummation remains. Has
not the first faith withered away in men? . . .

2. *We ought to understand thoroughly therefore, my brothers,
what is imminent or overhanging.* Already there have been
hunger and plagues, violent movements of nations and signs,
which have been predicted by the Lord, they have already been
fulfilled, and there is no other which remains, except the advent of the wicked one in the completion of the Roman kingdom. Why therefore are we occupied with worldly business,
and why is our mind held fixed on the lusts of the world or the
anxieties of the ages? Why therefore do we not reject every care
of earthly actions and prepare ourselves for the meeting of the
Lord Christ, *so that He may draw us from the confusion,
which overwhelms the world?* Believe you me, dearest brothers, because the coming of the Lord is nigh, believe you me, because the end of the world is at hand, believe me, because it is
the very last time. . . . *Because all saints and the Elect of the
Lord are gathered together before the tribulation which is*

about to come and are taken to the Lord, in order that they may not see at any time the confusion which overwhelms the world because of our sins [emphasis added]. And so brothers, most dear to me, it is the eleventh hour, and the end of this world comes to the harvest, and angels, armed and prepared, hold sickles in their hands, awaiting the empire of the Lord. . .

3. When therefore the end of the world comes, there arise diverse wars, commotions on all sides, horrible earthquakes, perturbations of nations, tempests throughout the lands, plagues, famine, drought throughout the thoroughfares, great danger throughout the sea and dry land, constant persecutions, slaughters and massacres everywhere. . . .

6. When therefore the end of the world comes, that abominable, lying and murderous one is born from the tribe of Dan. He is conceived from the seed of a man and from a most vile virgin, mixed with an evil or worthless spirit. . . .

7. But when the time of the abomination of his desolation begins to approach, having been made legal, he takes the empire. . . . Therefore, when he receives the kingdom, he orders the temple of God to be rebuilt for himself, which is in Jerusalem; who, after coming into it, he shall sit as God and order that he be adored by all nations . . . then all people from everywhere shall flock together to him at the city of Jerusalem, and the holy city shall be trampled on by the nations for forty-two months just as the holy apostle says in the Apocalypse, which become three and a half years, 1260 days.

8. In these three years and a half the heaven shall suspend its dew; because there will be no rain upon the earth . . . and

there will be a great tribulation, as there has not been, since people began to be upon the earth . . . and no one is able to sell or to buy of the grain of the fall harvest, unless he is one who has the serpentine sign on the forehead or the hand. . . .

10. And when the three and a half years have been completed, the time of the Antichrist, through which he will have seduced the world, after the resurrection of the two prophets, in the hour which the world does not know, and on the day which the enemy or son of perdition does not know, will come the sign of the Son of Man, and coming forward the Lord shall appear with great power and much majesty, with the sign of the word of salvation going before him, and also even with all the powers of the heavens with the whole chorus of the saints. . . . Then Christ shall come and the enemy shall be thrown into confusion, and the Lord shall destroy him by the Spirit of his mouth. And he shall be bound and shall be plunged into the abyss of everlasting fire alive with his father Satan; and all people, who do his wishes, shall perish with him forever; but the righteous ones shall inherit everlasting life with the Lord for ever and ever.

Let's summarize the key points in Ephraem's text on the last days:

1. Ephraem's manuscript lays out the events of the last days in chronological sequence. Significantly, he began with the rapture, using the word "imminent," then he described the Great Tribulation of three-and-a-half years duration under the Antichrist's tyranny, followed by the

second coming of Christ to earth with his saints to defeat the Antichrist.

2. Significantly, at the beginning of his treatise in Section 2, Ephraem used the word "imminent" to describe the rapture occurring before the tribulation and the coming of the Antichrist. "We ought to understand thoroughly therefore, my brothers, what is imminent or overhanging."

3. He clearly described the pre-tribulation rapture: "Because all saints and the Elect of the Lord are gathered together before the tribulation which is about to come and are taken to the Lord, in order that they may not see at any time the confusion which overwhelms the world because of our sins."

4. He then gives the purpose of God rapturing the church "before the tribulation"—so that "they may not see at any time the confusion which overwhelms the world because of our sins." Ephraem used the word "confusion" as a synonym for the tribulation period.

5. Ephraem described the duration of the "great tribulation" (the last half of the seven-year tribulation period) in sections 7, 8, and 10 as follows: "Forty-two months," "three and a half years," and "1260 days."

6. He summarized: "There will be a great tribulation, as there has not been since people began

to be upon the earth" and described the Mark of the Beast system.

7. He declared that Christ will come to the earth after the "three and a half years" tribulation period in Section 10: "And when the three and a half years have been completed, the time of the Antichrist, through which he will have seduced the world, after the resurrection of the two prophets . . . will come the sign of the Son of Man, and coming forward the Lord shall appear with great power and much majesty."

Dr. Paul Alexander, perhaps the most authoritative scholar on the writings of the early Byzantine Church, concluded that Ephraem's text *On the Last Times, the Antichrist, and the End of the World* taught that the Lord would supernaturally remove the saints of the church from the earth "prior to the tribulations that is to come." Ephraem wrote that the saints will be "taken to the Lord lest they see the confusion that is to overwhelm the world because of our sins." Dr. Alexander believed this text was written by some unknown writer in the sixth century but he concluded that it was derived from an original Ephraem manuscript (A.D. 373).

Other scholars, including the German editor Professor Caspari, who wrote a German commentary on this Latin manuscript in 1890, believed that Ephraem's manuscript was written by Ephraem himself in A.D. 373.

Writing on Daniel's Seventieth Week A question naturally arises in the mind of Bible students about how long Ephraem believed the Tribulation would last. Ephraem correctly stated that the "great tribulation" would last three and a half years, and his other writings reveal that he believed the whole tribulation period, "that sore affliction," would last "one week" of seven years. In a book about the genealogy of Christ, *The Book of the Cave of Treasures* (written about A.D. 373) Ephraem wrote that the sixty-ninth week of Daniel 9:24-27 ended with the rejection and crucifixion of Jesus the Messiah. He said, "The Jews have no longer among them a king, or a priest, or a prophet, or a Passover, even as Daniel prophesied concerning them, saying, '*After two and sixty weeks Christ shall be slain,* and the city of holiness shall be laid waste until the completion of things decreed' (Daniel 9:26). That is to say, for ever and ever" (page 235, emphasis added).

Daniel foretold that Jerusalem would be rebuilt "even in troublesome times" during the initial period of "seven weeks" of years (49 years). Daniel prophesied that this initial period of seven "weeks" of years would be immediately followed by a further period of 62 "weeks" of years ending with the cutting off of the Messiah (483 years). The combined total of 69 weeks of years (seven weeks plus 62 weeks) was to conclude with the rejection of Christ. As we saw earlier, Ephraem taught that Jesus Christ was slain at the end of the combined 69 weeks of years.

In the section of his book dealing with the future War of God and Magog, Ephraem wrote about the final (seventieth) week of Daniel as follows:

> *At the end of the world and at the final consummation* . . . suddenly the gates of the north shall be opened. . . . They will destroy the earth, and there will be none able to stand before them. *After one week of that sore affliction [Tribulation], they will all be destroyed in the plain of Joppa.* . . . Then will the son of perdition appear, of the seed and of the tribe of Dan. . . . He will go into Jerusalem and will sit upon a throne in the Temple saying, "I am the Christ," and he will be borne aloft by legions of devils like a king and a lawgiver, naming himself God. . . . *The time of the error of the Anti-Christ will last* two years and a half, but others say *three years and six months* (emphasis added).

Although there are some curious elements in Ephraem's description of prophetic events, it is clear that he believed that the final week of Daniel's prophecy about the seventy weeks would be fulfilled during the final seven years of this age, when the Antichrist will appear. This evidence of a belief in a "gap" or "parenthesis" between the sixty-ninth and seventieth week of Daniel 9:24-27 is highly significant; this belief was taught back in the fourth century of the Christian era! It is worthwhile to note that this teaching that there would be a gap or parenthesis was also taught by others in the early church, according to the Epistle of Barnabas (A.D. 110) and the writings of Hippolytus (A.D. 220).

Dr. John Gill Taught the
Pre-Tribulation Rapture in 1748

Dr. John Gill, a famous eighteenth-century Baptist theologian, published his commentary on the New Testament in 1748. He is considered a serious Calvinist scholar who wrote many volumes on theology. In his commentary on 1 Thessalonians 4:15-17, Dr. Gill points out that Paul is teaching a doctrine that is "something new and extraordinary." Gill calls the imminent translation of the saints "the rapture" and calls for watchfulness because "it will be sudden, and unknown before-hand, and when least thought of and expected." This is a clear, detailed 1748 teaching on the imminent pre-tribulation rapture (80 years prior to John Darby in 1830).

The apostle Paul, in 1 Thessalonians 4:15, said, "We say to you by the word of the Lord, and we who are alive and remain until the coming of the Lord will by no means precede those who are asleep" (1 Thessalonians 4:15). Gill's commentary on this passage is: "The apostle having something new and extraordinary to deliver, concerning the coming of Christ, the first resurrection, or the resurrection of the saints, the change of the living saints, and the *rapture both of the raised, and living in the clouds* to meet Christ in the air, expresses itself in this manner" (emphasis added).

A little later, in 1 Thessalonians 4:17, Paul wrote, "Then we who are alive and remain shall be caught up together with them in the clouds to meet the Lord in the air. And thus we shall always be with the

Lord" (1 Thessalonians 4:17). In his comments on this verse Gill revealed that he understood there would be an interval of time between the rapture and the return of saints with Christ at Armageddon:

Suddenly, in a moment, in the twinkling of an eye, and with force and power; by the power of Christ, and by the ministry and means of the holy angels; and to which *rapture* will contribute the agility, which the bodies both of the raised and changed saints will have; and *this rapture of the living saints* will be together with them; with the dead in Christ, that will then be raised; so that the one will not prevent the other, or the one be sooner with Christ than the other; but one being raised and the other changed, they'll be joined in one company and general assembly, and *be rapt up together: in the clouds;* the same clouds perhaps in which Christ will come will be let down to take them up; these will be the chariots, in which they'll be carried up to Him; and thus, as at our Lord's ascension a cloud received Him, and in it He was carried up out of the sight of men, *so at this time will all the saints ride up in the clouds of Heaven: to meet the Lord in the air; whither He'll descend* . . . here *Christ will stop* and will be visible to all, and as easily discerned by all, good and bad, as the body of the sun at noonday; *as yet He will not descend on earth, because not fit to receive Him; but when that and its works are burnt up, and it is purged and purified by fire, and become a new earth, He'll descend upon it, and dwell with His saints in it:* and this suggests another reason why *He'll stay in the air, and His saints shall meet Him there, and whom He'll take up with Him into the third heaven, till the general conflagration and burning of the world is over, and to preserve them from it:* and then shall all the elect of God descend from heaven as a bride adorned for her husband, and He with them . . . *then they shall be with Him, wherever He is; first in the air, where they shall meet Him; then in the third heaven, where they shall go up with Him; then on earth, where they shall descend and reign with Him a thousand years;* and then in the ultimate glory to all eternity.

As we examine Dr. Gill's 1748 teaching about the sequence of prophetic events it is vital to note that he declared:

1. The Lord will descend in the air

2. The saints will be raptured in the air to meet Him

3. Christ will stop in the air and will be visible to all

4. As yet Christ will not descend on earth, because it is not fit to receive Him

5. Christ will take up [the saints] with Him into the third heaven, until the general conflagration and burning of the world is over

6. He will preserve the saints from the conflagration

7. And then all the elect of God will descend from heaven to earth with Christ

Gill then summarizes the sequence:

1. They shall be with Him, wherever He is; first in the air, where they shall meet Him; then

2. In the third heaven, where they shall go up with Him; then

3. On earth, where they shall descend and reign with Him 1,000 years.

Therefore, in addition to Ephraem's pre-tribulation teaching from the fourth century, we have another clear statement of this doctrine from Dr. John Gill more than 80 years before John Darby in 1830. Those who have stated that the pre-tribulation rapture was never taught until 1830 are simply ignorant of these important Christian texts. The French writer Joubert once wrote, "Nothing makes men so imprudent and conceited as ignorance of the past and a scorn for old books."

Why is it important to teach the doctrine of the pre-tribulation rapture? The apostle Peter warned that in the last days, many people would challenge our Lord's promise of His second coming: "Knowing this first; that scoffers will come in the last days, walking according to their own lusts, and saying, 'Where is the promise of His coming?'" (2 Peter 3:3,4).

What does the Bible teach us about the attitude a Christian should have toward the subject of Christ's return? In 1 Corinthians 1:7, Paul wrote to us so that we might "come short in no gift, eagerly waiting for the revelation of our Lord Jesus Christ." One of the distinguishing characteristics of a true follower of Jesus is that he or she will be a faithful, waiting, and watching servant. Dr. Klink, one of the great students of the faith of the early church, wrote, "This constant expectation of our Lord's second coming is one of the characteristic features of primitive Christianity." Paul also commends a constant expectation of the rapture in Philippians 3:20, where he said, "Our citizenship is in heaven, from this we also eagerly wait for the Savior, the Lord Jesus Christ."

The great reformer, John Calvin, wrote about the vital importance of living in hope of the second coming: "It ought to be the chief concern of believers to fix their minds fully on His Second Advent." Martin Luther, in his *Sermon of Consolation*, declared that the hope of Christ's return is an absolute necessity for a Christian:

> If thou be not filled with a desire after the Coming of this day, thou canst never pray the Lord's prayer, nor canst thou repeat from thy heart the creed of faith. For with what conscience canst thou say, "I believe in the resurrection of the body and the life everlasting," if thou dost not in thy heart desire the same? If thou didst believe it, thou must, of necessity, desire it from thy heart, and long for that day to come; which, if thou doest not desire thou art not yet a Christian, nor canst thou boast of thy faith.

Throughout the New Testament we read exhortations to hold the hope of our Lord's soon return as the focus of our spiritual life. Far from being an unimportant issue limited to students of prophecy, the "blessed hope" of the rapture should be a cornerstone of every Christian's spiritual life.

The message and hope of the imminent return of Christ to rapture the saints has the following purposes:

1. It calls us to constant watchfulness for His return (1 Thessalonians 5:4-6).

2. It motivates Christians to witness to unbelievers in light of His imminent coming (John 9:4).

3. It reminds us to walk in holiness in an immoral world while we await His return (1 John 3:3).

4. It comforts the saints by reminding them of their eternal destiny with Christ (John 14:1-3).

5. It warns of the coming judgment on those who reject His salvation (2 Thessalonians 1:8,9).

6. It inspires us to persevere against opposition in light of His reward (2 Timothy 4:1-8).

7. It encourages sinners to repent and accept the Lord while there is still time (Acts 3:19-21).

Scripture's promise of the imminent second coming of the Messiah, Jesus Christ, is the last best hope of mankind. It is the promise of the ultimate vindication of God's plan to redeem mankind and the earth from the curse of sin and death. The final realization of Jesus Christ's claim that He is the promised Messiah and the fulfillment of prophecies about the coming Kingdom of God will culminate when the heavens open to reveal Christ coming in all His glory at the Battle of Armageddon.

Yet the Scriptures also teach that another event will occur before Christ comes to defeat the Antichrist and the armies of the world at Armageddon at the end of the seven-year tribulation period. This separate and earlier event is often called the rapture. The Bible passages that detail the revelation of Christ at the end of the tribulation period describe a totally different event than the passages that describe the coming of Christ in the air to take the saints home to heaven.

The longing for the rapture and the return of Christ has motivated generations of Bible students to examine the Scriptures in search of clues about the exact timing of His glorious appearing. Unfortunately, despite clear scriptural warnings against date-setting, many people have indulged in harmful speculation about the time of the rapture. Harold Camping's book, *1994*, for example, claimed that Christ would return on September 17, 1994.

Millions of people who have listened to these predictions have been deeply disappointed when the date-setters were proved wrong. However, despite these disappointments, we must not abandon our hope for an imminent rapture. We must simply be obedient to Christ's command that "when these things begin to happen, look up and lift up your heads, because your redemption draws near" (Luke 21:28).

In 1755, John Wesley de Fletcher wrote a fascinating letter to Charles Wesley that expressed the proper attitude we should have toward the return of Christ. In that letter he wrote, "I know that many have been grossly mistaken as to the year of His return, but, because they were rash, shall we be stupid? Because they say 'Today!'; shall we say 'Never!' and cry 'Peace, Peace,' when we should look about us with eyes full of expectation?"

The Bible warns us to live in holiness because Christ could return at any moment without warning. Jesus, in Luke 12:37,40, admonished, "Blessed are those servants whom the master, when he comes, will find watching. . . . "Therefore you also be ready, for the Son of Man is coming at an hour you do not expect." Peter, in his second epistle, said, "You therefore, beloved, since you know these things beforehand, beware lest you also fall from your own steadfastness, being led away with the error of the wicked" (2 Peter 3:17).

We must live in a dynamic spiritual balance. While we are commanded to live in holiness and urgently witness as though Christ will return before the dawn, we are also called to plan and work to fulfill the Great Commission as if He will tarry for another 100 years. We are to "do business ['occupy' in the Authorized Version] till I come" (Luke 19:13), fulfilling Christ's Great Commission to "go therefore and make disciples of all the nations, baptizing them in the name of the Father and of the Son and of the Holy Spirit, teaching them to observe all things that I have commanded you" (Matthew 28:19,20).

This discovery of texts written before 1820 brings us to the conclusion that, from the beginning of the early church until today, a remnant of the faithful have upheld the great precious biblical truth of pre-tribulation rapture. Ephraem the Syrian's A.D. 373 manuscript *On the Last Times* and Dr. John Gill's

1748 *Commentary on the New Testament* refute the dogmatic declarations that no scholar taught a pre-tribulation rapture before 1830. Also, in my book *Apocalypse*, I quoted from the early Christian writing called *The Shepherd of Hermas* (A.D. 110), proving that it, too, taught the pre-tribulation rapture as the hope of the church.

The Tombs of Mary, Martha, and Lazarus

Some writers have claimed that there is virtually no archaeological evidence to back up the historical claims of the Gospels. The truth is that much archaeological evidence has been discovered in Israel that proves the accuracy of the New Testament!

A hundred and twenty-five years ago a French Christian archaeologist named Charles Claremont-Gannueau wrote a little-known report dated November 13, 1873, from Jerusalem to the Palestine Exploration Fund. In this report he details his discovery, in a sepulchral cave near Bethany, of a group of Jewish ossuaries (stone coffins) from the first century of the Christian era. To his great surprise Claremont-Gannueau found that these ancient Jewish coffins contained the names of many people who are mentioned in the New Testament as members of the Jerusalem church. Despite its importance, this report was not published in the newspapers of the day. As a result, it was almost lost to history.

Several years ago I purchased, from a rare book dealer in London, material which contained this obscure report by Charles Claremont-Gannueau. The report, published by the Palestine Exploration Fund, included his translation of several of these inscriptions, which indicated that he had discovered the tombs of Mary, Martha, Lazarus, and many other Christians from the first-century church.

In the spring of 1873, Effendi Abu Saud, while constructing his house on the eastern slopes of the Mount of Olives near the road to ancient Bethany, accidentally discovered a cave that proved to be an ancient burial catacomb. Inside, he found 30 ancient stone coffins. Professor Charles Claremont-Gannueau examined these coffins, or ossuaries.

Some background information may prove helpful here: The Jews in the first century buried their dead either in the ground or in a tomb. Several years later they would clean the bones of the skeleton and rebury them in a small limestone ossuary, often 25 inches long, 20 inches wide, and 25 inches high. The lids of these ossuaries were triangular, semi-circular, or rectangular. Inscriptions with the name and identification of the deceased were painted or engraved on the sides or on the lids of the ossuaries in Hebrew or Greek.

Claremont-Gannueau was excited to note that several of the ossuaries he examined were inscribed with crosses or the name *Jesus*, proving that these Jewish deceased were Christians. Although he was unable to take photographs, he did use a special cloth to take squeezes of the ornamented surfaces as well as the inscriptions.

Engraved on the sides of three of these ossuaries from this cave were the names *Eleazar* (the Hebrew form of the Greek name *Lazarus*), *Martha*, and *Mary*. These names were followed by the sign of the cross, proving they were Christian. These names may have a connection with the Gospel of John, where we read the touching story about Christ raising His friend Lazarus from the dead: "Now a certain man was sick, Lazarus of Bethany, the town of Mary and her sister Martha" (John 11:1).

Claremont-Gannueau noted that this was one of the most important archaeological discoveries ever made concerning the origins of the early New Testament church. He wrote,

> This catacomb on the Mount of Olives belonged apparently to one of the earliest families which joined the new religion of Christianity. In this group of sarcophagi some of which have the Christian symbol and some have not, we are, so to speak, [witnessing the] actual unfolding of Christianity. Personally, I think that many of the Hebrew-speaking people whose remains are contained in these ossuaries were among the first followers of Christ. . . . The appearance of Christianity at the very gates of Jerusalem is, in my opinion, extraordinary and unprecedented. Somehow the new [Christian] doctrine must have made its way into the Jewish system. . . . The association of the sign of the cross with (the name of Jesus) written in Hebrew alone constitutes a valuable fact.

The archaeologist's report mentioned the following additional inscriptions found on ossuaries:

Hebrew inscriptions:

1. *Salome, wife of Judah*, engraved in very small characters . . . a cruciform sign.
2. *Judah, with the cross* +. Perhaps the husband of Salome.
3. *Judah the Scribe.* On another face of the sarcophagus, *Judah, son of Eleazar the Scribe.*
4. *Simeon the Priest* (Cohen).
5. *Martha, daughter of Pasach.* Perhaps the name is Jewish as well as Christian.
6. *Eleazar, son of Nathalu.* The form Nathai for Nathan is not uncommon.
7. *Salamtsion, daughter of Simeon the Priest.* The name of the woman, Salam Sion, is of the greatest interest. It is the name Salampsion of Josephus (daughter of Herod).

Greek inscriptions:

1. *Jesus.*—twice repeated, with the cross +.
2. *Nathaniel*, accompanied by a cross.

It is interesting to note that Claremont-Gannueau also found in one of the ossuaries

. . . three or four small instruments in copper or bronze, much oxidized, consisting of an actual small bell, surmounted by a ring. The Arabs thought they were a kind of castanets. Can we trace here the equivalent of the bells hung on the robe of the high priest? And do these ornaments come from the sarcophagus of our Simeon?

The French archaeologist realized that there was a high degree of probability that these tombs belonged to the family of Mary, Martha, and Lazarus, the close friends of Jesus. Claremont-Gannueau wrote,

What gives additional value to these short inscriptions, is that they furnish a whole series of names found in the Gospels, in their popular and local Syro-Chaldaic forms. The presence of the names of Jesus and Martha, of which we only knew historically that it was the feminine form of the Aramaic, would alone be sufficient to make this collection important from an exegetic point of view. By a singular coincidence, which from the first struck me forcibly, these inscriptions, found close to the Bethany road, and very near the site of the village, contain nearly all the names of the personages in the Gospel scenes which belonged to the place: Eleazar (Lazarus), Simon, Martha . . . a host of other coincidences occur at the sight of all these most evangelical names.

In addition, the Italian scholar P. Bagatti discovered another catacomb holding 100 ossuaries on the western side of the Mount of Olives, opposite the Temple Mount, near the Catholic chapel called Dominus Flevit. Coins minted by Governor Varius Gratus (A.D. 16) proved that these tombs were used for the burial of Christians before the fall of Jerusalem in A.D. 70. Several of the coffins in the cave belonged to a family of

priests buried in the first century. Based on the
inscribed crosses and the name *Jesus*, Baggatti concluded that several of these priests were followers
of Jesus Christ. Bagatti also found many ossuaries
containing the following names inscribed on their
sides together with the sign of the cross or the name
of Jesus: Jonathan, Joseph, Jarius, Judah, Matthias,
Menahem, Salome, Simon, and Zechariah. Many of
these names appear in the New Testament records of
the early church of Jerusalem. One ossuary had the
Greek inscription *Iota*, *Chi* and *Beta*, which reads,
"Jesus Christ, the Redeemer."

Without question the most fascinating ossuary
was the one inscribed with crosses and the name *Sapphira*. This is a unique name that has not been found
in contemporary Jewish literature outside the New
Testament passage Acts 5:1. Luke recorded the death
of this woman and her husband when they lied to
God and the church (Acts 5:1-10).

During the fall of 1945, Dr. Eleazar Sukenik of Hebrew University investigated another first-century
Jewish catacomb at the southern end of the Kidron
Valley on the road to Bethlehem. He found several
ossuaries with the sign of the cross, Greek inscriptions, and a coin minted in A.D. 41 for King Herod
Agrippa I—proving the tomb was sealed by A.D. 42.
Professor Sukenik concluded that the ossuaries
"contain almost the whole dictionary of names in
the New Testament."[3] One coffin had a surprising
dedication in Greek to "Jesus," followed by the ex-
clamation *y'ho*, meaning "Jehovah" or "the Lord."
The inscription reads: "[To] Jesus, the Lord."

In light of the A.D. 42 date for the sealing of this tomb, the presence of this dedication to "Jesus, the Lord" proves that Christians accepted Jesus Christ as God within ten years of His death and resurrection. Christian theologian Professor Alexander Hopkins commented on this significant inscription: "The inscription which was hidden for almost 2,000 years and inscribed at least two decades before any part of the New Testament was written . . . bears a personal testimony of faith . . . a message from the past with a very modern meaning for the present."

Several years ago another Jewish Christian ossuary was discovered in Jerusalem that contained the inscription, "Alexander, son of Simon of Cyrene." The Gospel of Mark refers to a person by this same name: "Now they compelled a certain man, Simon a Cyrenian, the father of Alexander and Rufus, as he was coming out of the country and passing by, to bear His cross" (Mark 15:21).

Miracles, Healing, and the Gifts of the Spirit

Many Christians have been told that the charismatic gifts listed in 1 Corinthians 12 were given to the early Christians solely to launch the church and that these supernatural signs ceased when the apostles died. Several writers have declared that a search of the writings of the early church confirms that there are no refcrences to these gifts continuing in operation beyond A.D. 100.

Recently I acquired a CD-ROM computer disk that contains the writings of the Ante-Nicene

Fathers, who lived in the period from the time of Christ till the Council of Nicea in A.D. 325. After an exhaustive search of these early Christian writings I can confirm that God did indeed continue to manifest His supernatural power through miraculous healings, raising people from the dead, and other charismatic gifts of the Holy Spirit during the three centuries following the resurrection of Christ.

There are brief references to the presence of these gifts in the early church manual known as the *Testimony of the Apostles—the Didache* (11:10-13 and 11:20), composed in A.D. 110. Additional references are found in the *Letter to the Corinthians* (2:1-5) by Clement, bishop of Rome, written in A.D. 100; and the *Shepherd of Hermas* (43:9, 24-33; 52-54), written in A.D. 110. In addition to those above, there are a number of other significant references to these supernatural gifts in the centuries following Christ's resurrection.

Irenaeus—Refutation and Overthrow of Knowledge Falsely So Called

The Christian teacher Irenaeus wrote a treatise called the *Refutation and Overthrow of Knowledge Falsely So Called* in A.D. 185. In that work he mentioned the continued operation of miraculous powers that were exercised by believers in his day. He demonstrated clearly that in his own time manifestations of divine and supernatural power were witnessed in some churches:

Some drive out demons really and truly, so that often those cleansed from evil spirits believe and become members of the church; some have foreknowledge of the future, visions, and prophetic utterances; others, by the laying-on of hands, heal the sick and restore them to health; and before now, as I said, dead men have actually been raised and have remained with us for many years. In fact, it is impossible to enumerate the gifts which throughout the world the church has received from God and in the name of Jesus Christ crucified under Pontius Pilate, and every day puts to effectual use for the benefit of the heathen, deceiving no one and making profit out of no one.

In addition, Irenaeus wrote:

Similarly, we hear of many members of the church who have prophetic gifts and by the Spirit speak with all kinds of tongues, and bring men's secret thoughts to light for their own good, and expound the mysteries of God.

Justin Martyr—*Dialogue with Trypho*

Justin Martyr wrote his *Dialogue with Trypho* in A.D. 165 and clearly referred to many gifts of the Holy Spirit appearing in the daily life of the second-century church (chapter XI). In chapter XXXIX Justin Martyr wrote:

Daily some of you are becoming disciples in the name of Christ, and quitting the path of error; who are also receiving gifts, each as he is worthy, illumined through the name of this Christ. For one receives the spirit of understanding, another of

counsel, another of strength, another of healing, another
of foreknowledge, another of teaching, and another of the
fear of God.

Tertullian—*The Passion of Perpetua and Felicitas*

Tertullian was a major theologian and Christian
writer from Carthage, North Africa. In A.D. 215, he
described these supernatural visions and prophetic
gifts of the Holy Spirit as operating normally in the
third-century church:

> Thus we who both acknowledge and reverence, even as we do
> the prophecies, modern visions as equally promised to us, and
> consider the other powers of the Holy Spirit as an agency of the
> church for which also He was sent, administering all gifts in
> all, even as the Lord distributed to every one.

Origen—Against Celsus

Origen was a Christian theologian who lived and
taught in Alexandria, Egypt from A.D. 185 to 254. In
his book *Against Celsus*, written in A.D. 250, Origen
describes the gifts of the Holy Spirit as still appearing, but he notes that these miraculous signs are beginning to diminish:

> Traces of the Holy Spirit who appeared in the form of a dove
> are still preserved among Christians. They charm demons
> away and perform many cures and perceived certain things
> about the future according to the will of the Logos (book I,
> chap XLVI, 2,8).

In book VII, chapter VIII of his book *Against
Celsus*, Origen noted that charismatic gifts were

diminishing, although some "traces of His presence" were still evident:

> Moreover, the Holy Spirit gave signs of His Presence at the beginning of Christ's ministry, and after His ascension, He gave still more; but since that time these signs have diminished, although there are still traces of His presence in a few who have had their souls purified by the Gospel and their actions regulated by its influence.

Novatian—*Treatise Concerning the Trinity*

In A.D. 270, Novatian of Rome wrote a strong defense of the doctrine of the Trinity and died as a martyr during the persecutions of the pagan Roman emperors. Novatian wrote toward the close of the third century about the key role of the Holy Spirit in empowering the church:

> They were henceforth armed and strengthened by the same Spirit, having in themselves the gifts which this same Spirit distributes, and appropriates to the church, the spouse of Christ as her ornaments. This is He who places prophets in the church, instructs teachers, directs tongues, gives powers and healings, does wonderful works, offers discrimination of spirits, affords powers of government, suggests counsels, and orders and arranges whatever other gifts there are of charismata; and thus makes the Lord's church everywhere, and in all, perfected and completed.

These documents from the first three centuries of the early church age tell us that God continued to empower the saints with supernatural gifts to demonstrate that the Holy Spirit's work among them was undiminished.

How You Can Be Assured of Eternal Life

Someday, each of us will meet Jesus Christ face to face. Hebrews 9:27 tells us, "It is appointed for men to die once, but after this the judgment." God declares that "all have sinned and fall short of the glory of God" (Romans 3:23). And it is impossible for a Holy God to allow an unrepentant sinner into a sinless heaven.

In light of the many signs that Christ's return is very near, each of us must make our final choice. Our sinful rebellion is leading us inexorably toward hell and an eternity without God. "The wages of sin is death, but the gift of God is eternal life in Christ Jesus our Lord" (Romans 6:23). However, God loves us so much that He sent His Son Jesus the Messiah to suffer the punishment for our sins. The gift of salvation is available to everyone who will confess his sin and ask forgiveness. In the Gospel of John, we read that "as many as received Him, to them He gave the right to become children of God, even to those who believe in His name" (John 1:12).

Final Warning, Final Choices

The holy Scriptures declare that the choice regarding eternal salvation is very clear. Who will be the god of our life? Jesus Christ or you? Either you will admit you are a sinner in need of a pardon and will accept Jesus to become your Lord, or you will insist on remaining the god of your life even though that decision will lead you to hell. If you insist on being your own god, you will succeed, but at the awful cost of an eternity in condemnation. Pride is the first and greatest sin; it is displayed in the stubborn attitude of many people who insist on having their own way even at the cost of an eternity without God. Milton, in his epic poem *Paradise Lost*, declared that in the end, either we shall say to God, "Thy will be done" or God will say to us, "Thy will be done."

Ultimately, it is your choice. You must choose heaven or hell as your eternal destiny. If you choose to commit your life to Jesus Christ, you will be assured that you will meet Him at the rapture as your Savior. If you reject His claims to be the Lord of your life, you will have chosen to meet Him as your final judge at the end of your life. In reference to Christ, the apostle Paul quoted Isaiah, saying, "Every knee shall bow to Me, and every tongue shall confess to God" (Romans 14:11; Isaiah 45:23).

In Acts 16, we read about a crisis that prompted the jailer of a Philippian prison to make his final choice. God used an earthquake to open the prison doors and break the chains that bound Paul and Silas. When the jailer awoke, he was afraid that the prisoners had escaped. As he drew his sword to commit suicide, the apostle Paul announced that the prisoners were still there. The frightened jailer recognized the power of Jesus Christ to save His servants. He called out, "Sirs, what must I do to be saved?" Paul gave him the key to eternal life: "Believe on the Lord Jesus Christ, and you will be saved, you and your household" (Acts 16:30,31). The Bible confirms that this man and his family found faith in Christ: "He rejoiced, having believed in God with all his household" (verse 34).

Jesus Christ's invitation to salvation remains open to anyone who is willing to repent of his sins. There is still time to accept Jesus as your personal Savior. "Behold, I stand at the door and knock. If anyone hears My voice and opens the door, I will come in to him and dine with him, and he with me. To him who overcomes I will grant to sit with Me on My throne, as I also overcame and sat down with My Father in His throne. He who has an ear, let him hear what the Spirit says to the churches" (Revelation 3:20-22).

If you have already chosen to follow the Lord, then I encourage you to obey the Great Commission of our Lord and Savior. In Matthew 28:19,20 Jesus commanded, "Go therefore and make disciples of all the nations, baptizing them in the name of the Father and of the Son and of the Holy Spirit, teaching them to observe all things that I have commanded you; and lo, I am with you always, even to the end of the age."

Our knowledge of the nearness of Christ's return should awaken a renewed love for Him and a passion to witness to those around us while there is still time. I have written this book together with my previous books to introduce non-believers to faith in

Christ and to encourage Christians in their faith. In addition, my goal is to provide believers with prophecy books and tapes that they can give to their friends and neighbors who do not yet have a personal faith in Christ.

The incredible events of the last decade are causing many people to ask what lies ahead for the earth. We receive letters daily from readers whose loved ones have come to know Jesus as their Messiah through reading this material. There is a growing fascination in North America with Bible prophecies regarding the last days. This tremendous interest provides us with the greatest opportunity we've ever had for witnessing. I trust my books and tapes will prove worthwhile to your personal study and help you to witness effectively to your loved ones.

The Lord has not left us in darkness concerning the general time of Christ's return. Although we cannot know "the day nor the hour in which the Son of Man is coming" (Matthew 25:13), the fulfillment of three dozen prophecies in our generation indicate that He is coming back to earth in our generation (for more on that, see my book *Prince of Darkness*). Someday soon the heavens will open "with a shout, with the voice of an archangel, and with the trumpet of God" (1 Thessalonians 4:16) announcing to the church the awesome news that our time of waiting is finally over. At that moment Jesus Christ will appear in the clouds to receive His bride, His faithful church. We will rise supernaturally in the air to meet our Lord and King.

Despite the dangers that lie ahead for mankind, those who love Jesus Christ as their Savior can rest in the knowledge that all these events are in the Lord's hands. The apostle John concluded his prophecy with the great promise of Christ: "He who testifies to these things says, 'Surely I am coming quickly.' Amen. Even so, come, Lord Jesus!" (Revelation 22:20).

If you are interested in ordering books, audiotapes, and videos from Grant R. Jeffrey, please refer to the order form on the last page of this book.

BIBLIOGRAPHY

Anderson, Robert. *The Coming Prince*. London: Hodder & Stroughton, 1894.

The Ante-Nicene Fathers. 10 Volumes. Grand Rapids: Eerdmans Publishing Co., 1986.

Auerbach, Leo. *The Babylonian Talmud*. New York: Philosophical Library, 1944.

Bullinger, E.W. *The Apocalypse*. London: Eyre & Spottiswoode, 1909.

Burkett, Larry. *The Coming Economic Earthquake*. Chicago: Moody Press, 1991.

Dean, L.R. *The Coming Kingdom—The Goal of Prophecy*. Philadelphia: Philadelphia School of the Bible, 1928.

Dunnan, Nancy. *Guide to Your Investments 1995*. New York: Harper Collins, 1995.

Elliott, E.E. *Horae Apocalyptic*. London: Seeley, Burnside, & Seeley, 1846.

Eisemann, Rabbi Moshe. *The Book of Ezekiel*. New York: Mesorah Publications, Ltd., 1988.

Feinberg, Charles. *PreMillennialism or Amillennialism?* Grand Rapids: Zondervan Publishing House, 1936.

Gill, Stephen. *American Hegemony and the Trilateral Commission*. Cambridge, 1990.

Hindson, Ed. *The New World Order*. Wheaton: Victor Books, 1991.

Kah, Gary H. *En Route to Global Occupation*. Lafayette: Huntington House, 1992.

Kurtzman, Joel. *The Death of Money*. New York: Little, Brown & Co., 1993.

LaHaye, Tim. *No Fear of the Storm*. Multnomah Press, 1992.

Larkin, Clarence. *The Book of Daniel*. Philadelphia: Clarence Larkin, 1929.

Leonard, Bernard. *The Book of Destiny*. Belleville: Buechler Publishing Co., 1955.

Lowth, William. *A Commentary Upon the Prophet Ezekiel*. London: W. Mears, 1773.

McAlvany, Donald S. *Toward a New World Order*. Oklahoma City: Hearthstone Publishing, 1990.

Malachi, Martin. *The Keys of This Blood*. New York: Simon & Schuster, 1990.

Medved, Michael. *Hollywood vs. America*. New York: Harper Collins, 1992.

Mesorah Publications. *Daniel*. Brooklyn: Mesorah Publications, Ltd., 1980.

Pentecost, Dwight. *Things to Come*. Grand Rapids: Dunham, 1958.

Peters, George. *The Theocratic Kingdom*. Grand Rapids: Kregel Publications, 1957.

Pusey, Rev. E.B. *Daniel*. New York: Funk & Wagnalls, 1887.

Sklar, Holly. *Trilateralism*. Montreal: Black Rose Books, 1980.

Tinbergen, Jan. *Reshaping the International Order—A Report to the Club of Rome*. Scarborough: The New American Library of Canada, 1976.

NOTES

Introduction

1. William R. Goetz, *The Economy to Come* (Beaverlodge: Horizon House, 1983), pp. 33–72; Joel Kurtzman, *The Death of Money* (New York: Back Bay Books, 1993), pp. 15–40.

2. Full documentation in Chapter 18, p. 489.

3. David Livingstone in *The Encyclopedia of Religious Quotations*, ed. Frank S. Mead (Westwood: Fleming Revell Co., 1975), p. 30.

4. Saint Augustine in Ibid., p. 50

Chapter 1: Daniel: The Prophet Who Saw Through Time

1. Isaac Newton, *Observations upon the Prophecies of Daniel and the Apocalypse of John* (London: J. Darby and T. Brown, 1733), p. 25.

2. Desmond Ford, *Daniel* (Nashville: Southern Publishing Association, 1973), p. 22.

3. Dr. David Williams, *Essays and Reviews*.

4. Dr. E. B. Pusey, *Daniel the Prophet* (London: John Henry and James Parker, 1864), p. xxv.

5. Ibid., p. 1.

6. Ibid., p. 5.

7. Ibid., p. vi.

8. Herbert Morris, *Testimony of the Ages* (Philadelphia: Bradley, Garretson, 1884), p. 563.

9. George Rawlinson, *Smith's Dictionary of the Bible* (London), p. 628.

Chapter 3: The Roman Empire will Rise Again

1. Gary H. Kah, *En Route to Global Occupation* (Lafayette: Huntington House Publications, 1992), pp. 23–65; Dennis Cuddy, *Now is the Dawning of the New Age and New World Order* (Oklahoma City: Hearthstone Publications Ltd., 1991), pp. 226–39.

Chapter 5: The New World Order

1. Quoted in Dennis Cuddy, *Now is the Dawning of the New Age and New World Order* (Oklahoma City: Hearthstone Publications Ltd., 1991), p. 244.

2. Ibid., p. 260.

3. *1993 Annual Report—Council on Foreign Relations* (New York: Council on Foreign Relations, 1994), p. 135.

4. Ibid., pp. 135–41.

5. Quoted in Gary H. Kah, *En Route to Global Occupation* (Lafayette: Huntington House Publications, 1992) p. 33.

6. Ibid., pp. 83–84.

7. *Trilateralism*, ed. Holly Skalar (Montreal: Black Rose Books, 1980), pp. 83–84.

8. Ibid., pp. 1–2.

9. Stephen Gill, *American Hegemony and the Trilateral Commission* (Cambridge: Cambridge University, 1990), p. 131.

10. Kah, *En Route to Global Occupation*, p. 39.

11. Cuddy, *Now is the Dawning,* p. 118.

12. Ibid., p. 246.

13. Eduard Pestel and Mihajlo Mesaroric, *Mankind at the Turning Point* (New York: E.P. Dutton and Co., Inc., 1974), pp. 9–10.

14. Peter Ustinov, *Chatham Daily News* (Chatham, Ontario, Canada: June 13, 1992), p. 24.

15. John Anderson, Ibid., June 13, 1992, p. 24.

16. *The European,* 29 September 1994 (London: The European newspaper, 1994), p. 8.

17. *A Vision for APEC* (Singapore: Asia-Pacific Economic Cooperation, 1993), p. 60.

18. Executive Orders, Presidental—U.S. Government, Library of Congress Internet Access.

19. Don McAlvany, *McAlvany Intelligence Advisor* (Phoenix: McAlvany Intellegence Advisor, Dec. 1993), p. 21.

20. "McAlvany Intelligence Advisor," 1995.

21. Don McAlvany, *Towards a New World Order* (Phoenix: Western Pacific Publishing Co., 1992), p. 277.

22. Don McAlvany "McAlvany Intelligence Advisor," 1995.

23. Ibid.

Chapter 6: Preparations for a One-World Government

1. Quoted in Norman N. Franz, *Monetary & Economic Review,* March 1993, p. 1.

2. Quoted in Boutros Boutros-Ghali, *An Agenda for Peace* (New York: UNDPI Publication 1247, 1992), para. 17.

3. *Toronto Star*, January 5, 1995, p. A3.

4. Ibid.

5. Ibid.

6. Paul Kennedy, *Toronto Star*, November 27, 1994, p. E4.

Chapter 7: Russia's Role in the Last Days.

1. Don McAlvany, "McAlvany Intelligence Advisor" (Phoenix: McAlvany Intelligence Advisor, Jan. 1994), p. 1.

2. Ibid., p. 215.

3. Ibid., p. 1.

4. Don McAlvany, *Towards a New World Order* (Phoenix: Western Pacific Publishing Co., 1992), p. 171.

5. *McAlvany Intelligence Advisor* (Dec. 1993), p. 22.

6. Jack Kemp, *National Review*, August 15, 1994, p. 6.

7. *Bereishis*, Vol. 1, (Brooklin: Mesorah Publications, Ltd., 1988), p. 311.

8. *The Pentateuch and Haftorahs* (London: Socino Press, 1961), p. 35.

9. *Ezekiel*, Art Scroll Tanach Series (Brooklin: Mesorah Publications, Ltd. 1988), p. 581.

10. Ibid., p. 583.

11. Flavious Josephus, *Antiquities of the Jews* (Grand Rapids: Kregel Publications, 1960), pp. 30–31.

12. Robert Young, *Analytical Concordance to the Holy Bible* (London: United Society for Christian Literature, 1971), p. 627.

13. *Eerdman's Handbook to the Bible*, ed. by David Alexander (Hertx, England: Lion Publishing, 1973), pp. 428–29).

14. Rev. William Jenks, *Comprehensive Commentary of the Holy Bible* (Brattleboro Typographic Co., 1839), p.743.

15. Ibid.

16. Rev. John Gill, *Commentary on the Old Testament*, vol. VI (Philadelphia: W. Woodward, 1748), p. 220.

17. J. Dwight Pentecost, *Things to Come* (Grand Rapids: Zondervan Publishing House, 1958), p. 327.

18. Gesenius, *Hebrew and Chaldee Lexicon* (Grand Rapids: Baker Book House, 1979), pp. 447–48.

19. Ibid., p. 162.

20. Ibid., p. 448.

21. George Rawlinson, *Five Great Monarchies* (New York: John Alden, 1885), p. 592.

Chapter 8: Israel's Role in the Coming World Government

1. Sidney Hook in *The Hero in History*, quoted by Moshe Kohn in the *Jerusalem Post*, 1995.

2. Joseph de Courcy, *Islamic Affairs Digest* (Gloucester: Intelligence Digest, 1995), p. 3–5.

3. Ibid.

Chapter 9: The Ecumenical World Church

1. Bernard F. Leonard, *The Book of Destiny* (Belleville: Buechler Publishing Co., 1995), p. 140.

2. Malachi Martin, The Keys of this Blood (New York: Simon and Schuster, 1990).

3. Ibid.

4. Ibid., p. 631.

5. Ibid., p. 632.

6. Ibid., p. 633.

7. Ibid., p. 639.

8. Nicholas O'Kearney, *The Prophecies of St. Malachy* (New York: D. & J. Sadlier & Co., 1859) p. 106.

9. Associated Press, Cotonou, Benin, from *Flashpoint* magazine, Living Truth Ministries, April 1993), p. 1.

10. Ibid.

11. Ibid.

12. Martin, The Keys of this Blood, p. 632.

13. Ibid.

14. *Presbyterian Layman*, January/February 1994.

15. Ibid.

Chapter 10: Living in Perilous Times

1. Quoted in Gary Bauer, *National Review*, August 15, 1994, p. 60.

2. Ibid.

3. Robert J. Bidinotto, *Reader's Digest*, November 1994, pp. 65–71.

Chapter 11: The Media Attack on Christianity

1. Michael Medved, *Hollywood vs. America* (New York: Harper Collins, 1992), pp. 22–23.

2. Ibid.

3. Ibid., p. 71.

Chapter 12: The Attack on Privacy and Freedom

1. Quoted in Luther M. Boggs Jr., *National Review*, August 15, 1994, p. 26.

2. Don McAlvany, "McAlvany Intelligence Advisor" (Phoenix: McAlvany Intelligence Advisor, Mar. 1994), p. 21.
3. Quoted in *Flashpoint* magazine, October 1994, p. 2.
4. Quoted in Michael Gratton, *Toronto Star*, November 4, 1994.
5. Ibid.
6. *Edinburgh Evening News*, June 20, 1994.
7. *Popular Science*, November 1994.
8. *New York Times*, September 6, 1994.

Chapter 13: The Secret Agenda of the New World Order

1. *The New American*, September 15, 1994.
2. Ibid.
3. Ibid.
4. Phyllis Schlafly, *Phyllis Schlafly Report*, June 1994.

Chapter 14: The Coming Economic Collapse

1. Quoted in Tom Bethell *The American Spectator*, September 1994, p. 16.
2. Ibid.
3. Gekko, *National Review*, October 1994, p. 34.

Chapter 18: Three Fascinating Discoveries

1. Dave MacPherson, *The Incredible Cover-Up* (Medford, State: Omega Publications, 1975), pp. 155–56.
2. John Bray, *The Origin of the Pre-Tribulation Rapture Teaching*, 1980.
3. Prof. Sukenik, *Jerusalem Christian Review*, vol. 7, issue 1, edition 2, May 1992, pp. 1,7.

Financial Information Resources

To obtain an objective report on the financial strength of your bank, savings & loan, or insurance company, call:

Weiss Group Inc.
4176 Burns Road, Palm Beach Gardens, Florida 33410
Phone: (800) 289-9222 or (407) 627-3300
Cost: $15.00 for a verbal report on your bank.
      $25 for a written Personal Safety Brief on your bank.

I highly recommend "The McAlvany Intelligence Advisor" as an excellent source of up-to-date financial, social, and political trends. This monthly report is edited by my friend Don McAlvany and provides a balanced financial perspective from a Christian viewpoint.

The McAlvany Intelligence Advisor
166 Turner Drive, Durango, Colorado 81301
Phone: (800) 525-9556 or (970) 259-4100
Cost: $115.00 annual subscription

Would you like to receive an up-to-date prophetic research and intelligence report every month from Grant R. Jeffrey?

You can join hundreds of other students of prophecy by becoming a member of

Destiny Dateline
Tape-of-the-Month Club

$69.95 plus $4.95 shipping for one year

We will immediately send you your first monthly audiotape by Grant R. Jeffrey with a cassette album made to hold 12 tapes.

You may order your Tape-of-the-Month subscription by phone with your credit card.

Call our toll-free number
1-800-883-1812

or mail your check and order form from the following page.

Speaking Engagements
or Teaching Seminars

Grant R. Jeffrey is available for seminars and speaking engagements throughout the year for churches, conferences, and colleges.

Please contact:

**Grant Jeffrey Ministries
Box 129, Station "U"
Toronto, Ontario M8Z 5M4
Canada**